Paul Gerhardt. — P. 264

CHRISTIAN SINGERS
OF
GERMANY

BY
CATHERINE WINKWORTH

1545 : HANS . SACHS . ALTER 51 IAR

Essay Index Reprint Series

BOOKS FOR LIBRARIES PRESS
FREEPORT, NEW YORK

First Published 1866
Reprinted 1972

Library of Congress Cataloging in Publication Data

Winkworth, Catherine, 1827-1878.
  Christian singers of Germany.

  (Essay index reprint series)
  Reprint of the 1869 ed., which was issued as v. 6
of The Sunday library for household reading.
  1. Hymns, German--Bio-bibliography. 2. German
literature--History and criticism. I. Title.
II. Series: The Sunday library for household reading,
v. 6.
BV480.W5 1972   264'.2   72-1295
ISBN 0-8369-2878-4

PREFACE.

THE hymns of Germany are so steadily becoming naturalized in England that English readers may be glad to know something of the men who wrote them, and the times in which they had their origin. Scarcely one of the numerous hymn-books which have been compiled here within the last fifteen years is without its proportion—sometimes a considerable proportion —of German hymns. This is, in fact, one of the many ways in which the literature of each nation now tends to become, through the medium of translations, the common property of both. But hymns form only a part, though an important part, of the religious poetry of Germany, which itself constitutes but one sharply defined branch of the general literature of the country. Yet it is impossible to trace the course historically of even this one channel of national expression, without being brought into contact with those great movements which have stirred the life of the people, and finding the passing fashions of each successive age, in thought or phraseology, reflected from its surface. Such a work as the present cannot attempt more than an outline of a subject which is thus linked on the one side to the general history and literature of Germany, while on the other it has a separate history of its own, full of minute and almost technical details. Only the principal schools and authors are described, and specimens are selected from their works ; but other writers of secondary rank are mentioned, to enable readers who may be inclined to do so, to fill up the picture of any particular school or period more completely for themselves. The choice of the specimens has been determined partly by their intrinsic merits, partly by their novelty to the English public; hence nearly all the great classical hymns are named as illustrating the spirit of certain times, but they are not given in full, because they have been previously translated, and are in many instances familiar to us already. A very few, which it was impossible to pass over, form the only exceptions to this rule.

In reading the poems scattered through the following pages, it must be remembered that they suffer under the disadvantage of being all translations and from one hand, which inevitably robs them of somewhat of that variety of diction which marks, in the original, the date of the composition or the individuality of the author. Still, as far as possible, their characteristic differences have been carefully imitated, and the general style and metre of the poem retained. Verses have been occasionally omitted for the sake of brevity, and once or twice a Trochaic metre has been altered into an Iambic, where the change did not seriously affect the shape of the poem, whilst it enabled the English version to reproduce certain striking expressions in the German. Single rhymes have been throughout substituted for double ones, except where the latter constitute an essential element of the metre ; this modification necessitates the addition or the omission of a syllable in the line, but makes it possible to give a more faithful and spirited rendering than can be managed within the very limited range of English dissyllabic rhymes. The frequent recurrence of particular phrases and rhymes is not accidental, but is a peculiarity of all German popular poetry from the Niebelungen Lied downwards. Besides the specimens given in this volume, many of which are rather poems than hymns, between three and four hundred German hymns in English dress may now be found in various collections of translations. Of these the chief are " Hymns from the Land of Luther ;" " Sacred Hymns from the German " by Miss Cox ; the " Spiritual Songs of Luther " and " Lyra Domestica " of Mr. Massie ; " Hymns for the Church of England " by Arthur Tozer Russell ; the " Lyra Germanica " and the " Chorale Book for England." Nearly all the German hymns in our ordinary hymn-books are drawn from some one of these sources or from John Wesley. Where only the first English line is mentioned in this work, the complete hymn may generally be met with in the "Lyra Germanica," or is one of Wesley's well-known versions.

It seems out of place in a work like this to give a list of authorities, which would necessarily be long. German hymns, like our own, have undergone many revisions, and are to be met with in very varying forms; of course these specimens have been taken from what appeared to me the most trustworthy sources at my command. But I may be allowed to express my obligations to the following important works :—Wackernagel's great work, " *Das Deutsche Kirchenlied*," both in the edition of 1842 and the one now in progress ; his lives and editions of Heermann and Gerhardt, and his brother's " *Altdeutsches Lese-buch ;*" the " *Geschichte des Kirchenliedes und Kirchen-gesanges*," by Dean Koch of Wurtemberg, to which I owe many details of the biographies of the chief hymn writers; the " *Geistliche Volkslieder*" of Hommel ; Von Hagenbach's " *Kirchengeschichte ;*" Gervinus' " *Geschichte der deutschen Dichtung ;*" and Gustav Freitag's charming series of sketches of German life, " *Bilder aus der deutschen Vergangenheit.*"

CLIFTON, *April* 1869.

CONTENTS.

CHAPTER IX.

CHAPTER X.

CHAPTER XIII.

LIST OF ILLUSTRATIONS.

"A PREFACE TO ALL GOOD HYMN-BOOKS."

By Dr. Martin Luther, 1543.

Lady Musick speaketh.

Of all the joys that are on earth
Is none more dear nor higher worth,
Than what in my sweet songs is found
And instruments of various sound.
Where friends and comrades sing in tune,
All evil passions vanish soon ;
Hate, anger, envy, cannot stay,
All gloom and heartache melt away ;
The lust of wealth, the cares that cling,
Are all forgotten while we sing.
Freely we take our joy herein,
For this sweet pleasure is no sin,
But pleaseth God far more, we know,
Than any joys the world can show ;
The devil's work it doth impede
And hinders many a deadly deed.
So fared it with King Saul of old ;
When David struck his harp of gold,
So sweet and clear its tones rang out,
Saul's murderous thoughts were put to rout.
The heart grows still when I am heard,
And opens to God's Truth and Word ;

So are we by Elisha taught,
Who on the harp the Spirit sought.
  The best time o' the year is mine,
When all the little birds combine
To sing until the earth and air
Are filled with sweet sounds everywhere;
And most the tender nightingale
Makes joyful every wood and dale,
Singing her love-song o'er and o'er,
For which we thank her evermore.
But yet more thanks are due from us
To the dear Lord who made her thus,
A singer apt to touch the heart,
Mistress of all my dearest art.
To God she sings by night and day,
Unwearied, praising Him alway;
Him I too laud in every song,
To Whom all thanks and praise belong.

CHAPTER I.

A.D. 800—900.

EACH Christian people has brought its own characteristic tribute to the vast treasury of devotional thought and literature, which is the common property of the whole Christian Church. The tribute of Germany is pre-eminently that of sacred song, of verse and music in combination and adapted for use in the Church and among the people. Her literature begins with a work of religious poetry, and from that time onwards has been always remarkably rich in productions of this class. The very genius of the people —its inborn love for music, especially for part-singing, its bent towards the expression of feeling in the lyrical form—peculiarly fitted it for this work; and the result has been the creation of a literature of hymns and hymn-tunes, which has had a wide influence not only within but beyond Germany. The hymn-books of Denmark, Sweden, Norway, and Iceland, and in part those of Holland, consist, to a large extent (until recently it would have been correct, we believe, to say, almost entirely), of translations and adaptations from the German; which have, however, become so completely naturalized among the people that their alien origin is forgotten, and they have furnished the model on which the hymns of native growth have been composed. In Switzerland, in the Protestant Church of France, and to some extent in Holland, the spread of the German hymns has been checked by the influence of the Calvinistic Churches, which have always feared to give a prominent place to art of any kind in the worship of God—rather indeed have allowed it to creep in on sufferance, than delighted to introduce it as a free-will offering of beauty. Yet here, too, hymns adopted from the German, or of the German type, have gradually made their way. In England the national character of our Reformation has left less scope for the influence of foreign elements. Our Church has distinguished its services more by the beauty of its prayers than its hymns, while our Nonconformist sects have been strongly imbued with those Calvinistic views of worship of whose influence we have just spoken. But a people with so marked a genius for poetry as the English, could not but use their gift in the service of religion as well as in secular ways; though the fact that hymns occupied a less important place in the religious worship of England than Germany, produced a marked difference in form in the compositions of the two countries. Germany's preeminence is in her hymns; but in sacred poetry not of this class, she has had no names of equal rank with those of Milton or Herbert of old, or Keble, Coleridge, and Wordsworth in the present day. In course of time, however, her hymns reached us too. There can be no doubt that the acquaintance of the Wesleys with the stores of her hymnology led them to see both the beauty of this form of poetry and the immense advantages that might be drawn from it, in spreading a knowledge of the truth among the common people, and in increasing the warmth and attractiveness of worship. They not only translated many German hymns, but wrote a large number themselves in the same style ; and it is from their time that the impulse dates which has led to the study of hymnology, not only of English or German, but also of Latin and Eastern growth, and to the rise among us of a large number of new and very good hymn-writers and hymn-books.

The story of the hymnology of Germany in the sense we have here given it, begins properly speaking with the Reformation. It was not until the people possessed the word of God and liberty to worship Him in their own language, that such a body of hymns could be created, though vernacular hymns and sacred lyrics had existed in Germany throughout the Middle Ages. But it was then that a great out-burst of national poetry and music took place which reflected the spirit of those times; and on a somewhat smaller scale the same thing has happened both before and since that time at every great crisis in the history of the German people. The most marked of these periods are the twelfth and thirteenth centuries—the era of the Crusades abroad and the rise of the great cities at home ; the Reformation ; the great struggle for religious liberty in the seventeenth century.; and the revival of literature towards the close of the eighteenth century, after the exhaustion that followed the Thirty Years' War.

As far back, however, as we hear anything of the

German race, we hear of their love for song. They sang hymns, we are told, in their heathen worship, and lays in honour of their heroes at their banquets ; and their heaven was pictured as echoing with the songs of the brave heroes who had fallen in battle. The first dawn of Christianity came to the Gothic races from Greece, but in Southern Germany it seems to have proceeded from the many missionaries who were sent out by the British and Irish monasteries in the sixth century, who sought no special authorization from Rome, and did not carry with them the Roman liturgy. But the chief instruments in the conversion of the remoter regions were the Anglo-Saxon monk Winifred, better known as St. Boniface, who was martyred in 755, and Charlemagne. Both these great men saw the imperative need of some centre of unity and order to restore society and preserve anything of faith or of letters in those times of utter chaos and discord, and believed that they had found the means to this end in the unity of the Church. That they greatly promoted civilization there is no doubt, but their work, even that of Boniface, had its darker side, where it came in contact with an already existing Christianity, and forcibly repressed what was national and distinctive in its character. For wherever they went they introduced at once not only the · Christian religion, but the hierarchy and liturgy of Rome, and with it the Gregorian Church music and the Latin hymns.

This style of music owes its origin to Pope Gregory the Great, who ascended the papal chair in 590, and thenceforward devoted his extraordinary abilities and energy to securing the unity and independence of the

Church. Here, however, we are only concerned with his influence on Church music. Before his time the Ambrosian style had been widely prevalent through the Western Church. It was founded on the Greek system of music, and was introduced by St. Ambrose, with the assistance of Pope Damasius, into the Great Church of Milan in the year 386. A true instinct taught St. Ambrose to adopt for his hymns the most rhythmical form of Latin verse that was then in use, and for his tunes a popular and congregational style of melody, and thus both spread rapidly through the Western Church, and became a powerful engine for affecting the minds of the people of all classes. In a well-known passage of his " Confessions,"[1] St. Augustine tells us (he is addressing our Lord) :— " How did I weep, in Thy Hymns and Canticles, touched to the quick by the voices of Thy sweet-attuned Church! The voices flowed into my ears, and the Truth distilled into my heart, whence the affections of my devotion overflowed, and tears ran down, and happy was I therein. Not long had the Church of Milan begun to use this kind of consolation and exhortation, the brethren zealously joining with harmony of voice and hearts. For it was a year, or not much more, that Justina, mother to the Emperor Valentinian, a child, persecuted Thy servant, Ambrose, in favour of her heresy, to which she was seduced by the Arians. The devout people kept watch in the Church, ready to die with their bishop, Thy servant. Then it was first instituted that after the manners of the Eastern Churches, hymns and psalms should be sung, lest the people should wax

---

[1] Library of the Fathers. St. Augustine's "Confessions," p. 166.

faint through the tediousness of service; and from that day to this the custom is retained, almost all The congregations throughout other parts of the world following herein."

One tune from the Ambrosian period is still preserved in Germany to the present day, in connexion with Luther's German version of St. Ambrose's great hymn, *Veni Redemptor gentium.* It is a simple, dignified, somewhat quaint melody.[1]

In course of time, however, there is no doubt that Church music had become deteriorated by the introduction of a more secular style, and that this was one cause of the reaction under Gregory the Great. Yet another may perhaps be found in the fact that the Ambrosian style was an intrinsically *congregational* method of singing, which enabled all the people to bear a part, and not a small one, in the service; while the Gregorian, which had less melody and rhythm, and was extremely difficult to acquire, was necessarily restricted to the clergy and the trained choir, and therefore harmonized better with the hierarchical principles of Gregory. It was natural, therefore, that from this period onwards, as the hierarchical element in the Church gained strength, this system should have rapidly supplanted its rival; nor would it be fair to say that this was altogether without its advantage, for in those distracted times the impulse towards unity in the Church was in many ways a true instinct towards self-preservation, and a common liturgy is one of the strongest bonds of a common

[1] It may be found in German tune-books under the name of "Nun kommt der Heidenheiland," and is No. 72 in the Chorale-Book for England.

religious life. There is, too, undoubtedly much grandeur and beauty in this style, which adapt it for certain forms and occasions of worship; but its stiffness and monotony, and its aptness to degenerate into a nasal unmusical chant in the hands of un-trained singers, unfit it for truly popular and common use. It has maintained its place in the Roman Church to the present day, and has exerted a strong influence on the music of the reformed Churches. During the eighteenth century this influence showed itself markedly in Germany in the adoption of a certain slow and uniform style of singing the old chorales, admitting only notes of equal length, and in "common" time. Recently there has again been a reaction towards the freer and more varied rhythm of the sixteenth and seventeenth centuries, when the laity delighted to assert their right to a share in the Christian priesthood, by bearing a part in the public service of God.

One thing that helped to make the Gregorian chanting an affair of the learned, was the very com-plicated method of notation then employed, and it was soon found necessary to establish schools, in which singers went through a training that lasted often for years. Gregory founded a famous school in Rome, with a prior and four masters, and for many generations afterwards the sofa was shown on which he used to recline while himself examining the scholars. They were mostly orphan boys who were entirely maintained here, and afterwards received appointments from the Pope. In the days of King Ethelbert, forty of them came to England, and intro-duced the Gregorian music into this country.

Charlemagne, like our own Alfred, was an enthusiastic lover of Church music, and especially of this style which he had learnt to know in Rome.   In his own chapel he carefully noted the powers of all the priests and singers, and sometimes acted as choir-master himself, in which capacity he proved a very strict, often severe master.   He extinguished the last remnants of the Ambrosian style at Milan, and it was with his approval that Pope Leo III. (795—810) imposed a penalty of exile or imprisonment on any singer who might deviate from the orthodox *Cantus firmus et choralis*.   He not only founded schools of music in France, but throughout Germany, at Fulda, Mayence, Treves, Reichenau, and other places.   Trained singers from the famous choirs in Rome were sent for to take charge of these institutions, and seem to have been not a little shocked at first by the barbarism of their pupils.   One says that their notion of singing in Church was to howl like wild beasts ; while another, Johannes Didimus, in his Life of Gregory, affirms that—" These gigantic bodies, whose voices roar like thunder, cannot imitate our sweet tones, for their barbarous and ever-thirsty throats can only produce sounds as harsh as those of a loaded waggon passing over a rough road."

The new style of Church music naturally found its most zealous promoters in the cloisters, among whom we may name Rabanus Maurus, a pupil of Alcuin, and abbot of the great convent of Fulda, and Walafrid (nicknamed Strabo), abbot of Reichenau. The Benedictine monasteries which were henceforward founded in increasing numbers north of the

Alps, were for the next two or three centuries, the asylums where arts and letters were preserved through the storms of those stormy times. Every convent, in fact, constituted a little town in itself when it had attained its full proportions. It began generally in the humblest manner. The abbot of some considerable monastery would send a small band of missionary monks to some spot, chosen either for its natural advantages, or from the needs, or perhaps the earnestly-expressed wishes, of the surrounding population. First, the monks would fell the trees, and erect temporary huts for themselves; then the chapel was built and service celebrated; then more permanent abodes were constructed, and gardens and fields were brought into cultivation. Then, if possible, the relics of some saint were procured, and deposited within the altar to give a special sanctity to the place, and attract worshippers in the hope of obtaining miraculous cures, and henceforward the number of monks and dependants would rapidly increase. When the institution was completed, we know by plans still preserved in the archives of St. Gall, that it would consist of the church as centre, the monks' dwellings, the cloisters, and the convent school within the inner inclosure; around which clustered handsome buildings for the abbot's and physician's houses; for the secular school, the hospital, the lodgings for travellers, whether monks or laymen; and the smaller abodes and workshops necessary for the various artificers whose crafts here found employment. The whole of this little town, so to speak, was itself inclosed within a ditch, and in later times fortified with walls and towers.

Among the most complete and famous of these monasteries was that of St. Gall. In that lonely but sheltered spot on the lower slopes of the Alps, and not far from Lake Constance, which gave access to Southern Germany, there was cherished for centuries a sacred fire of true enthusiasm for learning, which spread its light by degrees into many a half-barbarous court and distant convent. Here the earliest and most strenuous efforts were made to tame the rough mother-tongue of the Germans, and teach it to express as far as might be the shades of thought and feeling which the languages of Greece and Rome had so marvellously embodied, and all that the Christian faith had to say besides. There exists in its archives a very ancient Latin and German dictionary traditionally ascribed to St. Gall himself (died 638), and many other glossaries, paraphrases, and interlinear translations from the Latin. Among those who thus occupied themselves in the ninth century was a monk named Notker, whom Walafrid, then Dean of St. Gall's, strongly urged to devote himself to sacred poetry. He wrote, however, in Latin, and his hymns therefore concern our subject only because he was the originator of a form of Latin hymnology, which when translated into German gave rise to the earliest German hymns, properly so called, with which we are acquainted. This was the Latin Sequence or Prose. It was customary in all cases where a Hallelujah was introduced to prolong the last syllable, and to sing on the vowel "ah" a series of elaborate passages intended to represent an outburst of jubilant feeling. These were termed Sequences, because they followed the Hallelujah and repeated its notes,

and were of course sung without words. What
Notker did was to write words for them, and he tells
us himself how he came to do it, in a letter addressed
to Bishop Luitward, to whom he dedicated a volume
of these compositions. " When I was yet young and
could not always succeed in retaining in my memory
the long-drawn melodies on the last syllable of the
Hallelujah, I cast about in my mind for some method
of making them easier to remember. Now it happened
that a certain priest from Gimedia came to us who
had an Antiphonarium, wherein were written some
strophes to these melodies, but indeed by no means
free from faults. This put it into my mind to
compose others for myself after the same manner.
I showed them to my teacher, Yso, whom they
pleased on the whole, only he remarked, that as many
notes as there were in the music, so many words
must there be in the text. At this suggestion I
went through my work again, and now Yso accepted
it with full approbation, and gave the text to the
boys to sing." These Sequences spread rapidly, for
they supplied the want that was beginning to be
felt of melodies in which sometimes the people could
join, and words which could be adapted to special
occasions beyond the ordinary service of the mass.
They increased in number therefore more quickly
than the hymns properly so called, and gradually
assumed a strictly metrical form, which at first they
did not possess. Notker himself composed thirty-
five of them ; and one which still finds a place in
our own Burial Service, the " *Media vita in morte*,"
is traditionally ascribed to him, and said to have
been written while watching some workmen building

the bridge of St. Martin at the peril of their lives. It cannot however be certainly traced beyond the eleventh century, but from that time onwards it was in use in the Latin, and afterwards in a German version as a battle-song, which was supposed to exert magical influences.

It is to this same ninth century, and in one instance, to the teachings of the convent of St. Gall, that we owe the two earliest specimens of German sacred poetry. They are both Harmonies of the Gospels, and it strikingly shows the affinity of the Teutonic mind for the Jewish Scriptures, that the earliest monuments of its written literature are all drawn from this source— the translation of the Bible into Gothic by Ulphilas, the great Bishop of the Goths, who died in 388, and the two books now before us. The earliest of them is called "The Heliand," or the Saviour, and is written in Saxon, therefore in the ancient Low German dialect. It is said to have been suggested by Louis the Pious to teach the newly-converted Saxons something of the faith they had accepted, and to have been carried out by a peasant who heard in his sleep a voice summoning him to the undertaking. About thirty years later, a similar task was achieved by Otfried, a monk probably of Alemannic race, who had been educated at first at Fulda under Rabanus Maurus, then had lived many years in St. Gall, and finally removed to Weissenburg in Alsace, another of the numerous monasteries scattered along the borders of Switzerland, where the mountains break down to the lakes and cultivated country of Northern Europe. Though they thus belong to the same period of time, these works were composed under widely different circumstances. In Southern Germany the Romans had founded large cities, and Roman and Celtic elements were mingled with the Teutonic blood. Christianity had early made its way there, and a considerable amount of it existed before the earliest missionaries from Rome came thither. In the seventh century St. Emmeran found a multitude of priests and churches in Bavaria; the land had already gloried in several native saints before the time of Charlemagne; and culture must have made no inconsiderable progress, when we are told that the noble lady Theudelinde was able to maintain a pious and learned correspondence with Pope Gregory the Great. In Northern Germany, on the other hand, little had been done for the introduction of Christianity until Charlemagne converted the people by force, and the country long remained scantily populated and unsettled. Vast tracts of forest or heath were interrupted by solitary farmsteads of immense extent, where cattle and sheep were the chief source of wealth; for, until the close of the tenth century, there was but little agriculture; towns and monasteries existed but in small numbers and at great distances, and it was long before any churches except the convent chapels were built. Slowly the new religion permeated this wild and scattered people; but as it did so, it rooted itself the more deeply in the popular life, and bore less of the impress of the hierarchical and Roman element than the religion of Southern Germany, a distinction which has maintained itself even to the present day.

The form of the two works is contrasted as we might expect from their origin; the Heliand is written in the alliterative measure of the ancient ballads, but without strophes ; the work of Otfried is composed in four-lined verses with rhyme.   Rhyme is a peculiarly Christian ornament of verse, and the struggle was long between accented and rhymed forms of poetry, and the ancient forms of classical metre.   Otfried's is the first rhymed poem we possess, and thus has always marked an important epoch in European literature.   The Heliand is not so much a Harmony of the Gospels as a Saxon epic on the life of our Lord, and it seems to have been intended to form part of a larger work embracing the whole course of Scripture History.   The style is simple and *naïve :* the writer nowhere brings forward his own personality, but is evidently inspired by a strong love to his subject.   The relation of the disciples, and implicitly the relation of all Christians to their Lord, is conceived after the true Teutonic type as that of followers bound by an oath to their duke or leader ; all that expresses personal loyalty and obedience on the one hand, or affectionate condescension on the other, is brought out with quick insight and strong feeling. In general, the writer keeps very close to his authorities, but in some passages, where the heathen lays may have been recalled to his mind, he permits himself a more excursive description, and echoes of the old Scandinavian ballads float through his verse. The Sermon on the Mount specially attracts him, and he gives it with fulness and evident predilection.

Otfried, on the other hand, continually betrays his acquaintance with classical models, and the self-consciousness of the educated barbarian in the presence of a higher culture.   He is constantly lamenting his own incompetence and the barbarism of the German tongue ; he gives fewer facts and less of the distinctly ethical discourses than his Saxon contemporary ; but he much more frequently introduces episodes, sometimes similes or allegories from ecclesiastical works, sometimes mystical and moral reflections of his own. But there are passages where he rises to warmth and true poetry, as where, in describing the journey of the Magi, he speaks of the longing of the soul for its heavenly fatherland ; and the very idea of thus endeavouring to make the grounds of their faith intelligible to the common people, marks him out as no common man.

The following is a version of the passage just mentioned. The rhyme and metre of the original are very irregular, and here and there a rhyme is wanting altogether ; still, as its structure constitutes a marked difference between this poem and its predecessors, it seemed best to imitate, as far as possible, its rhythm, while keeping close to the meaning ; but in such a process somewhat of the poetical element is apt to vanish.

MYSTICE DE REVERSIONE MAGORUM AD PATRIAM.

> Now warneth us the Wise Men's fare
> That hereof we be well aware,
> How we should to ourselves take heed,
> And seek our native land with speed.
>
> Ye wot·not what I say, I wis ;
> That land is hight the Paradise :
> I verily could laud it sore,
> For wordès fail me nevermore.

But if of all my members each
Were gifted with the gift of speech,
Yet could not any words avail
To tell out all its wondrous tale.

Never couldst thou believe it right
Save thou shouldst see it with thy sight,
Nor couldst thou well, not even then,
Tell what thou saw'st to other men.

For there is life withouten doom,
And there is light withouten gloom ;
There wonneth the angelic race,
And everlasting blessedness.

We have forsaken it, alas !
Well may we rue that came to pass ;
Well may we never stay to weep
After the home we did not keep.

We fared forth hastily from thence
Misled by pride and arrogance,
Lured in some fond and secret guise,
By lusts that tempted us with lies.

Ah ! then we list not to obey,
And bear the mark thereof alway !
Now here as exiles we must stand
Sore weeping in an alien land :

Unused, alas ! from age to age
Lieth our proper heritage,
Untasted what it hath of good,—
So wrought for us our haughty mood.

We now must suffer and be sad
For lack of joy we might have had ;
We now must bear, as best we may,
Sore want and many a bitter day.

Now full of sorrow we bemoan
Our lot in this land not our own,
And bear the wounds that sin doth smite,

And many griefs of our sad plight.
 Here many a trial night and day
Lurketh in wait beside our way,
And yet we orphans sad and weak
Not yet our home are fain to seek.
 Ah, well-a-day, thou stranger land!
Hard art thou truly to our band,
Heavy art thou and hast no ruth,
I tell thee this in very truth.
 Sore griefs do here the heart beset
That for its home is pining yet:
Well have I found this true in me,
Nought joyous have I met in thee.
 The only gifts thou dost bestow
Are a heart laden with its woe,
A mood that aye is fain to weep,
And sorrows manifold and deep.
 But if into our mind it come
That we once more will seek our home,
And if our hearts would swift return,
And with a dolorous longing yearn:
 Then like the Wise Men shall we fare
By a new road to bring us there,
Seeking the true way that will lead
Back to the home we sorely need.
 That path, I wot, is fair and sweet,
But must be trod with washen feet:
Such is the manner, well I ween,
Of men that would thereon be seen.
 Kindness must in thy soul be bred,
And great and willing lowlihead;
And, most of all, within thy heart
True love must live in every part.
 Learn thou to find thy joy in guise
Of fair and ready sacrifice;

Yield to the good thy will alway,
And never thine own lusts obey.

Within the love-shrine of thy heart,
Let love of this world have no part ;
From things of passing time now flee,
Their very loss shall profit thee.

Remember what I erst did say,
This is that new and other way ;
Choose thou to tread it, as I rede,
And surely to thy home 'twill lead.

And when thou dost that life possess,
And knowest all its blessedness,
To God Himself wilt thou be dear,
And nevermore know harm or fear.

CHAPTER II.

THE two centuries we have now reached are a very barren period for literature. Charlemagne had given an impulse to arts and letters of which the effects are traceable as long as there were any pupils left of the circle of learned men whom he gathered round his court. But these gradually died out, and his vast empire fell to pieces. Then came a time when men had something else to do than to read or write ; had too often to fight or flee for their lives to have much leisure or thought for more peaceful tasks. The frontiers of Germany had to be secured, its lands brought under cultivation, its towns built, its social polity developed. It was not until the great defeat of the Normans in 891 by Arnulf, at Loven on the Dyle, that Germany was delivered from their attacks, and its eastern portion was kept in constant alarm by the incursions of the Hungarian and Slavonic tribes, until nearly the close of the eleventh century. Thus on one occasion, early in this century, the whole of Germany between the Elbe and the Oder was ravaged ; the most horrible cruelties were practised, especially against monks and priests, and all the churches were burnt down. The cause of offence was that the chief had asked in marriage the daughter of the Duke of Saxony, and had received the scornful reply that it was not meet to give a Duke's daughter to a dog,—a play on the words *Hun* and *Hund*, or hound.

A vivid description of one of these incursions is left us by Eckhard IV., a monk and chronicler of St. Gall. In the year 924, an invasion of the Hungarians took place, which lasted for two years. The wild hordes first burst into Bavaria, swept over all the south of Germany, and then vanish from our story as they pass down the Rhine. They carried with them cattle, and carts containing their plunder. At night they placed their carts in a circle, lit watch-fires, and stationed watchmen outside the barrier, while within it they encamped on the ground. By day they ravaged the country, plundering and burning on all sides; so that their approach was heralded by the red glare of burning villages on the horizon. When the abbot of St. Gall heard of them, he assembled the brethren and all the dependants, and commanded that they should at once begin to make spears, and shields, and other weapons, and also prepare a fortified asylum in case of attack. He himself and the other monks put on their coats of steel, and drew over them the monk's cloak and cowl, and laid their own hands to the work of fortifying the point he had chosen, a spot at the junction of three streams, which could only be approached by a narrow way. The monks and servants would not believe in the coming danger, and so it was but just in time that they transported their valuables to this retreat. The very next day the Huns appeared. Only two persons had

been left in the convent, a holy woman who had made
a vow of seclusion and refused to leave her cell, and
a half-witted monk who could not be induced to
accompany his brethren into their fortress. The
former was murdered, the latter was treated with a
rough good-nature, and given as much wine and
meat as he could take,—"though of a truth the dis-
courteous people, when I had drunk enough, forced
me to drink more with blows," he said afterwards.
The Hungarians took all they could find, and
observing that the highest point of the building,
the vane, was crowned by a shining cock, they con-
cluded this to be the god of the place, and supposed
his image would be of gold. Two men therefore tried
to ascend the tower and bring down the weathercock,
but both fell and were killed. Their companions,
enraged, next endeavoured to burn down the church,
but its thick walls defied their efforts, on which they
withdrew to the gardens, saying that the god was
too strong for them. They then sent spies to examine
the abbot's place of refuge, but these reported
that its natural strength and the determination of
its defenders seemed so great, that it would be
best to leave it alone ; and so, after a long and
wild banquet in the convent gardens, the barbarians
gradually drew off, and fell upon the neighbouring
villages. For some weeks, however, the abbot could
not venture to leave his fort, fearing their return, but
every day he and some of the bolder monks stole
down to the abbey, and said mass at its altar. At
last he heard that the enemy was really gone. One
of the suburbs of Constance had been burnt down,
but the town itself and the abbey of Reichenau,

which had been next attacked, had been successfully defended, and the barbarians were on their way to the Rhine.

By very slow degrees these wild people were either subdued and converted to Christianity, or pressed back into the vast plains and thick forests and morasses of Central Europe, and the frontiers of Germany became at peace. But within them was constant fighting still. All the great nobles claimed the right of private war; there was no regular administration of justice; trial by ordeal was practised; and a revolt against the Emperor himself appeared to his powerful vassals the most natural thing to be undertaken when they had any grievance to avenge, or when his absence in Italy offered a fair opportunity. These early Othos and Henrys of the Saxon and Salic lines, were indeed, for the most part, men of ability and energy, who strove hard to establish order and promote civilization; but their power in the State depended almost entirely on their personal character and the wealth and consequence of their families, and was weakened by their frequent absences in Italy.

In Germany itself, the clergy, on the whole, frequently sided with the Emperor as against the nobles, and to some extent thus constituted themselves protectors of the common people. They treated their dependants more mildly than other lords did, and their methods of agriculture were superior to any other; they gave employment, too, to many handicrafts, and thus it was not unnatural that towns gradually grew up or rapidly increased round the great abbeys and bishops' sees. It was to

two assemblies of bishops, moreover, that the distracted world owed that Truce of God, proclaimed in
the year 1032, which gave breathing-time to the poor
down-trodden peasant or townsman, and was the
beginning of a more settled state of society. It was
an agreement that no violence or weapons of any
kind should be used from sunset on Wednesday to
sunrise on Monday, nor on any high festival of the
Church, and whosoever violated this peace was to
pay his fine or *wehrgeld*, or suffer excommunication.
Many of the nobles at first refused to submit to this,
and declared their intention of adhering to the good
old customs of their forefathers, and fighting on every
day in the week : but a succession of bad harvests and
a great dearth which occurred about this time was
pointed out to them by the bishops as a sign of God's
anger with their conduct; and even the turbulent
Normans of France yielded to this argument. Nor
indeed was it untrue, for it is evident that the local
scarcities of food, which were of terribly frequent
occurrence at this period, were in great measure due
to the evil passions and ignorance of men. From this
time onwards, however, we can trace an increase in
the extent of land brought under cultivation ; mining
was introduced in the Harz district, and the towns
steadily grew in wealth and importance. But how
much of heathen superstition still lingered in the
most Christian and civilized places, is curiously shown
by a Mirror of Confession written by a Bishop Burchardt of Worms, early in the eleventh century. There
we find penances assigned for worshipping the sun,
the moon, the starry heavens, the new moon, or an
eclipse, and for trying to restore the moon's light

when eclipsed, by wild outcries, "as though the elements could help thee, or thou couldst help them." So, too, offering prayers and sacrifices by a well, at a cross-road, or to stones is forbidden, and so is the old wives' custom at the birth of a child, of placing food and drink and three knives on the table to propitiate the Parcæ or Three Sisters. The good old bishop believes in trial by ordeal, but we cannot but feel a great respect for him when we find the belief in the possibility of witchcraft and in divination classed among utterly vain and empty superstitions; and when we observe the heavy penalties affixed to slaying a bondsman even at the command or by the hand of his lord, unless he were a thief and a murderer; and to selling or entrapping any human being into slavery. To the former of these offences it seems no secular penalty was then attached, the lord possessing the power of life and death over his bondsman. Yet side by side with these superstitions there was a great deal of genuine Christian faith, among the laity as well as the clergy. The separation between these two classes was not indeed so marked as it afterwards became. Many of the secular clergy were married—Bishop Burchardt imposes a penance on any one who should despise or refuse the ministrations of a married priest,—and the monks often vied with the knights in field sports, as they did with the farmer in agriculture. When the need arose of defending land or faith by arms, the abbot raised his troops like the lord of any other fief, and could even on occasion, as we have seen at St. Gall, put on his own coat of mail and become general himself. On the other hand, many knights rivalled the monks in pious exercises, and the cloister was their natural refuge when pressed by conscience or the troubles of a restless life. It was in the secular school of the convent that their children were educated, and it was among the higher clergy that the princes sought for State-advisers and secretaries.

Throughout this period the literature of Germany remained exclusively in the hands of the clergy, and was written in Latin, the then universal medium of communication for the learned class. Even so truly popular a subject as the story of " Renard the Fox" was treated in Latin, for the earliest existing MS. of it is a Latin version, which it is, however, supposed was based on a Flemish original now lost.[1] This was indeed a sort of flowering time of mediæval Latin poetry, while native German poetry was almost extinct. Only a very few German poems remain from these centuries, and these are not remarkable except for their date. The principal are two long poems, by Ezzo, a learned canon of Babingberg, on the miracles of Christ, and on the mysteries of redemption and creation.

In the public services of the Church the people's share was confined to uttering the response, " Kyrie Eleison, Christe Eleison," at certain intervals during the singing of the Latin hymns and psalms. These words were frequently repeated, sometimes two or three hundred times in one service, and were apt to degenerate into a kind of scarcely articulate shout, as is proved by the early appearance, even in writing, of such forms as " Kyrieles." But soon after Notker had created the Latin Sequence, the priests began to

[1] The earliest German version dates from 1170.

imitate it in German, in order to furnish the people with some intelligible words in place of the mere out-cry to which they had become accustomed. They wrote irregular verses, every strophe of which ended with the words, "Kyrie Eleison," from the last syllables of which these earliest German hymns were called *Leisen.* They were, however, never used in the service of the mass, but only on popular fes-tivals, on pilgrimages, and such occasions. The most ancient that has been handed down to us is one on St. Peter, dating from the beginning of the tenth century, of which we give an imitation, as well as we can manage it, in English ; and also of a prayer from the tenth century, which is found at the close of a copy of Otfried's work, inscribed, " The Bishop Waldo caused this Evangelium to be made, and Sigi-hart, an unworthy priest, wrote it." The language of both differs so widely from modern German, as to be unintelligible without a glossary ; but both are written in irregular metre, and in rhyme, though the rhymes are very imperfect.

ST. PETER.

Our dear Lord of grace hath given
To St. Peter power in heaven,
That he may uphold alway,
All who hope in him, and say
    Kyrie eleison !
    Christe eleison !

Therefore must he stand before
The heavenly kingdom's mighty door ;

There will he an entrance give
To those who shall be bid to live :
    Kyrie eleison !
    Christe eleison !

Let us to God's servant pray,
All, with loudest voice to-day,
That our souls which else were lost
May dwell among the heavenly host :
    Kyrie eleison!
    Christe eleison !

PRAYER.

Thou Heavenly Lord of Light,
Guide us with grace and might
To Thine own realm, to be
For ever like to Thee.
Lord Christ, from heaven above
Send us Thy Father's love,
That we to heaven may go,
Nor suffer the least woe.

ANOTHER PRAYER (*Ninth Century*).

God, it is Thy property
Ever merciful to be ;
Hear the prayers we now outpour,
For we need Thy mercy sore.

We are bound without, within,
With the heavy chains of sin ;
Tenderly and speedily
Let Thy pity set us free.

CHAPTER III.

A.D. 1100—1250.

A WONDERFUL change came over Germany during the next two centuries. There was a great change in the mere external aspect of the country. The peasant who looked out from the door of his farmstead saw a very different landscape from that which greeted his forefather's eyes. The forest indeed still skirted the horizon, but the cleared spaces were wider, and the monotonous green of the broad stretches of pasture land was broken up by the more varied colouring of arable crops. The villages were far more thickly studded over the land, and nearly every one had its wooden church with its one tinkling bell; while farther off, by the river-side, stood some great abbey with its stone buildings, round which a busy town was rapidly growing up, where the village found a market for its produce and employment for its superfluous population. But one new feature would not please the peasant quite so well: on any neighbouring height which commanded the fertile meadows beneath, there was almost sure to be perched a new stone dwelling inhabited by some armed follower of the prince or great lord of the country, and from these

strongholds a lawless crew often issued to carry off
the fruits of peaceful industry. During the next two
hundred years, indeed, the most marked changes in
the social aspect of the age were the growth of the
great towns in size, wealth, political power, and all
the arts of life; and the rise of a large class of armed
and mounted followers of the great lords of the
empire, whom the institution of chivalry placed, in a
certain sense, on a level with their chiefs, while it
constituted a barrier between them and the unknightly
classes—an order which in after-times developed into
the lesser nobility of the empire.

But it was altogether an era of rapid growth, one
of those times when men's minds are awake and alive,
and full of energy to attempt new enterprises in any
field. Germany was ruled by the Hohenstauffens, a
vigorous, ambitious, warlike race, whose dream it was
to prove themselves true heirs of Charlemagne by
re-establishing the Empire of the West, and who fell
at last in that struggle with the popes of which the
real basis was the question whether the headship
of Western Christendom was to belong to the State
or the Church. The noblest of them, Frederick Barbarossa (1152–1189), had all the qualities that made
him the darling hero of the people : brave, handsome,
able in war and in council—a liberal patron of the
singers and builders, whose arts were beginning everywhere to flourish on the German soil—the champion
of his country against the Papal chair—the conqueror
of the warlike Normans of Southern Italy,—he stirred
the hearts of the people with an enthusiasm that was
in itself an education. The very manner of his death
threw a legendary halo round his memory. That

their monarch should at last have taken the Cross in his old age, and far away in the Eastern land, when a river had to be crossed, should have plunged in on horseback before his whole army, to show the way, and perished in the attempt, seemed a fitting end for so brave a life ; yet the mass of the people would not believe he was dead : in the popular imagination he became confounded with his great predecessor Charlemagne, and the legend was transferred to him, of the sleeping monarch in a hidden cave who was to start to life again in his country's utmost need. But not only did the frequent expeditions of the Hohenstauffens into Italy bring the Germans into contact with the more refined culture of the Lombard cities and the southern Normans, yet wider fields were opened to them by the Crusades. It was at this period that one mighty impulse thrilled through Western Christendom, and drew men, women, and children even, nobles and peasants alike, to the service of the Cross. It was no wonder that men's hearts were attracted to a service which in this new form touched the springs of loyal allegiance to the invisible Lord, and of reverent compassion for His earthly sufferings, and also of worldly ambition and love of adventure, and opened to the soldier a means of securing as high a place in the heavenly kingdom by his own craft of fighting, as the monk could gain by prayer and mortification. And so for the next two hundred years there was a constant stream of Crusaders going to and returning from the East, and rendering the intercourse between the East and West almost as close as that between Europe and America in our own day. If these expeditions wrought much harm and misery by their terrible drain on the strongest part of the population, by the wild habits and unknown forms of disease (such as the Oriental leprosy and plague) which were brought home by returning bands of pilgrims, they also wrought much good. Many joined them from a true impulse of devotion, and came back trained and tempered knights and warriors who had learned letters and refinement from the Normans and Provençals ; the priest and scholar brought back new ideas and new manuscripts from Greece ; the merchant discovered new channels for commerce, and carried home new fruits and luxuries to his native fields and city. Germany, however, was less affected by the universal enthusiasm than the other European nations : it was longer before the fire was kindled in the slow hearts of the people : the struggles with the popes made enterprises patronised by them less popular ; and there were never wanting men who looked on them with a disenchanted eye. " If it were of a truth so grievous to our Lord Christ," says one of the Minne-singers, " that the Saracens should rule over the spot of His entombment, could not He alone humble the power of the heathen nation, and would He need our hands to help Him ?" An old monkish chronicle of Wurz-burg begins its narration of the second crusade under the Emperor Conrad III., by declaring that in the year 1147, "there came into the country false prophets, sons of Belial, sworn servants of Antichrist, who by their empty words seduced Christiâns, and by their vain preaching impelled all kinds of men to go forth to deliver Jerusalem from the Saracens." It goes on to describe the mixed multitude that was

D

gathered together for this purpose, and the very
mixed motives that actuated them. " The one had
this, the other that object. For many were curious
after new things, and went forth to behold a strange
land ; others were constrained by poverty and the
meanness of their circumstances at home, and these
were ready to fight not only with the foes of the
Cross of Christ, but with any good friends to Christendom, if thereby they might but get rid of this
their poverty. Others again were burdened with
debt, or hoped secretly to escape from the services
they owed to their lord, or they feared the merited
punishment of their misdeeds ; all these simulated
great zeal for God, but they were zealous only to
throw down the heavy load of their own troubles.
Scarce a few could be found who had not bowed the
knee to Baal ; who were guided by a pious and
meritorious intention, and were so inflamed by the
love of the Divine Majesty, that they were ready to
shed their blood for the Most Holy Place. But we
will leave this matter to Him who can read all hearts,
only adding, that God best knoweth who are His."
Similar judgments are expressed by many other
writers throughout the twelfth century ; and even
where the poet or chronicler is filled with enthusiasm
for the great idea embodied in these enterprises, we
find a curiously frank and shrewd exposure of the
defects in their execution. This mood of mind, a
sort of slow practical good sense and perception of
actual facts, may explain the circumstance noticed by
many of their contemporaries, that the Germans were
the last to join and the first to discontinue the Crusades.
Still there is also a great capacity for enthusiasm in

the German people, and they by no means stood apart altogether from what constituted the great life of Europe in those days. Four of their emperors took the Cross, and were followed to the East by immense armies, and many knights joined in other expeditions.

The immediate fruit of this participation in the common life of Christendom was the rapid development of the institution of chivalry, and of a national literature—the first great outburst of German poetry and song. It came almost suddenly. We seem to pass at a bound from an age when literature was almost exclusively Latin and in the hands of the clergy, to one when it is German and chiefly in the hands of the knightly order. A few compositions indeed remain from the early part of the twelfth century which mark the period of transition; for though in language and subject they approach the new school, they are still the work of the clerical class. Such in religious poetry are the "Life of Jesus," by a nun who died in 1127, the version of the Pentateuch, and in secular poetry the Lays of Roland and of Alexander, &c., written by priests. But very soon a whole large[1] class of lyrical poets ang up who are known to us as the Minne-singers; their works are in German, and show a wonderful mastery over the language. Instead of the imperfect rhymes and halting metre of the previous age, we have long poems in intricate metre and crowded with rhymes, which occur often in the middle as well as at the end of each line. It became the fashion to compose if possible, at least to learn and sing these poems. They flew over the country on the wings of the tunes attached to them;

[1] More than two hundred are known to us still by name.

wandering knights and grooms taught them to each other; they were sung at village-wakes, and at courts and tournaments; and ladies had collections of them written on slips of parchment and tied together with bright-coloured ribbons. The subjects of this new poetry were, except in some rare cases, limited in range. It concerned itself almost entirely with ladies' love, with feats of arms, and with that contrast between the bright and dark side of human life which was so strongly felt throughout the mediæval times, and never more so than at this period. It was, unlike that which had preceded it, an age when there was great enjoyment of life,—delight in adventure, in social intercourse, and knightly pastimes; delight in natural beauty, such as the glow of summer and the song of birds, in the beauty of women, of costume, of verse, of stately buildings. There is a strain of almost childlike gaiety to be heard in most of these old poets. But it was also a time when life was peculiarly uncertain; when long partings from home and friends, strange vicissitudes of fortune, or death, might overtake at any moment those in highest place; while the Christian faith had awakened in the thoughtful Teutonic race that sense of the incompleteness and inadequacy of all finite beauty, of remorse for sin, of mysterious awe in face of the eternal destinies of man, which once roused could never be wholly laid to sleep again. The very changes of the seasons came with a sharper contrast to those men in their rude uncomfortable abodes than we in our ceiled and glazed houses can well imagine. Winter was a time of darkness, discomfort, and isolation; spring brought life and hope, and was welcomed all over the country by symbolic festivals at which the prince and princess of May and their followers encountered and overcame the representative of savage Winter. Summer brought the happy out-of-doors toil to the husbandman; the tournament, or the real combat, or the wandering life to lady, and knight, and squire. No wonder then, that in the poetry of these days, the alternation of joy and sorrow, " Freud und Leid," meets us in every form; in the happiness of greeting and the pain of parting; in the gloom of winter and the joyousness of the May-time; in the praise of pleasure, and in meditations on penitence and death.

In the Church, too, the voice of native song now made itself heard. The German Sequences, " Leisen," or " Leiche,"[1] as they were also called, became much more common, and at the highest festivals were sung even at the service of the mass itself. One for Easter, which we meet with in many various forms, and another for Whitsuntide, were thus used, and have descended to the present day as the first verses of two of Luther's best-known hymns :—

> " Christ the Lord is risen,
> Out of Death's dark prison,
> Let us all rejoice to-day,
> Christ shall be our hope and stay :
>   Kyrie eleison.
>   Alleluia, Alleluia, Alleluia !
> Let us all rejoice to-day ;
> Christ shall be our hope and stay.
>   Kyrie eleison."

[1] The origin of this term is uncertain, but it is thought to have denoted at first a certain dance measure. It is often applied to very long poems of somewhat irregular structure.

Or in other forms—

> " Christ hath risen again,
> Broken every chain ;"

Or,

> " Christ is risen again,
> Out of all that pain."

And for Whitsuntide, " here singeth the whole Church,"
as an old manuscript says,—

> " Now let us pray the Holy Ghost
> For that True Faith we need the most,
> And that He may keep us when death shall come,
> And from this ill world we travel home.
>
> Kyrie eleison."

These are attributed to Spervogel, a writer of the
twelfth century, of whom we only know that he was
a priest, of a burgher family, and a favourite sacred
poet of that time.   He composed many short didactic
poems, almost epigrammatic in brevity and condensed
thought, which were the beginning of a class of religious poetry that was much loved and practised in
the next two or three centuries.

Another " Leich" or " Sequence" of his, which
became extremely popular, is

THE PRAISE OF GOD.

> All growth of the forest,
>   The deep-hidden gold,
> All secret abysses,
>   Thine eye doth behold ;
> In Thy Hand all things lie.
>   All the hosts of the heavens
> Cannot fill up the meed of Thy praises on high.

Another of his poems is called

HEAVEN AND HELL.

He is full of power and might
Who was born on Christmas night,
The holy Christ is He ;
Praised of all things that be,
  Save the devil, whose lothely pride
Brooked not once to bow the knee,
  So must he in hell abide.

In that hell is mickle woe,
Well doth he who dwells there know ;
Shineth not the sun so bright,
Helpeth not the moon by night,
  Not a star he there may see,
Foul is all that meets his sight,
  Ah how fain in heaven were he !

But in heaven there stands a Home,
A golden way thereto doth come,
The pillars are of marble fair,
Set about with jewels rare,
  That our Lord for it doth win :
But no man may enter there,
  Save that he be pure from sin.

He who goeth to church full fain,
Pure from envy and from stain,
Gladsome life he well may have ;
Him await beyond the grave,
  Angel friends and blithesome morn,
Heavenly life so fair and brave ;
  Well for him that he was born !

> Alas ! that I have served so long
> A lord that is both fell and strong ;
> Evil wage fiom him I win,
> Ah I rue me of my sin !
> Holy Ghost, now succour me
> Ere my woes in hell begin,
> Break his bonds and set me free.

Several of the great Latin hymns were also translated into German at this time ; and that these hymns and sequences were used in church is proved by a passage in a Life of St. Bernard by a contemporary and disciple, in which it is expressly mentioned that in the cathedral at Cologne the people broke out into hymns of praise in the German tongue at every miracle wrought by the saint ; and the writer regrets that when they left the German soil this custom ceased, as the nations who spoke the Romanic languages did not possess native hymns after the manner of the others. Still undoubtedly their use in church was very restricted, and was always regarded with suspicion by the more papal of the clergy ; but there were many other occasions in life on which they were employed : they seem to have been commonly sung at the saints' festivals and special services which were frequently held outside the church, and on pilgrimages. So St. Francis, in an address to his monks in the year 1221, says : "There is a certain country called Germany, wherein dwell Christians, and of a truth very pious ones, who as you know often come as pilgrims into our land, with their long staves and great boots ; and amid the most sultry heat and bathed in sweat, yet visit all the thresholds of the holy shrines, and sing hymns of praise to God and all His saints."

It may give us some idea of the quantity of poetry
written from this time onwards, that the great collection by M. Wackernagel of religious poetry prior
to the Reformation, contains nearly 1500 pieces, and
the names of 85 different poets, while many of the
poems are anonymous, and much no doubt has
perished. Among the names still left a large number
are secular, others are those of monks and priests, and
the vanity of the world forms not unnaturally their
frequent theme. Here is a graceful little poem of this
kind by a monk of the thirteenth century, entitled

THE BEAUTY OF THIS WORLD.

O Rose! of the flowers, I ween, thou art fairest,
But thorny and worthless the stem that thou bearest,
   Fleeting thy beauty, unlovely thy fruit ;
World, I would liken thee unto the roses,
Sweet are thy flatteries, sad are their closes,
   Virtue and goodness in thee have no root.

Red is the berry, O Rose! on thy bushes,
Harsh is its inside, though fairly it blushes ;
   So, World, dost thou lure us and mock us with lies :
Outside thy seeming is gracious and sunny,
Outside thy greetings are sweet as the honey,
   Bitter thy kernel ;—O man, then be wise !

But in the list we also find the greatest of the
knightly Minne-singers, Hartmann von der Aue,
Reinmar von Hagenau, Gottfried von Strasburg,
Wolfram von Eschenbach, and the noble singer
Walther von der Vogelweide.

Hartmann "of the Meadow," as he calls himself

has left us several crusaders' songs, and among them
the following :—

CRUSADER'S HYMN.

My joy was ne'er unmixed with care
  Until the day
I took this sign that now I bear,
  Christ's flower of May :
It tells us of a summer-time,
  That will not wither,
A lovely, eye-delighting clime :
  God bring us thither !
Up to the numerous choirs,
From which to deepest fires,
His falsehood hurled the Prince of Ill ;
But to the good stand open still.

For so the world with me hath dealt,
  My mind no more
Longs for her gifts ; what once I felt,
  Thank God, is o'er !
God hath been very good to me
  O'er many another,
Since He from cares hath set me free
  That choke and smother
Love in the heart, and bind to home
The foot that fain afar would roam ;
While I exultant onward fare,
The triumphs of Christ's hosts to share.

Another crusading song, which was very widely
used on pilgrimages in these days, was sung to a
melody which has been preserved to the present

time by its connexion with one of Luther's hymns ;[1] it is this :—

PILGRIM'S SONG.

Now in the name of God we go,
His grace be round us evermo ;
God's strength be with us every hour
And fill us with His mighty power.
          Kyrie eleison.

And may the Holy Cross be still
Our shield from every ghostly ill,
The Cross where Christ endured such woe ;
O thence shall all our gladness flow !
          Kyrie eleison.

And also from the Holy Tomb,
Where He Himself lay wrapped in gloom,
With the five wounds He deigned to bear ;
Rejoicing, let us onward fare
          Toward thee, Jerusalem.

Kyrie eleison, Christe eleison !
O help us now, Thou Holy Ghost,
O Thou most blessed Voice of God,
To tread with joy the toilsome road
          Toward thee, Jerusalem !
              Kyrie eleison !

Another crusader and Minne-singer of those days, Sir Reinmar of Hagenau, gives us a glimpse of the struggle that must have gone on in many minds between the love of pleasure and the self-control that befitted a soldier of the Cross, a struggle of which we

---

[1] That on the Ten Commandments.

may still use his own words, "full many another feels it too :—"

UNRULY THOUGHTS.

E'er since the day this Cross was mine,
　　I set a guard upon my thought,
As well beseems the Holy Sign,
　　And as a faithful pilgrim ought ;
To God I raise my thoughts by night and day,
That from His service ne'er my foot may stray ;
　　But they would have their will, and roam
　　　　Unchecked as they were wont to do ;
　　Nor is this trouble mine alone,
　　　　Full many another feels it too.

All other things were lightly borne,
　　If but my thoughts would keep true ways ;
The God whom I to serve have sworn
　　They help me not enough to praise,—
Not as I ought, and for my soul were well.
On the old stories they are fain to dwell,
　　And lure me back to pleasures past
　　　　That I was eager once to seek ;
　　Christ, Thou forbid them, turn them thence ;
　　　　For my own strength is all too weak.

But I would not forbid them quite
　　　　To seek by times their native land ;
Awhile I let them take their flight,
　　　　Then want them swiftly here at hand ;
So there to greet our friends they oft are sent,
Then back they come to help me to repent,
　　To win forgiveness for us both,
　　　　For sins that all my past beset ;—
　　Yet fear I their deceitfulness,
　　　　Fear they may oft mislead me yet.

Farewell then, Pleasure ! well for him
  To whom thou comest harmlessly ;
Thou haunt'st me still in visions dim,
  Though of thy bondage I am free :
The days, the nights, when once I shunned thee not,
By many an effort have I now forgot,
  Closed are the paths that toward thee lead ;
    Let no man point the way to thee
    Afresh,—I count him else a foe
  To my sworn service and to me.

A little anonymous poem of the same date, the last
verse of which appears, from the metre, to be incom-
plete, surprises us by what seems to us the modern
tone of its tender and passionate

LAMENT.

Alas for my sorrow !
  My heart is in pain ;
Where is hope for the morrow ?
  To whom now complain ?
O God, take compassion
  On me lying low,
And comfort, O comfort me,
  Through Thine own woe.

Keenly regretful,
  I call to my mind
How we are forgetful,
  How He is so kind !
Who gladly, yet painfully,
  Yielded His breath,
Only to ransom us
  Ever from death.

> Where shall I find Him,
>   Him dearest to me,
> Who let His foes bind Him
>   That we might be free ?

But among all these singers, Walter von der Vogelweide (of the Birds' nests or the aviary) may be singled out as their highest type. He was the darling of his own times, and is constantly referred to by other poets as "their master in the lovely art of words and tones," "the sweetest of all nightingales," &c. It is not known what part of Germany was his birthplace, but he travelled all over it in the course of his life; he was a welcome guest at its courts, especially those of Thuringia and Austria, and he was a crusader. His poems give us the picture of a life such as we can well understand in these days, however different the circumstances may be,—a life full of travel, and of interest in questions of politics and religion, and even of literature. For the frequent reference to each other's works by these Minne-singers, with criticism or with praise, shows that those days too had their literary world. A large number of his poems are like those of the other Minne-singers, filled with praises of his lady, and of the May-time,—graceful, tender, often quaint and naïve lyrics. So one begins :—

> " When the flowers out of the grass are springing,
>   And seem to laugh at the glorious sun,
>   On an early morning in May,
> And the little birds are all loudly singing
>   Their very best, because summer's begun,
>   'Tis half heaven itself in the May."

And again—

MAY MIRACLES.

Would ye see the lovely wonder
   Wrought us by the May?
See how all are laughing yonder,
   Whether priest or lay.
   Mighty magic doth she hold,
Whence it cometh who shall tell?
But so far as reigns her spell,
   No one feeleth old.

We are full of joy and springing,
   Welcoming the May
With our dancing, laughing, singing :
   No sad dumps to-day !
   Heavy looks were now to blame ;
Since the birds in happy throngs
Carol forth their sweetest songs,
   Let us do the same !

Gentle May, thou showerest fairly
   Gifts afar and near ;
Clothest all the woods so rarely
   And the meadows here :
   O'er the heath new colours glow ;
Flowers and clover on the plain,
Merry rivals, strive amain
   Which can fastest grow.

     *   *   *   *

Lady ! part me from my sadness,
   Love me while 'tis May :
Mine is but a borrowed gladness
   If thou frown alway ;

> Look around and smile anew !
> All the world is glad and free ;
> Let a little joy from thee
> Fall to my lot too !

But others treat of higher and more serious themes, and show us a man deeply engaged in the political and religious life of his day. He was a warm lover of his country, but he does not hesitate to rebuke and satirize his countrymen, whether clergy or laity, for their faults and shortcomings. In the great struggle between the Pope and the Emperor, he is heart and soul on the national side, and writes such stern reproofs and bitter epigrams on the Head of the Church, as startle us from one of its sons. But he is an earnest Christian, sometimes lamenting his own sins with simple penitence, sometimes expressing a strong and manly faith. He preaches the Crusade, and so heartily that he refuses the meed of a poet's praises to the archangels themselves, if they come not to the succour of Christendom.

We give first one of his famous patriotic songs, then three of his religious poems, and then a crusader's hymn.

THE PRAISE OF GERMANY.

> Ye should raise the cry of "Welcome
> To the bearer of tidings"—for I am he !
> All that ye have heard aforetime
> Was merely a wind ;—now ask of me !
> But my guerdon must not fail ;
> If ye make me now good cheer,
> I have that to say ye will love to hear ;
> Look, what bid ye for my tale ?

I will tell to German ladies
Such gentle tidings in this fair land,
    As on earth may none be sweeter ;—
Nor great the guerdon I demand.
        Ah what could I from them require ?
        They are too high for me, I trow ;
    I am modest, nor ask them to bend so low,
        Fair greetings only I desire.

    I have seen full many a country,
And sought out the best in every part,
    But if alien scene or customs
Could ever like German please my heart,
        May evil hap that heart befall !
    I speak the truth, for of what avail
To strive unfairly with words or in mail ?
        German breeding surpasseth all.

    From the Elbe stream to the Rhine,
And back to the far Hungarian ground,
    Dwell the best and sweetest women
That I in all the world have found.
        If my skill be true and keen
    In noble breeding and beauty rare,
Better the women are here, I swear,
        Than high dames I have elsewhere seen.

    German men are brave and modest,
Like angels in truth their women seem ;
    He who blames them is deluded,
No otherwise of him I deem.
        Noble Virtue, constant Love,
    Let him come hither who seeks for these,
They dwell in this land, with joy and ease :
        Long may I live there, no more to rove !

A MORNING PRAYER.

In safety may I rise to-day ;]
Lord God, defend Thou all my way,
Where'er I go or ride throughout the land.
O Christ, now suffer me to prove
The mighty power of Thy dear love,
And for Thy mother's sake guard me on every hand:
As holy angels from on high
Once guarded Thee when Thou didst lie,
Thou ancient God, a babe of days,
Before the ox and ass so meek and still ;
When Joseph ever good and true
To Thee and them gave tendance due,
With faithful care that still hath praise :
So care Thou, Lord, for me, in me fulfil
Thine own commands, and keep me in Thy ways.

EQUALITY BEFORE GOD.

Lord God, if one without due fear
Repeat Thy ten commandments here,
And break them then,—not true His love to Thee.
So if one call Thee Father, yet
His brethren own not, or forget,
Sick is his heart, though sound his words may be.
Thou madest us of self-same blood,
We eat alike, and live by food ;
If one should find a heap of bones
From which the worms have stripped the fleshly pall,
How could he lord from servant tell,
Though once he might have known them well ?
God sits above all earthly thrones,
And feeds all living creatures great and small ;
Jews, Heathens, Christians, are His servants all.

REPENTANCE.

How seldom praise I Thee, to whom all lauds belong !
Yet since from Thee I hold both speech and song,
How dare thy vassal do Thy rule such wrong ?
Alas ! nor rightful works, nor proper love is mine
To Thee, my Father, nor my fellows here,
None yet to me as my own self was dear :
Father and Son, one God, Thy Spirit in me shine !
How shall I love him who hath wrought me ill ?
He who hath done me good must aye be dearer still.
Forgive my sins, I yet towards this will set my will !

IN THE HOLY LAND.

Now at last is life worth living,
  Since my sinful eyes behold
This pure land, where One forgiving
  Wrought such mighty deeds of old !
What I prayed for now I have,
I behold the soil, the grave,
Where God dwelt as Man, to save.

Lovely Land, so rich in story,
  Far above all I have seen
Dost thou bear the palm of glory ;
  Ah what wonders here have been !
That a Virgin bare a Child
Lord of angels, yet so mild,
Sounds it not a wonder wild ?

Here baptized was He most holy,
  Purity for us to win,
Stooped to bondage sore and lowly,
  To set free the slaves of sin.

E 2

But for Him were we forlorn,
His sharp spear and crown of thorn ;
Heathen, dare ye Him to scorn ?

Ah how far His pity stretches,
    Tasting death in very deed,
He the rich for us poor wretches,
    But to save us in our need !
That He shrank not from such woe,
Willingly could bend so low,
Greater wonder could one know ?

Here the Son to hell descended
    From the grave wherein He lay,
By the Father still attended
    And the Spirit, whom none may
Sever from Him.   They are One,
Sole and glorious as the sun ;
So it was ere time begun.

There He hath the devil vanquished,
    Whom no Kaiser e'er could quell,
Freed those who in prison languished ;
    Then sore griefs the Jews befell,
He whom they had wrought such woes
Broke their strictest watch, and rose
Living Conqu'ror o'er His foes.

Forty days this land beholds Him,
    Forty days, and then He went
Where the Father's light enfolds Him,
    Whence His Spirit He hath sent,—
May He keep us in His grace !
Holy is this land and place
That hath seen God face to face !

Here He told of that expected
   Day of terrors, long deferred,
When the prayers, by men rejected,
   Of the widow shall be heard,
And the oppressed shall find a friend,
And the wise no arts defend ;
Chasten now, ere comes that end !

Then that Judge's righteous sentence
   No lament hath power to stay ;
Here, O here may be repentance,
   Wait not for the final day ;
Pledge nor hostage then avail,
Thou must answer without fail,
And thyself meet bliss or bale.

But if what I now have spoken
   Seemeth not to you too long,
List one moment yet, ere broken
   Fails the current of my song.
All God's mightiest works for man
Here in this fair land began,
Here too ends the wondrous plan.

Christians, Heathens, Jews assever
   Each that it is theirs of right ;
God alone, the bless'd for ever,
   Must decide it with His might.
All the world is fighting here,
Ours the rightful cause, no fear
God will make its justice clear !

The Minne-songs, which form a purely lyrical
poetry, were soon followed by poems of the narrative
and didactic class. Early in this same thirteenth
century the Nibelungen-Lied received its present

shape; and the old legends, some like this taken from the heathen times, others of purely Christian origin, became the favourite subjects of the poets. The stories of Tristram, Percival, and the quest of the Holy Grail—knightly romances and histories of saints that were half mystical and symbolical, half legendary—must have filled the imaginations of youths and ladies in those days as novels do in ours. Most of these stories were connected with that circle of legends of which King Arthur and his Round Table form the centre, and were thus derived from a foreign, generally from a French or Provençal source, but their treatment was entirely German. It soon betrays two opposite tendencies, one of which takes up the external side of these romances, that of love of adventure and worldly success; while the other brings into relief their religious element and the development of character, and anticipates in the latter respect somewhat of the characteristics of the modern novel. Of these schools the representative types are Gottfried von Strasburg and Wolfram von Eschenbach. The former chose for the subject of his longest poem the story of Tristram and Iseult, and makes it the vehicle of depicting the knightly life of his own times on its most stirring and fascinating side. The latter selects the quest of the Holy Grail by Sir Percival, and embodies in his poem those grave and high conceptions of knightly duty and religious faith, which characterise the more serious thought of his day. Wolfram von Eschenbach was a Bavarian by birth, of ancient and noble family, but being a younger son, he possessed but little worldly wealth, and seems to have led a wandering life,

welcome as knight and poet alike at the German
courts and castles. From the frequent allusions in
his principal poem to the court of Thuringia, he no
doubt formed one of the band of knights, poets, and
adventurers, who gathered round the Landgrave
Hermann of Thuringia, and made that little court at
once brilliant and disturbed. Wolfram's lifetime coincided with the brightest period of the German Empire
under the Hohenstauffens, for he was born under
Frederick Barbarossa, and died under Frederick II.
German chivalry was then at its highest point,
and religious fervour was kindled to enthusiasm by
the Crusades ; thus it is but natural that these should
form the moving springs of his romance. It opens
with the history of Gamuret, the father of Percival, a
younger son of the noble house of Anjou, a knight of
the adventure-loving order, who can never enjoy life
but in stirring action. He takes service at one time
under the Caliph of Bagdad, and wins the hand of a
Saracen princess. But he soon leaves her to seek
new conflicts, and after his departure she bears him a
son, who grows up a heathen, but a very brave and
noble knight. At last in Spain he obtains, as victor
in a tournament, the hand of the queen and a large
territory, and for a time lives happily with his wife ;
but hearing that his former sovereign is in need of his
services, he sets out for the East, and is slain by the
way. The queen almost dies of grief for his death,
but lives at last for the sake of her little son Percival.
Fearing, however, lest he should inherit his father's
spirit and meet with his father's fate, she retires with
him into a deep forest, where she brings him up
in perfect seclusion, and forbids the few faithful

attendants who had followed her, ever to name chivalry or knighthood in his presence :—

> " Each morn he bathes him in the stream ;
>   Of care or harm he does not dream ;
>   But when the birds' delicious song
>   Held ear and heart in magic strong,
>   His breast swells with a longing deep ;
>   The child runs to his mother's side ;
>   But when she asks, ' What makes thee weep ? '
>   He cannot tell and will not bide,
>   As children wont at every tide.
>   His mother, filled with wakeful care,
>   Watches his footsteps everywhere,
>   Till once, unseen, she sees her boy
>   Lost in a dream of vaguest joy,
>   Listening to that sweet song.   Then she
>   Swore the birds' enemy to be ;
>   She bade her squires to catch and kill
>   All birds they found, the good and ill.
>   But ah ! the birds were craftier yet ;
>   They slipped away from bow and net,
>   And sweeter still o'er copse and corn
>   Rang their dear song at break of morn.
>   The boy then asked her wherefore she
>   To harmless birds was enemy,—
>   ' Dear mother, let these murders cease,
>   And let us live with them at peace.'
>   The mother kissed her lovely boy ;
>   ' How could I thus break God's command,
>   Who made them but for purest joy ! '
>   Awhile the boy doth musing stand ;
>   ' Who is God ? mother mine,' he saith.
>   ' My child, receive my words in faith :

God dwells above us bright as day ;
Mercy and love are His alway :
Cry to Him in the hour of need ;
He loves to help, and that with speed.
But there is one, His direst foe,
Faithless and cruel ; far below
That Black one dwells in darkest night :
Heed not his lures, nor fear his might,
But even in thought from him, O flee ;
From him and Doubt, O keep thee free."

But her precautions are unavailing. One day three
shining knights come riding through the green forest.
The boy thinks they must be gods, they are so bright,
and kneels to them. They tell him they are knights,
show him their weapons, and, when he wants to
know how he may become like them, tell him to seek
King Arthur's court. Now nothing can detain the
boy, his mother finds her tears are useless, and gives
permission for his departure ; but hoping to drive him
back to her through disgust with the world, she
sends him forth in a fool's dress, bidding him to wear
it for her sake, to honour old men, and to prize a
woman's kiss and her ring. So he sets out, and
meets with various adventures to which his simplicity
and unknightly dress give a half-comic air ; he makes
his way, however, by dint of courage and straight-
forwardness, and comes at last to King Arthur's
court. Here he undertakes a combat with a knight
in red armour, Ither, and slays him ; but though
Arthur and Guinevere receive him kindly, touched
by his beauty, his courage, and his simplicity, he
finds himself an object of derision to the other
knights and ladies, and makes his escape carrying

with him the armour and horse of the Red Knight.
After a while he reaches the castle of a grey-haired
noble knight, and, remembering his mother's instructions to ask the counsel of old men, he goes
up to the knight and requests from him shelter and
advice. Here he remains for some time, and speedily
becomes proficient in knightly exercises and de-
meanour, assisted partly by a flying fancy that he
feels for his host's fair daughter, Liasse. But he
knows that he has not yet earned the right to a
lady's love, and moreover the longing for action is
upon him, and so once more he departs :—

> " In dress and manners now need he
> Ne'er blush in noblest company ;
> Yet had his master's teachings stirred
> Thoughts that till then had slept unheard,
> That made his heart beat restlessly.
> Too small his world seems now to him,
> Too strait its bounds, its light too dim ;
> A mist before his eyes seemed spread,
> No charm was in the verdant mead,
> In him and round him twilight grey ;—
> His ignorance had passed away."

In time he meets with a most beautiful princess,
Konduiramir, who is besieged by cruel foes; he
rescues her, falls deeply in love with her, and is at
last rewarded by her hand and crown, and lives for
a time happily with her. The land flourishes under
his wise and mild sway, and all seems going well,
till he remembers how long it is since he has had
news of his mother, and sets forth to find her once
more.

Riding alone beside a lake in the deep forest, he meets with the sick king, Amfortas, disguised as a fisherman, who directs him to a wondrous castle, Monsalvas, which is in truth the abode of the Sangreal, or as it is always called in this poem, "the Holy Grail." The Holy Grail was said to be a vessel of pure emerald, belonging to Joseph of Arimathæa, from which our Lord had partaken of the Last Passover, and which had received the blood that flowed from His wounded Side. Since then it was said to dwell in a certain palace, guarded and served by knights and ladies. Wherever it appeared it bestowed what was needed for earthly wants, and for the soul's salvation; but none could see it except by special grace, and none were admitted to its service except the pure and devoted. Sir Percival is now put to the test, by being permitted to behold the Holy Grail. He is admitted to the splendid castle, and treated with hospitality; he sees the sick King Amfortas, who is suffering acute anguish from a poisoned wound. The Holy Vessel is borne through the banqueting hall by its train of beautiful virgins, but Sir Percival remains unmoved; he asks not the meaning of what he sees, he asks not why Amfortas is suffering thus. So he goes to rest; when he wakes the next morning, the castle is still and deserted; in the courtyard he finds his horse ready saddled and bridled, but no one is to be seen. As he leaves the castle a groom calls after him from one of the towers, bidding him depart as hateful to the sun. Percival turns in anger, but the window is closed, and not a creature is visible. A little further he meets his cousin Sigima, who is mourning in the forest over the death of her lover, and the story of whose faithful love and grief forms a touching episode. She hears where he has been, and explains to him all he has witnessed, but when she finds that neither pity nor wonder had moved him to speak, she cries woe upon him and drives him from her.

Percival rides on "with a thorn in his heart," but without clearly seeing what he has done wrong, nor does he for some time experience any ill effects from it. On the contrary, after various successful adventures, he reaches King Arthur's court, where he is received with acclamations; a splendid banquet is prepared in his honour, and Gawain, the King's nephew, shows him especial friendship. But in the midst of the banquet, when the festivity is at its height, his fate overtakes him. Kundria the sorceress, a terrible messenger from the Sangreal, rides into the hall, tells the knights that they and their Round Table are dishonoured by the fellowship of Percival, relates the story of his visit to Monsalvas, then tells them of another quest of the Castle Merveilleux, in which also honour is to be won, and disappears. She is followed by a strange knight, who accuses Gawain of wrong, and challenges him fiercely. All the knights rise from table, and gather round Gawain and Percival to console them. But Percival is inconsolable:—

* * * *

> " There stunned and mute sits Percival,—
> Ah, what avails the manhood now
> Of that brave heart, its chastity,
> Its lofty aims and aedent glow?

He is disgraced before them all.
    Yet innocent and pure is he,
No vice can in his life be found,
Ne'er have his steps transgressed the bound
Of modesty, the soul's true prize
And fairest crown in noble eyes.

      *   *   *   *

" Gawain embraced the valiant man,
And strives to cheer him as he can,
    ' O friend, thy journey well I know
    Will bring thee many a toil and woe :
    God give thee luck, and grant to me
    In time of need to succour thee.'
But Percival cried, ' What is God ?
Would He haye suffered such a load
Of scorn to fall on thee and me
Were He so good and great and free ?
The fountain of His might is dry.
Him truly served my arm and heart,
My recompense is this sore smart ;
Henceforth His service I resign,
If He hath wrath, that wrath be mine.
O friend, thou go'st to war and strife,
Take for thy aid a faithful wife,
A woman fair and chaste and good,
Complete in tender womanhood ;
Be she thy guide, thy strength, and guard,
Her love will be thy best reward.' "

He determines to start at once on the quest of the
Holy Grail, and not to return until his honour is
restored. Gawain undertakes the quest of the Castle
Merveilleux, and so the two depart. From this
point the story divides, sometimes following the

fortunes of one, sometimes of the other hero. But the story of Gawain is not a mere episode: he represents the child of this world; brave, ready, untroebled by deeper thoughts, he meets with difficulties indeed, but with far more good luck and brilliant success than Percival, until the latter accomplishes his object at last. Percival, on the contrary, encounters life in a much more dreary and commonplace aspect; for five years he wanders on, never reconciled to God, taking no pleasure in anything, meeting with no brilliant adventures, but carrying in his heart an intense longing to behold once more the Holy Grail, repair his fault, and then to be reunited to his wife, whom he never forgets. At last he meets with a hermit, Trevizrent, a brother of Amfortas, to whom he tells all his sorrows, and whose instructions at last restore him to faith. Percival says:—

> " Like to a dream my joy is fled,
>   A weight of grief is on my head;
>   Where church and minsters fairly rise,
>   I ne'er am seen by mortal eyes;
>   In strife and combat am I known,
>   Yet hate I none but God alone;
>   For He, revengeful, sends me scorn
>   And sorrows scarcely to be borne.
>   If God would give us help indeed,
>   No anchor else my life would need,
>   But jealous of my just renown,
>   Fate all my deeds with thorns doth crown;
>   And *could* God help it, *could* He right:—
>   Let men praise as they will His might;—
>   I cry aloud unjust is He
>   Who leaves me bound by misery."

Trevizrent replies by making Percival see how his conduct at Monsalvas proved him unworthy of the honour that had been done him in admitting him to the vision of the Holy Grail; how his youthful impetuosity had been the cause of his mother's death, who had expired of grief for his long absence; and how his love of strife had led him to kill the Red Knight, who was his own cousin, a man of great virtue and purity, and would have been his friend. Towards God his sin is defined as *disloyalty*, the forsaking his rightful allegiance on the touch of trial. Throughout the poem we find that man's highest duty is conceived as *loyalty* to the various relations in which he may be placed, whether towards God or man. Doubt, fickleness, inconstancy are the deepest stains on a knight. Trevizent thus vindicates the justice of God in punishing him, and then goes on to speak of the help he may yet expect from Him :—

" Eternally shall sound His praise
  Who showed to man such wealth of grace,
  His noble nature bowed to us
  And stooped to wear our likeness thus.
  God's name and nature is pure Truth,
    He hateth all disloyalty ;
  Then think upon thy life with ruth,
    And let thy firm decision be
  Never from Him to turn aside,
  Who still is true whate'er betide.

      *   *   *   *

" He is the Father far above,
  Whose essence is unfaltering Love ;'

Yet love or wrath the world may choose ;
Ah woe ! if thou that love refuse !

    *   *   *   *

But God is also radiant Light,
Piercing the thickest walls with might ;
No secret impulse stirs the breast
But stands before that eye confest ;
The swiftest thought He sees and tries
Ere it from heart to lips can rise.
If God so judge each thought that lurks
Within thee, on thy own vain works
How wilt thou dare to found a claim ?
Must thou not bend with inward shame
Before that Perfect Purity,
And ask His grace to succour thee ?
Thou hast thy choice, or love or wrath,
But choose, oh choose, the better path ;
Changed be thy mind, then shalt thou prove
That God can look on thee with love."

Percival now becomes reconciled to God ; he remains
fifteen days sharing the hermit's fare, and learning
from him the true history of the Holy Grail, and the
meaning of all he saw, and then once more sets out
on his quest. In course of time he arrives at King
Arthur's court, just at the moment when Gawain has
returned from his successful expeditions, bringing
with him the beautiful Duchess Orgueilleuse, who
has consented to become his wife. Once she had
attempted to lure Percival from his allegiance to
Konduiramir, but in vain. Gawain has now invited
the whole Round Table to witness his nuptials, and
his combat with Gramoflanz. Early in the morning
he rides out to try his powers, he meets with Percival,

and, not recognising him, attacks him; they fight long. Just as Percival is about to win the victory an exclamation of the squire's betrays to him his opponent's name; he instantly flings away his sword, dismounts, and reproaches himself for having fought with his friend. The combat with Gramoflanz is postponed to the next day, to give Gawain time to recover. Percival however contrives at dawn to take it upon himself, in order to spare Gawain, and overthrows Gramoflanz. He gives him his life; Gawain and he are reconciled, and three marriages are arranged at once. Percival is restored to his place at the Round Table, and treated with the highest distinction. Many a lady would fain try to console the stately knight, who never smiles except in courtesy; but he cares for no one but Konduiramir, and all the happy love around him only quickens his longing after her. He lies awake till dawn, then

> " His eye doth on the armour rest
> That lies before him, and his breast
> Anew is filled with heavy sighs :
> ' If Fate for aye to me denies
> What on her favourites she bestows,
>   The joy of happy love, whose power
> Can put to flight the sorest woes,
>   Nought else I ask that she can shower.
> But God wills not such happiness !
> If we had loved each other less,
> The tie might break, and I might find
> Some solace elsewhere to my mind.
> But *her* love hath such hold on me,
> Who never from my griefs am free,

> No love or joy can in me dwell,
> My sickness is incurable.
> Fate loves to give in lavish measure
> To those who strive for earthly pleasure !
> God give sweet joy to all men here !
> But from their host I disappear."

But his time of trial is now nearly at an end. Not far from the camp he encounters his half-brother the heathen Feirefiss; they fight : Percival is almost overcome, but his strength is restored by prayer, and he is on the point of conquering, when his sword breaks in his hand. The relationship is now discovered; Percival returns to Arthur's camp with his brother, and in the midst of the rejoicings Kundria the sorceress appears once more to tell him that he is accepted as the monarch of the Holy Grail. He sets out for Monsalvas, heals Amfortas by the power of prayer, and then is suffered to meet with Konduiramir.

> " So Percival rode all night through
> To meet that lady sweet and true ;
> Till with the earliest blush of day
> A host of tents before him lay,
> Pitched on the dewy flowery sward,
> Bright banners floating all abroad.
>
>   * * * *
>
> He finds the tent where sleeps the Queen
> Among her women, and between
> Her beauteous twins ;—Ah, now at last
> His joy is come, his griefs are past !
> There on the bed of whitest snow
> Three lovely heads like roses glow,

Lit by the morning beam they sleep,
Smiling in slumber calm and deep.

  *   *   *   *

Till the Queen wakened, opes her eyes,
Beholds him there with glad surprise,
And springs to her great hero's breast,
By joy itself o'ercome, opprest,
With kisses covers all his face,
And holds him in a close embrace.
She cries : ' Thee now my God doth send,
 My heart's delight, my only joy ;
At last, at last there is an end
 Of mournful days and long annoy ;
I have my heart's most fervent prayer,
And fled is every thought of care.' "

They now all proceed to Monsalvas. Feirefiss receives
baptism, which enables him to behold the Holy
Grail ; he marries the royal virgin who has hitherto
borne it, and the two return to the far East to spread
the true faith there. The younger of Percival's twin-
sons is sent back to the world to become the king of
his temporal dominions, and Percival himself with
Konduiramir and his elder son are left reigning at
Monsalvas.

 " So I, Wolfram von Eschenbach,
  Following the Master whom I trust,
  Have told the story true and just
  Of the great deeds of Percival,
  His noble race, his children all ;
  I leave him in that lofty place
  Where he was called by Heaven's high grace.

And he whose life shall end like this,
Whose soul no guilt or bitterness
From God above hath power to part,
Whose valiant arm and noble heart
Earth's homage too of right obtain,—
I trow he hath not lived in vain."

Such is a slight sketch of the finest and most earnest of these early German romantic epics. The style is at times long-winded and prolix,—thus we have two pages full of all the remedies tried by Amfortas for his wounds,—but the poem is pervaded not only by a lofty tone of thought and feeling, but by much grace, tenderness, and imagination, with touches of humour, and half-sarcastic, half-courtly allusions to the life and the writings of his own times.

But as dark days came over Germany, after the fall of the Hohenstauffens, the bloom of her knightly poetry faded, and another style, chiefly didactic or mystical, but of much lower poetic merit, took its place.

CHAPTER IV.

PERPLEXED and troubled indeed must have been many hearts in the trials that now fell on Germany. Frederick II., the last of the Hohenstauffens, a wise and brave prince, a patron of the large cities and of learning, and a successful crusader, died in 1250; and for twenty-three years Germany was without a settled head, until the choice of the princes devolved on Rudolph of Hapsburg. To a great extent every man did that which was right in his own eyes; and as there existed a numerous class of returned crusaders and unemployed soldiers, the smaller castles all over the country were soon transformed into robber-strong-holds, whose inhabitants lived by levying a sort of black-mail on the merchants and peasants whom they despised. The great cities alone were able to protect themselves; they purchased or assumed their freedom from the lords who still asserted manorial rights over them, and leagued together to defend it, forming the Swabian league in the South and the Hanseatic in the North; and from this time onwards we find them sending deputies to the diet, and recognised as an independent portion of the empire. Rudolph of Hapsburg did his best to restore order, and destroyed,

it is said, in Thuringia alone seventy of the robber-
castles, whose ruins still add to the picturesqueness of
that region of wooded hills and romantic glens. But
the twenty years of his reign were but an interval
of peace amid a succession of storms. During the
first half of the fourteenth century the distractions
of Germany reached their height. There were rival
emperors at home, rival popes abroad, and bitter
conflicts between the civil and ecclesiastical powers.
On the 25th November, 1314, two emperors, Frederick
of Austria and Louis of Bavaria, were crowned at once ;
and for eight years, until the battle of Mühldorff in
1322, a desolating warfare between their respective
partisans was carried on all over the country. While
the struggle lasted the Pope declined to pronounce
decisively in favour of either candidate, but was supposed to lean to the side of Louis of Bavaria. When,
however, Louis was left master of the field, the Pope
refused to acknowledge him, unless he consented in
the fullest terms, to hold the empire as a fief of the
Holy See. To this Louis would not accede, and he
was supported by the diet, who gave him their undi-
vided vote, and at last declared that the unanimous
choice of the country was the true source of the
imperial dignity, and sufficed to bestow it without
any consent of the Pope. The Pope now laid Germany under an interdict, which was not removed
from some districts for twenty-six years. During an
interdict all the ordinary ministrations of religion were
suspended ; no church was open, no bell was heard, no
sacrament but those of baptism and extreme unction
was administered. To these social and spiritual calamities were added, as is often the case in times of

political convulsion, natural ones. Germany was visited with earthquakes, plagues of grasshoppers or locusts, and bad harvests, in the train of which came that fearful pestilence known as the Black Death, which swept over Europe in the middle of this century, and the full extent of which we are only now beginning to appreciate. It passed over Germany in 1348, bringing the usual accompaniments of such terrible visitations, in lawlessness, outbursts of despair, and some scattered examples of heroic devotion. It was no wonder that men's minds grew unsettled. Some believed that the last times had come, and that the end of the world was at hand. Some looked for a Messiah in the person of the " Priest-hater," Frederick II., who was to rise from the dead, do justice, humble the clergy, and lay down his crown on the Mount of Olives. Some thought only of averting the wrath of God in the present, and so that strange epidemic of religious frenzy sprang up, which brought into all the highroads and market-places of Europe the ghastly processions of the Flagellants and the White Hoods. Hundreds of either sex wandered in bands from town to town, half-naked, or clothed in white shirts spotted with blood. On reaching a town they proceeded to the church, and after a service, if they could have one, formed into a circle, in which they paced round in pairs singing their wild chant :

> " Now raise your hands to God, and cry
> That this great death may pass us by :
> Now raise your arms to God, and call
> That He have mercy on us all."

They then adjured the crowd of spectators to imitate

their penance, and finally, casting themselves on the ground, scourged each other till they were weary. On their way from town to town they sang hymns and sequences in German, exhorting the people to repentance ; and it is certainly a fact that the use of hymns in the vernacular becomes much more common from this time onwards, no doubt partly from their being thus introduced into many parts hitherto unacquainted with them. The mode of life of these Flagellants, however, led in some cases to acts of license, which by degrees turned the popular feeling strongly against them, and so they vanish from our sight.

In such times as these it must have been difficult for men not to be either fanatics, like these poor Flagellants, or altogether indifferent to the religion which presented itself in such a shape as it wore then, when rival Popes disputed the Headship of Christendom, and the Papacy appeared as the enemy of civil authority and political liberty ; while the bishops and most of the richer monastic clergy lived lives of self-indulgence and worldly ambition. But, like the remnant in old days that had not bowed the knee to Baal, so now there grew up in various parts of the country a set of men who formed themselves into no sect, but who kept alive the flame of love and faith and hope in many hearts where it had else died out. The names best known to us (though many others are still preserved) are those of Eckhardt and Tauler, especially the latter, and in the next century the same tone of thought and piety meets us again in the works attributed to the more famous Thomas à Kempis. Tauler was a Dominican monk of Strasburg, a man of the deepest piety, and of great courage and ability, whose sermons were the delight of Luther, and are full of instruction to us now. The Dominicans and Franciscans had for some time availed themselves of the privilege early granted to their order of cele- brating mass during a time of interdict, and had thus earned themselves a high place in the popular favour; but after the open breach between the Emperor and the Pope in 1338, they too, in many instances, refused to say mass. Tauler was one of the few who steadily adhered to the national side; and, believing that the Pope himself had no right to deny the guidance and consolations of religion to the people, considered it his duty to disregard the inter- dict. Throughout this period, therefore, and espe- cially when the Black Death was raging, he laboured assiduously, not only in Strasburg, but in all the great cities along the Rhine to Cologne; and being a mighty preacher, he was followed by grateful crowds, his sermons were taken down by listening friends, and with his letters widely circulated over Germany.

Tauler and those who thought like him were called Mystics, because they spoke often of a mystical or hidden life of God in the soul, and the worthlessness of the creature and outward things. But though there is much in their phraseology and turn of thought which belongs to their age, and seems at first alien to us now, the real core of their faith, which made them of such help and use in their day and the beginners of a work that has lasted to our own, was their strong grasp of the truths, that an immediate and personal relation may and ought to exist between each individual soul and the living God; and that since God is absolute goodness, the highest welfare and happiness of His creatures must lie in the voluntary blending of their will with His. Outward helps had indeed failed these men utterly, and so they fell back on that which no outward privation could take away, the presence of God himself in the heart as the ground of all belief, and held this faith with an intense realization proportioned to the difficulties and discouragements around them. What seems to us morbid and exaggerated in their depreciation of all outward things, and sometimes even of the affections of ordinary life, was but the result, partly of their being thus thrown in so absolutely on their own consciousness, partly of their circumstances; and when all this is eliminated, there remain in their writing some of the truest piety, and of the deepest and wisest thoughts on the relation of God and Christ to the human soul, on the nature of sin and of salvation, that we can meet with anywhere.[1]

This school encouraged the study of the Scriptures, and the first complete German version of the Bible was made by Matthias of Beheim, as early as the fourteenth century. They also promoted both preaching and singing in German, and a large number of mystical and didactic poems were written by them. Tauler himself wrote several, which were widely known, and we give two of them :—

WHAT I MUST DO.

From outward creatures I must flee,
  And seek heart-oneness deep within,
If I would draw my soul to Thee,
  O God, and keep it pure from sin.

---

[1] The " Theologia Germania " was long attributed to Tauler, but was probably written by his friend and teacher, Nicholas of Basle.

The senses I must all control,
 If I the Highest Good would know :
For virtue strive with all my soul,
 If I would feel Love's living glow.

And I my hasty tongue must bind,
 Must straighten what it's said amiss,
If I true peace with God would find,
 Or ever hope to reach true bliss.

ONLY JESUS.

O Jesu Christ, most Good, most Fair,
More fragrant than May's flowery air,
Who Thee within his soul doth bear
 True cause for joy hath won !
But would one have Thee in his heart
From all self-will he must depart,
God's bidding only, where Thou art,
 Must evermore be done.
Where Jesus thus doth truly dwell,
His presence doth all tumults quell,
And transient cares of earth dispel
 Like mists before the sun.

He who despiseth vanity,
And dwells in free simplicity,
So Jesus in his heart may be,
 No vexing cares need know.
His comforter the Saviour is,
Sole Comfort of the comfortless ;
A cross unstained and bright is his
 Whose patience conquers woe.
Have inward oneness, Faith's clear sight
Bid all distracting forms take flight,
Gaze on Christ's image day and night,
 Then He is thine below.

Give place to nought that can misguide,
Be thine own self whate'er betide,
What is not thine cast thou aside,
  So shalt thou freely stand.
From hasty judgment, oh refrain,
We weigh in balance false and vain;
Christ and His love seek thou amain
  In all that thou hast planned :
He who doth undertake too much,
The goal of Truth will rarely touch;
A ship o'erdone with sail is such,
  That scarce shall reach the land.

But he who this world's solace leaves,
Whose heart to God in secret cleaves,
And all things as from Him receives,
  Shall find his griefs are o'er;
He who hath conquered in the fight,
Serves Christ alone with all his might,
And follows where Christ leads aright,
  Hath a bright crown in store.
God help us then to reach that bliss
Christ hath prepared above for His !
Thee, Triune God, we praise and bless,
  Oh help us evermore !

During the remainder of this century and the next,
the political and social conditions of Germany became
more tranquil as the constitution of the empire
became more fixed.   In the cities especially life
grew settled and sheltered ; it crystallized indeed
into very rigid forms, in their internal polities and
in the guilds which governed that large part of life
occupied by industrial interests ; even the domain of
private life was invaded by the sumptuary laws which

regulated the dress and the table of each class, but were probably never very strictly obeyed. But the sense of being a member of an important and politically free community made up for the loss of much of that personal liberty of action which the Teutonic race had so highly valued ; and the activity of mind produced by constant association with their fellow-men, rendered the citizens now the great patrons of art and letters. Town schools became usual, and before the end of the fifteenth century as many as eight great universities had been founded. And so, too, poetry now passed into their hands from those of the knightly order. It did not at first profit by the change. It was enrolled among the crafts of which the guilds had the control, schools for verse and song-making were set up, and the Minne-singers were succeeded by the Master-singers. For the most part it was but poor mechanical work that they turned out, generally moral and didactic, often directly religious in tone, but very prosaic in quality. Yet there must have been a great deal of reading and reciting of this poetry such as it was, for the Master-singers are counted by hundreds, and their verses by thousands. By far the best of them are the first and last (of any note) in their ranks,—Heinrich Frauenlob and Hans Sachs. The latter belongs to the period of the Reformation, and marks the transition to modern thought ; the former (1250—1318) belongs to the close of the crusading age, and marks the transition of poetry from the knightly to the burgher order. In spirit and form he belongs to the Minne-singers, and is frequently counted among them ; he is reckoned

among the Master-singers because he was the first
to found a sort of guild of poets. He was a very
voluminous writer, greatly admired in his own day,
and from his constant praise of women won for
himself the title of Frauenlob (Praise-the-ladies),
and the honour of being borne to his grave by them.
A very large proportion of his poems are love-songs,
but there are many more serious; many prayers and
pious reflections, many lamentations over the degeneracy of the times, and praises of Brother Berthold, a
famous Franciscan preacher, who travelled about the
country, heard gladly by the common people, and
was a sort of forerunner of Tauler. From his religious poems we choose two, one evidently written
when he was fighting with the fear of death; the
other expressing the confidence that helped him
through it. In style Frauenlob is graceful and
fluent, but often too prolix and elaborate. The
mode in which the following is rhymed is an instance
of his love of an intricate arrangement of rhymes.

DEATH WILL CONQUER.

My joy is wholly banished,
Now listen to my sad complaint :
The sins of days departed
Weigh on me sore and I wax faint,
For they are many well I know,
And now dark Death will bring me all to nought.
My life will soon have vanished,
For bitter Death my end hath sworn,
My gifts, my prayers sad-hearted,
On him they are but all forlorn,
When once he bids me with him go :
Ah woful prospect with sore sorrow fraught !

Now nought avails a generous mind,
Nor skill, nor art, nor aught of pride,
Nor that all dames to me were kind :
All gifts and powers of heart and sense
That once were mine are lost to me ;
I must seek other company,
Death is my fellow, and he drives me hence.

Grim Death the end is bringing
Of joy to this poor heart in me ;
Ah sorely doth he grieve it !
O Lord my God, I cry to Thee,
Receive my soul for pity's sake ;
My body to the earth and worms I give.
My lovely art, my singing,
Grows dim within my bosom's shrine;
To whom shall I now leave it ?
Ah God, it will no more be mine !
'Twas Thou didst give it, who dost take.
Grant me Thy mercy now while yet I live!
Yes, I have done with sweetest song,
This is the last, my sad complaint,
Death comes and brings a silence long :
Then list to me, my fellows all,
Women and men alike, I mean,
None can say aught 'gainst this, I ween,
See that from righteousness ye never fall.

O Mary, Mother purest,
Now through the death of thy dear Son
Remember all thy kindness,
And all that He for us hath won
Upon the cross, where once was seen
A sharp spear bent against His holy side.
Lord Christ ! Thou this endurest
And yet Thou canst the Jew forgive,
For it was done in blindness !

Pray Thou for me too then, while yet I live,
Thou wilt be not less good to me, I ween;
Show Thy dear grace to me at this sad tide.
Farewell to all that glads mine eyes !
Now, Death, dost thou thy work begin ;
Lend me, ye friends, your tears and sighs,
And be not Frauenlob forgot,
Whom Death, alas ! hath conquered here !
Ah God, my latest hour is near,——
Courage, my heart, and go : 'tis but the common lot !

NO MORE DESPAIR.

Now will I nevermore despair of heaven,
Since it is Thine, my Father, who hast given
Thy glorious kingdom to the poor indeed.
Yea, mighty God, since Father is Thy name,
Christ for my brother I may dare to claim,
And He for all my sins will help me plead.
A brother's truth to us He swore
When on Himself He took humanity,
For us alone that form He wore,
For us alone hung high upon the Tree.
Look in what cruel sorrows there He pined !
Dear Lord, I bid thee call those woes to mind,
And, brother-like, entreat Thy Father, who is mine,
To give me, too, my lot in that blest heritage of Thine.

It was at this time that dramatic poetry made its
appearance in Germany; and just as lyrical and
narrative poetry had first been awakened to life by
the religious sentiment which thus made for itself a
voice, so our earliest examples of this style also
are religious—the mystery and morality plays. It
is curious that the first beginning of the drama should

be in a convent, and the work of a nun, a certain Hros-
vitha, who lived in the Abbey of Gandersheim, about
980. Her works, however, hardly concern our subject,
as they were written in Latin, though one of them was
afterwards translated into German for performance ;
and we do not encounter any further dramatic attempts till we reach the thirteenth and fourteenth
centuries, when we meet with mysteries on the life
of our Lord. No doubt these took their rise in the
wish to set vividly before the people the chief in-
cidents of Scripture history, and the mode of doing
so is by some thought to have been derived from
the symbolical games which ushered in the spring,
or from the processions of returning crusaders, who
often re-entered their homes in quaint and symbolical
array. The Passion and Resurrection and the
Lamentation of the Virgin form the subjects of the
earliest mysteries, and to these ere long were added
similar representations of scenes from the infancy of
the Saviour, which were performed about Twelfth
Night. At first they were written partly in Latin
and partly in German, and a considerable portion
consisted of action unaccompanied by words, while
other parts were sung, not recited, but gradually
the German element preponderates and the Latin
disappears. Scenes from the Old Testament or the
Apocrypha, which were held to typify events in our
Lord's life, were introduced between the acts of the
principal drama, and from the necessity of compression
were generally given in a more vigorous and dramatic
form than the original piece itself, which is often
extremely prolix. The stories of Joseph and
Samson, of David and Goliath, of Esther, of Susannah

and the Elders, were the favourite subjects of these *entr'actes*. Next the comic element found its way into these pieces, especially into those which were performed about Twelfth Night, a time of merry-making and often of licence. The first example of it, however, that is now extant, is in an Easter mystery of the fifteenth century, where the merchant who sells precious ointment, first to Mary Magdalene, and afterwards to the three Maries on their way to the grave, quarrels with his servant and his wife, and ends with striking the latter, who repays him by a sound rating. This element of grotesque fun afterwards became much more developed, but it never in Germany attained anything like the proportions that it assumed in France and Italy. On the whole the representation of these dramas was a serious, and in its way a religious, act. A city or a village, or perhaps some great guild, or the students of a university, undertook to give one of these mysteries. The performance, in the summer, frequently took place out of doors, in the winter, in the church or the guild-hall; it often lasted for more than one day, and people came to see it from far and near. The performers who personated such characters as those of our Lord, His mother, or His disciples, were expected to prepare themselves by religious acts for their work, and to abstain from all licence while it was in progress. Of course a more secular tendency gradually showed itself; still on the whole the drama was a plant of very late growth in Germany, and it was long before it attained as much importance in its purely secular shape as it possessed in the Middle Ages in its religious form. The mystery has never quite died out there ; many of us are probably aware that once in ten years a genuine ancient mystery is still performed in a little village of the Bavarian Tyrol.

Another style of poetry sprang up in these centuries which had the most genuine life in it of any type that we have yet met with, and that has continued characteristic of the German people to this day. It is that of the "Volkslied," or popular song, and in these far-back days it holds somewhat the same place in German literature that the ballad does in our own. The narrative form of the ballad seems to have been less congenial to the German mind than to the English. We find, indeed, some poems on contemporary events—like that on the Battle of Sempach, by Halbsuten—but they are wanting in the life, terseness, and swing of the ballad. The German popular song, on the other hand, even in its rudest days, is full of freshness and vigour, often of sweetness and pathos, though lax and unpolished in form and marked by abrupt transitions and quaint similes. But it has the true breath of the people's life in it, which it deals with in its most varied forms—in songs of love, of dancing, of drinking, of wandering and parting, of spinning and weaving, and of the huntsman's and forester's crafts, which are some of the best of all. It furnished the type that, in Luther's hands, was refined and strengthened into the congregational hymn which became so powerful an instrument in the spread of the reformed religion ; and at this period the best of its sacred poems are those which more or less partake of this character.

It was natural that poetry of this simple and direct

style should concern itself more with the great facts of the Christian faith than with the minor phases of spiritual experience; and, accordingly, we find most of the poems of this kind are composed for one or other of the chief festivals of the Church. That of Christmas was an especial favourite with the warm-hearted, child-loving Germans, and for it Tauler wrote the following symbolical little poem, which soon became one of these popular songs :—

CHRISTMAS CAROL.

A ship comes sailing onwards
  With a precious freight on board;
It bears the only Son of God,
  It bears the Eternal Word.

A precious freight it brings us,
  Glides gently on, yet fast;
Its sails are filled with Holy Love,
  The Spirit is its mast.

And now it casteth anchor,
  The ship hath touched the land;
God's Word hath taken flesh, the Son
  Among us men doth stand.

At Bethlehem, in the manger,
  He lies, a babe of days;
For us He gives Himself to death,
  O give Him thanks and praise.

Whoe'er would hope in gladness
  To kiss this Holy Child,
Must suffer many a pain and woe
  Patient like Him and mild;

Must die with Him to evil
And rise to righteousness,
That so with Christ he too may share
Eternal life and bliss.

Another Christmas carol of this date is the following on

THE ROSE OF SHARON.

A spotless Rose is blowing,
Sprung from a tender root,
Of ancient seers' foreshowing,
Of Jesse promised fruit;
Its fairest bud unfolds to light
Amid the cold, cold winter,
And in the dark midnight.

The Rose which I am singing,
Whereof Isaiah said,
Is from its sweet root springing
In Mary, purest Maid;
For through our God's great love and might
The Blessed Babe she bare us
In a cold, cold winter's night.

A favourite song, or we might almost call it a ballad
for Easter, was this one:—

THE THREE MARIES.

There went three damsels ere break of day,
To the Holy Grave they took their way;
They fain would anoint the Lord once more
As Mary Magdalene did before.   Alleluia.

The damsels each to other made moan,
" Who will roll us away the stone,
That we may enter in amain
To anoint the Lord as we are fain?"

Full precious spices and salve they brought,
But when they came to the spot they sought,
Behold the grave doth open stand,
An angel sitteth on either hand.

" Ye maidens, be not filled with fear,
He whom ye seek, He is not here ;
Behold the raiment white and fair
Which the Lord was wrapped in, lieth there.

" Ye maidens, do not here delay,
Ye must to Galilee away ;
To Galilee ye now must go,
For there the Lord Himself will show."

But Mary Magdalene could not depart,
Seeking the Lord, she wept apart ;
What saw she in a little while ?
She saw our Lord upon her smile.

In garb and wise He met her there
As were He a gardener, and did bear
A spade within His holy hand,
As would He dig the garden land.

" O tell me, gentle Gardener thou,
Where hast thou laid my Master now ?
Where thou hast hidden Him bid me know,
Or my heart must break beneath its woe."

Scarce could He speak a single word,
Ere she beheld it was the Lord ;
She kneeleth down on the cold bare stone,
She hath found her Lord and she alone.

" Touch me not, Mary Magdalene,
But tell the brethren what thou hast seen ;
Touch me not now with human hand,
Until I ascend to my Father's land."   Alleluia.

The Easter and Whitsuntide sequences which were
introduced in the previous period were now expanded
into longer hymns, of which many variations are still
preserved.   One of the best is this :—

AN OLD EASTER HYMN.

Rejoice, dear Christendom, to-day,
   For Christ hath overcome,
His bitter pains have passed away,
   And empty stands His tomb ;
   Those bitter pains had been our lot,
   If Christ for us had borne them not,
Great bliss hath risen on us to-day :
                 Alleluia.

O Easter Day, our voices ne'er
   Can praise thee fittingly,
Since God, whose power all things declare,
   Such glory puts on thee ;
   But let us keep thee as we can,
   Angels to-day rejoice with man,
When rose that Sun so wondrous fair :
                 Alleluia.

O Jesus Christ, our blessed Lord,
   We share Thy joy to-day !
All those who hear and keep Thy Word
   Are glad with Thee to-day !
   All Christian people now rejoice
   With freshened hearts and gladsome voice,
Glory to Thee our Blessed Lord :
                 Alleluia.

Praise to the Father and the Son,
   And to the Holy Ghost ;

For all the sins that we have done,
　To-day forgive us most ;
　And give us peace and unity,
　From now to all eternity,
So sing we as the ages run :

　　　　　　　　　Alleluia.

A sequence found about the same date is called in old manuscripts

THE COMMON MAN'S PROCESSIONAL.

So holy is this day of days
No man can fill its meed of praise,
　Since the Holy Son of God
Now hath conquered Death and Hell,
And bound the Devil who there doth dwell,
　So hath the Lord delivered Christendom ;
This was Christ Himself :

　　　　　　　　　Kyrie Eleison !

We have a testimony to the use of Easter hymns in church in the following poem by Conrad von Queinfurt, belonging to the fourteenth century (he died in 1382 in Silesia), which is quite in the style of the Minne-singers both in thought and the carefully varied metre.

EASTER SONG.

Fair Spring, thou dearest season of the year,
　Thou art brimful of sweet delights ;
The creatures robbed of joy by winter drear
　Thou dost repay for cold and gloomy nights.
　　I feel thy airs are soft and mild,
　　Thy winds are balmy and not wild,

O how unlike the wintry blast !
What Frost had bound in fetters fast,
   Now feels the prison-time gone by,
     For 'tis unbound and free ;
   Whether it climb or swim or fly,
     Whatever kind it be,
   Whether of water, earth, or sky,
     'Tis happy now we see.
The sun smiles with his lovely rays,
And sing, dear little birds, sing out your Maker's praise !

So many joys hath Spring, but most of all
   She hath one day above the rest,
That Christendom with one glad voice doth call
   Of all bright days the first and best.
   We hail thee, then, O chosen Day,
   With many a loud and gladsome lay,
   Thou art the day that God hath made,
   Well may our joy be now displayed !
     Thou art the Pascha to the Greek,
       And still we hear the Jew
     Of thee as Passover doth speak,
       And Latins know thee too
     As Transitus, that crowns the Holy Week ;
   But thou, where'er is heard the German tongue,
Art holy Easter-tide, when life from Death hath sprung.

We hail thee, blessed Day, we greet thee well,
   We praise thee ever, we adore
The Christ who triumphed over death and hell,
   Whose death slew Death for evermore.
     O sweetest day, that saw'st Thee rise,
     Our Paschal Lamb, our Sacrifice,
     Our Brother who hath won for us
     A heritage most glorious !

Forest and foliage, corn and grass and flowers,
   Would show their love to Thee !
The birds sing in the greening bowers,
   Christ, they are praising Thee !
Thou wouldst not lack, had they our powers,
   A song more worthy Thee !
For Thou art Conqueror, O Christ, to-day,
Who madest Death's great power itself give way.

    *   *   *   *   *   *

So Christians triumph as your heart desires ;
   In chorus sweet and clear and strong,
Ye laymen in the church, ye priests in choirs,
   Answer each other in your song.
     Sing, " Christ the Lord is risen again,
     Christ hath broken every chain."
   The year of jubilee He bringeth in,
   True freedom for all faithful hearts to win ;
     So to His table go thou solemnly,
       Where in His flesh and blood
     The Paschal Lamb itself is offered thee—
       The Lamb slain on the rood.
     Praise the true Christ with happy hearts and free,
     Praise Him, for He is good !
Thus, Spring, thou well may'st speak of joy to man,
Thou hast the Easter Day that ended Death's dark ban.

Many also of the popular songs were translated, if
one may so call it, into a religious form, often in the
most tasteless and absurd manner, but occasionally
with so much success, that the religious entirely super-
seded the secular version. This was the case with
the following little hymn, the idea of which was taken
from the song of a wandering artisan, that begins,
" Innsbruck, I must forsake thee." In its sacred

form, however, it speedily became very popular, and many other hymns were afterwards written on its simple and pathetic melody.

FAREWELL.

O World, I must forsake thee,
And far away betake me,
　To seek my native shore ;
So long I've dwelt in sadness
I wish not now for gladness,
　Earth's joys for me are o'er.

Sore is my grief and lonely,
And I can tell it only
　To Thee, my Friend most sure !
God, let Thy hand uphold me,
Thy pitying heart enfold me,
　For else I am most poor.

My Refuge where I hide me,
From Thee shall nought divide me,
　No pain, no poverty :
Nought is too bad to bear it,
If Thou art there to share it ;
　My heart asks only Thee.

Henry of Loufenburg, who was a priest at Freiburg, and afterwards a monk in the convent of St. John in Strasburg, was the chief sacred poet of the fifteenth century in Germany, and furnished a large number of these transformations of secular into religious songs, and he also translated many of the great Latin hymns. He was himself a fertile composer, and some of his hymns are very graceful and sweet, but many

are prolix and fantastic ; and though they seem to
have been liked in the religious world of his own
day, they scarcely bear transplanting to ours.   One
of the best is

HOME-SICKNESS.

I would I were at last at home,
And all earth's trials overcome :

At home in that calm, happy place
Where I shall see God face to face !

Then thither, Heart, for refuge flee,
Where angel-hosts are waiting thee.

If earth for thee be only gloom,
Thou wilt but get the sooner home.

At home is Life that never dies,
And perfect joy unmixed with sighs ;

And perfect health, untouched by pain,
That perfect ever shall remain.

A thousand years are as a day,
For weariness hath there no sway.

Rise thither, heart and soul of mine,
And seek that blessedness divine.

The treasure that is stored not there
Will only bring thee woe and care.

Thou hast no resting-place below,
To-day, to-morrow, thou may'st go.

Then since it may not other be,
From earth's deluding phantoms flee :

Repent thy sins, prepare for home,
To-morrow may the Voice say, Come.

Farewell, O World, now home I fare ;
God guide all true hearts safely there !

Another tenderly-conceived little poem of his is this :—

CRADLE SONG.

Ah Jesu Christ, my Lord most dear,
As Thou wast once an infant here,
So give this little child, I pray,
Thy grace and blessing day by day :
  Ah Jesu, Lord Divine,
  Guard me this babe of mine !

Since in Thy heavenly kingdom, Lord,
All things obey Thy lightest word,
Do Thou Thy mighty succour give,
And shield my child by morn and eve :
  Ah Jesu, Lord Divine,
  Guard Thou this babe of mine !

Thy watch let angels round it keep
Where'er it be, awake, asleep ;
Thy holy Cross now let it bear
That it Thy Crown with saints may wear :
  Ah Jesu, Lord Divine,
  Guard Thou this babe of mine !

Now sleep, O sleep, my little child,
Jesus will be thy playmate mild ;
Sweet dreams He sendeth thee, I trow,
That full of goodness thou may'st grow :
  Ah Jesu, Lord Divine,
  Guard me this babe of mine !

So He who hath all love and might,
Bids thee good-morrow and good-night.
Blest in His name thou daily art,
My child, thou darling of my heart :
  Ah Jesu, Lord Divine,
  Guard me this babe of mine !

Henry of Loufenburg also wrote and widely introduced the use of many hymns in mixed Latin and German. Verses of this kind had long been a favourite amusement among the monks, and they seem now to have acquired a general popularity. The best-known of them all was a Christmas carol dating from the fourteenth century, which is found in many various versions, and of which the following is an imitation :—

CAROL.

In dulci Jubilo　　　　　　*In sweet joy*
Sing and shout all below !
He for whom we're pining
Lies *in præsepio ;*　　　　　*In a manger ;*
Like the sun is shining
Matris in gremio.　　　　　*In His mother's lap.*
Qui est A et O.　　　　　*Who is Alpha and Omega.*
Qui est A et O.

O Jesu parvule,　　　　　　*O infant Jesus,*
How my heart longs for thee !
Soothe the sad and ailing,
O Puer optime,　　　　　　*Child most excellent,*
With Thy love unfailing !
O Princeps gloriæ,　　　　　*O Prince of glory,*
Trahe me post Te,　　　　　*Draw me after Thee !*
Trahe me post Te !

Mater et filia,　　　　　　*Mother and daughter,*
O Mary, virgin aye,
Hadst thou not gained for us
Cælorum gaudia,　　　　　*The joys of heaven,*
Death still had reigned o'er us
Per nostra crimina.　　　　*For our sins.*
Quanta gratia !　　　　　　*How great the grace !*
Quanta gratia !

Ubi sunt gaudia ?	*Where are those joys ?*
Only there where alway	
Stand the angels singing	
Nova cantica,	*New songs,*
Their sweet voices ringing	
In regis curia.	*In the King's court.*
Would we were there to-day !	
Would we were there to-day !	

This latter class of mixed hymns has been commonly, but erroneously, attributed to Peter Dresdensis, who died in 1440, as rector of Zwickau. His real work with regard to hymnology lay in the strenuous efforts he made to introduce hymns in the vernacular more freely into public worship, especially into the service of the mass. No doubt he had been led to this by his acquaintance with Huss, whose assistant he had been at Prague. It was in 1467 that the followers of Huss formed themselves into a separate and organized Church, known as that of the Bohemian and Moravian Brethren, one of the distinctive peculiarities of which was the free use of hymns and prayers in their mother tongue. Many such hymns were already in existence, and others were soon written, and in 1504 they were collected and published by their archbishop, Lucas—the first example of a hymn-book composed of original compositions in the vernacular to be found in any Western nation which had once owned the supremacy of Rome. Somewhat earlier than this book, however, towards the end of the fifteenth century, we find two or three collections of German versions of the Latin hymns and sequences. For the most part they are of such inferior merit that they quite lose the grandeur of the original, and so we need not linger over them.

But there is one large class of sacred poems very characteristic of the mediæval period, which has not yet been mentioned—the poems addressed to saints, and, above all, to the Virgin Mary. The former class is not very important, either as to number or quality; but not so the latter. "Marien-lieder," and, in a minor degree, "Annen-lieder," hymns to St. Mary and to St. Anne, constitute a very large and well-known class among the poems of the ante-Reformation times in Germany. It is in the age of the Crusades and the Minne-singers that they first assume a prominent place in its literature. The intercourse of Christians with Saracens tended to intensify the devotion paid to the Virgin, just because such a sentiment towards a woman was a most distinctive peculiarity of the Christian mind. Again, the chivalry which òwed so much to the Christian idea of womanhood, had in its turn a reflex action on religious thought, favourable to the worship of a feminine ideal. The hymns addressed to the Virgin at this time form a sort of spiritual counterpart to the minne-songs or love-songs addressed to his earthly lady by the knight. It was easy to transfer the turn of expression and tone of thought from the earthly object to the heavenly one, and the degree to which this is done is to us often very startling. After this period, for a while these poems become less frequent, but in the fifteenth century they revive in the most extra-vagant forms. The honours and titles belonging to our Lord Jesus Christ are attributed to His mother; God is said to have created the world by her and to have rested in her on the seventh day ; she is said to have risen from the grave on the third day and ascended into heaven ; she is addressed, not only as a persuasive mediator with her Son, but as herself the chief source of mercy and help, especially in the hour of death and at the day of judgment. By degrees, her mother is invested with some of her own attributes; for it is said, if Christ would obey His own mother, ought not she much more to obey hers ? And so a set of hymns to St. Anne sprung up, in which she is entreated to afford aid in death, and obtain pardon for the sinners from Christ and Mary, who will refuse her nothing. Some of the earlier hymns to the Virgin, especially those on her lamentation beneath the cross, are very sweet and touching ; but the greater number of such as we have now been speaking of have not much poetical merit. They are often mere lists of titles, or word-play on her name or on the relation of the words "Ave" and "Eva." As Wackernagel says, "The existence of so many godless hymns addressed to the Virgin and the saints, or teaching the whole doctrine of indulgences, is a perfectly irrefragable testimony to that degeneracy of the nation which rendered the Reformation necessary; the existence of so many breathing an unstained Christianity is a witness to the preservation of so much true religion as made the Reformation possible."

H

CHAPTER V.

THE opening of the sixteenth century marks the commencement of one of the great transitional eras of history, and its changes were not in one direction only. Men's horizon on the physical earth had been suddenly widened by the discovery of a new world ; their mental horizon by the re-discovery of an old one, in the revival of letters consequent on the fall of Constantinople and the invention of printing. An intellectual eagerness and a trust in the unbounded possibilities of the future had taken possession of their minds, and they were not likely to be satisfied with such a present as they saw around them. It was for the schools and universities that reformers first sprung up in Erasmus and Reuchlin ; then, almost at the same time, an Ulrich von Hutten began to call on his countrymen to feel and to assert their national unity and their ancient rights against Italian priests and Spanish mercenaries, and to reform their own lives. His vigorous appeals, expressed, not in Latin, but in clear and trenchant German, made themselves heard by all classes, and helped to pave the way for the reformation that was coming. The following

Ulrich von Hutten.—P. 98.

poem, written when he had been forced to seek an asylum in the castle of his friend Franz von Sickingen, was ere long circulated all over the country on broadsheets, and became a favourite song of the earliest adherents of the Reformation.

ULRICH VON HUTTEN'S SONG.

I've ventured[1] it of purpose free,
　Nor yet my deed I rue ;
I may not win, but men will see
　My heart and life were true.
'Tis not my own I seek alone,
　This they must know at least ;
'Tis good of all, though me they call
　A foe to Church and priest.

But I will let them spread their lies
　And chatter as they will ;
If I would but the truth disguise,
　And tongue and pen keep still,
Flatterers enow were mine, I trow,
　Now I'm a banished man ;
Yet think not I afar to fly,
　Time yet may change the ban.

But nought of pardon will I pray,
　For nought of guilt I own ;
I would have bowed to Justice' sway,
　Here Passion reigns alone,
Nor grants my cause by ancient laws
　A hearing fair and free ;—
But God ordains and need constrains
　That thus they deal with me.

" Ich habs gewagt," " I have ventured it," was Hutten's motto.

H 2

Yet oft ere now it hath been seen
    When rich men felt secure,
They yet have lost the game, I ween,
    They deemed their own full sure.
A mighty flame from sparks oft came ;
    Who knows, my turn may come ?
I've played my stake, the risk I'll take,
    And here abide my doom.

And 'midst it all my solace is
    A conscience void of spot ;
My direst foes must grant me this,
    My honour hath no blot.
For there is nought I've said or sought,
    But it doth well appear,
That all was done before the sun
    In honour bright and clear.

Now if my nation's gallant youth
    Will not my warning take,
And bravely stand for Right and Truth,
    It grieves me for her sake,
I must depart, with heavy heart ;
    Yet deem not all is o'er,
Come foul or fair I'll not despair,
    But mix the cards once more.

No courtiers' crafts shall me affright,
    Though deep the game they've played ;
An honest heart that loves the Right
    Can never be dismayed.
Full many a name will join the game,
    Nor life nor wealth will cherish ;
Up ! burghers grave, and horsemen brave,
    And let not Hutten perish !

But a far deeper ground of dissatisfaction lay behind than any discontent with the education or politics of the time ; religion, which touches the life of all classes in its inmost springs, had fallen into a deep degeneracy. If the common man had a hard life of it in this world, compelled to incessant toil, subject to pestilence, bad harvests, and the exactions of his superiors, what was there to raise him above his troubles or give him hope for the future? That conception of an inward self-surrender to God which He would inspire, and to which He Himself would respond by His helping presence now, and heaven hereafter—the conception which had been the very kernel of religion to Tauler and his school—was preserved but in few hearts. To most men, religion was an outside thing of rules and ceremonies ; God was a harsh judge, whom all the sacrifices and merits of the saints could scarce propitiate ; while their appointed instructors, the clergy, were in popular estimation the very types of a proud, idle, often sinful life, led at the expense of other people. Once the clergy had been the preservers of learning, the protectors of the common people, and the assertors of justice against oppressive custom ; now their luxury, their ignorance in many cases, their avarice, and their often impure lives, were the favourite themes of the satirical poems, which are the most important productions of the secular literature of this period.[1] The way in which such men adapted the consolations of religion to the wants of the common people, shows a state of mind which it is very difficult for us to realize at all. Pious brotherhoods were

[1] This is the era of "Renard the Fox," "Till Eulenspiegel," Brant's "Ship of Fools." and the poems of Rosenblüt.

formed for accumulating a stock of spiritual treasures, the benefits of which were to secure to each member eternal salvation. Thus, for instance,[1] that of the Eleven Thousand Virgins, called St. Ursula's Ship, to which the Elector Frederick the Wise belonged, had a stock of 6,455 masses, 3,550 whole psalters, 200,000 rosaries, 11,000 prayers to St. Ursula, 630 times 11,000 Paternosters and Ave Marias, &c. &c. &c. All these were available to wipe out the sins of the individual members of the brotherhood. But in one respect this association was one of the best : a man could become a member by the mere repeating of a certain number of prayers, and it was therefore open to the poor ; where payment of money was required, as was frequently the case, of course the poor man was excluded.

It is easy to understand how in a country where such societies already existed, Tetzel, the German Dominican, to whom Leo X. had confided the sale of indulgences in Germany, should have found there a good market for his wares. He rode from town to town, everywhere received with great pomp and ceremony by the clergy. His great red cross was set up in the nave of the parish church, and day by day he preached and exhorted the people not to lose such an opportunity of securing heaven, resorting often to the coarsest and most profane expressions and devices. On his way he came to a village near Wittenberg, where the sale of indulgences was to begin on All Saints Day, the festival of the dedication of the church ; but the night before, another monk of the Augustine order had affixed to the church-doors his famous

[1] Freytag, " Bilder aus der deutschen Vergangenheit," vol. i. p. 90.

" Ninety-five theses on the power of indulgences," and henceforward their sale was to be checked.

Luther, born in 1483 in the village of Eisleben, sprang from the people, for he was the son of a pious and honest, but stern peasant. He had known want and hardships in childhood, and terrible mental conflicts in later years. One of these drove him into a monastery, and there they did not cease. " Of a truth I was a pious monk, and kept the rule of my order more strictly than I can tell. If ever a monk got to heaven by monkery, I was determined to get there. I strained myself to the very utmost, and tormented and plagued my body with fastings, vigils, prayers, and other exercises, far more than my bitterest enemies can torment me now. I, and others too, have toiled to the utmost, with a deadly sincerity, to bring our hearts and consciences to rest and peace before God, and yet could never find that same peace amid such horrible darkness." " For I knew Christ no more, save as a severe judge, from whom I sought to escape, and yet could not." In this distress of mind he was comforted by an aged monk, who taught him that Christ was the atonement for all our sins, and that this was proclaimed by the Church in the Apostles' Creed, and directed him to the study of the Epistle to the Romans.

From this time he was a zealous preacher and professor of theology, and he had always been an earnest Romanist. Even his visit to Rome in 1510, though he had been greatly shocked at the infidelity and immorality he met there, had not led him to think for a moment of such a thing as setting himself in opposition to the Papal authority. Nothing short of seeing that the authorities of the Roman Church in that day countenanced a practice so clearly contrary to the Gospel, and ruinous to men's souls, as this sale of indulgences, could have moved him to take a step of such tremendous import. Many years afterwards he said, "I entered on this affair with great fear and trembling. I was alone, and had entangled myself in the contest without forethought, and on many and weighty points I gave way to the Pope ; not only because I could not draw back, but because I sincerely and earnestly worshipped him from the bottom of my soul . . . . How and what my heart suffered and underwent in those first two years, and in what a sense of unworthiness (not false and affected, but true and sincere), nay, in what sheer despair I was plunged, is little conceived by those who have since assailed the Pope's majesty with great pride and arrogance. But I, alone in the breach, was none so joyous and sure of my cause."

It was in 1517 that he published his Theses, and during the next three years, while engaged in disputes with Cajetan and Eck, he wrote and brought out several of his most important works, among them his Commentary on the Galatians, his Address to the Christian Nobles of Germany, and his sermon on the Liberty of a Christian Man. In 1520 came his open breach with the Pope, when he burnt the Papal bull of excommunication. Then followed his appearance before the Diet of Worms in 1521 ; his concealment on the Wartburg, and return to Wittenberg in 1522 ; his marriage in 1525 ; and his life at Wittenberg, until the year 1546, when he died on a journey, at Eisleben, at the age of sixty-three.

Luther was a true representative of the German people, in the depth and force and honesty of his nature, in his keenness of intellect and his occasional coarseness, in his love of art and humour and domestic life. Hence all he said and did was caught up by the people with an enthusiasm which can scarcely be conceived. " His Theses flew over Germany," says a contemporary, Myconius, " as if the angels of God had been his messengers, and carried them to all men's eyes." The works that so quickly followed them, seemed to utter the very words for which men's souls were thirsting. His great doctrine of justification by faith in Jesus Christ, the one Mediator between God and man, gave peace to the conscience by delivering it from the burden of past sins, and a new spring of life to the soul by showing men that their dependence was not on anything in themselves, no works of their own performance, but on the infinite love and mercy of God which He had manifested to all mankind in His Son. And again, his doctrine of the universal priesthood of all believers put a new spirit into the Church, by vindicating for every member of it his right and duty to offer for himself the sacrifice of praise and prayer, and to study for himself God's word in the Scriptures.

It was on the Wartburg that he began his translation of the Bible, the first part of which, the New Testament, was published in 1522, and the whole Bible in 1534. " In this work," says Grimm, "Luther has made use of his mother-tongue with such force, purity, and beauty, that his style, from its powerful influence on our whole language, must be considered to have been the germ and laid the basis of the modern high German language, from which, up to the present day, but few deviations have taken place, and those mostly to the detriment of its force and expressiveness." His next effort was to give the people the means of worshipping God in their own language. In 1523 he published a treatise "on the ordering of Divine Service in the Church;" and at Christmas 1525, service was celebrated in the parish church of Wittenberg according to this new German rendering of the mass. In 1526 came out a complete new German liturgy, and now was felt the want of German psalms and hymns to fill the place of the Latin hymns and sequences. Luther at once set to work to supply it. He was intensely fond of both music and poetry, and was himself a master of vigorous and simple German. What he thought of music may be seen from the preface to this work; and long before Shakespeare he had said, "He who despises music, as all fanatics do, will never be my friend." He would have all children taught to sing: "For I would fain see all arts, specially music, in the service of Him who has given and created them."

From this time onwards, throughout his life, he was an active reformer of church music and hymns, and enlisted in the same work the large circle of friends whom he gathered round him. At Wittenberg he kept open house, and many who came from a distance to see and consult with the great reformer, or poor students who came to attend his lectures, found a place at his table. After dinner, whether he dined at home or abroad, it was his custom to take a lute and sing and play for half an hour or more with his friends. In 1524 he invited Conrad Rupf, choir-master to the Elector of Saxony, and Johann Walther, then choir-master to Frederick the Wise at Jorgau, to live with him until the work of reforming and readapting the liturgy for popular use should be completed. With this "house-choir," as he calls it, he studied the old stores of church music, with which he had already a considerable acquaintance from his own education as a chorister, and selected those tunes which lent themselves best to their new purpose. A large number of chorales belonging to the old Latin hymns, others of German origin—whether sacred, or, in some cases, secular—were thus appropriated ; a still larger number of new tunes were composed. Luther himself composed several ;[1] among others, the splendid chorale to his own hymn, "A sure stronghold our God is He," and that to his Christmas carol, " From heaven above to earth I come." But it was in the composition of the hymns that his own chief work lay. " It is my intention," he writes to his friend Spalatin, " after the example of the prophets and the ancient fathers, to make German psalms for the people ; that is, spiritual songs, whereby the Word of God may be kept alive among them by singing. We seek, therefore, everywhere for poets. Now, as you are such a master of the German tongue, and are so mighty and eloquent therein, I entreat you to join hands with us in this work, and to turn one of the psalms into a hymn, according to the pattern (*i.e.* an attempt of my own) that I here send you. But I desire that all new-fangled words from the Court should be left out ; that the words may be all quite plain and common, such as the common

---

[1] He is the undisputed author of three chorales, and about fifteen may in all probability be ascribed to him.

people may understand, yet pure, and skilfully handled ; and next, that the meaning should be given clearly and graciously, according to the sense of the psalm itself." Luther himself had recourse to this most ancient treasury of sacred song, and wrote versions of various psalms, choosing them, as we may observe, from their adaptation to his own circumstances and feelings. He also translated afresh many of the Latin hymns, which he counted among the good things that God's power and wonderful working had kept alive amid so much corruption, and gave new versions of several of the early German hymns.

Altogether he wrote certainly thirty-seven hymns. More are frequently ascribed to him, but with doubtful accuracy. Of these, twelve were translations from the Latin, and four were new renderings of the old German *Leisen ;* the remainder were purely original compositions. The intention with which they were written is clearly enough to be discerned. They were not so much outpourings of the individual soul, as the voice of the congregation meant for use in public worship, or to give the people a short, clear confession of faith, easily to be remembered. But they are not written from the outside ; Luther throws into them all his own fervent faith and deep devotion. The style is plain, often rugged and quaint, but genuinely popular. So, too, was their cheerful trust and noble courage ; their clear, vigorous spirit, that sprang from steadfast faith in a Redeemer. All the many conflicts, inward and outward, of Luther's life, had only deepened his experience ; they had by no means damped his courage or his power of enjoyment. Since he himself had once found peace in Christ,

and could trust in God, he was at leisure to feel all
the delightfulness of music, of children, of birds and
flowers, of the society of pleasant friends; he had,
too, a strong sense of humour, which, in his polemical
writings, shows itself in very downright, and often
coarse forms, but which gives a peculiar raciness and
life to his letters and sayings.

In the years when he was composing most of
his hymns, four printers in Erfurt alone were entirely
occupied in printing and publishing them. Nor could
they be prevented from penetrating where his printed
works were carefully excluded; they were carried
over the country by wandering students and pedlars,
and here and there found their way even into Roman
Catholic churches. "The whole people," writes a
Romanist of that day, "is singing itself into this
Lutheran doctrine." Collections of hymns sprang up
at this time with astounding rapidity, and in several
of these Luther took part. The four principal ones,
which have prefaces written by him, and contain most
of his hymns, passed through many editions, and are
known by the names of their printers.[1] Of these, the
earliest, the "Énchiridion," published at Erfurt in
1524, was at first placed in the people's hands for
reading while the choir were singing, for the congregation was so unused to joining in the public
service, that they could not at once adopt the new
practice. It was some four or five years before
Luther taught the people in his own parish church of
Wittenberg to sing in church, but then the custom
spread very swiftly.

[1] They are the "Erfurter Enchiridion," the hymn-book of Johann
Walther, that of Joseph Klug, and that of Valentin Babst.

The best known of all Luther's hymns is that founded on the forty-sixth Psalm, which has been already mentioned. It is supposed to have been written on his way to the Diet of Worms, from the coincidence of the third verse with Luther's answer to Spalatin, who tried to dissuade him from the journey: " If there were as many devils in Worms as there are tiles on the roofs, I would go, and would not be afraid. If Huss was burnt to ashes, the truth was not burnt with him." Some, however, think that it was composed at the close of the Second Diet of Spires—that in 1529, which revoked the religious liberty granted in the previous one of 1526, and against which five sovereign princes and fifteen free cities *protested*, and so earned the name of *Protestants*, a title which is, however, very rarely used in Germany, as " Evangelical" is the word used there in contradistinction to Roman Catholic.

THE STRONGHOLD.

A sure stronghold our God is He,
    A trusty shield and weapon ;
Our help He'll be, and set us free,
    Whatever ill may happen.
        That old malicious foe
        Intends us deadly woe ;
        Armed with the strength of hell,
        And deepest craft as well,
On earth is not his fellow.

Through our own force we nothing can,
    Straight were we lost for ever,
But for us fights the proper Man,
    By God sent to deliver.

Ask ye who this may be?
Christ Jesus named is He,
Of Sabaoth the Lord,
Sole God to be adored,
'Tis He must win the battle.

And were the world with devils filled
  All eager to devour us,
Our souls to fear should little yield,
  They cannot overpower us.
      Their dreaded Prince no more
      Can harm us as of yore;
      Look grim as e'er he may,
      Doomed is his ancient sway;
A word can overthrow him.

Still shall they leave that Word its might,
  And yet no thanks shall merit;
Still is He with us in the fight
  By His good gifts and Spirit.
      E'en should they take our life,
      Goods, honour, children, wife,
      Though all of these were gone,
      Yet nothing have they won—
God's kingdom ours abideth!

Still more popular in its own day was the second
hymn that Luther ever wrote; no doubt from its containing in short compass a complete epitome, at once
of the reformed doctrine of salvation, and of the
actual experience of those who had passed through
the same conflicts as Luther himself. An eye-witness
of the Reformation says: "Who doubts not that
many hundred Christians have been brought to the
true faith by this one hymn alone, who before, perchance, could not so much as bear to hear Luther's

name. But his sweet and noble words have so taken their hearts that they were constrained to come to the truth." A curious use was made of it in the year 1557, when a number of princes belonging to the reformed religion being assembled at Frankfort, they wished to have an evangelical service in the church of St. Bartholomew. A large congregation assembled, but the pulpit was occupied by a Roman Catholic priest, who proceeded to preach according to his own views. After listening for some time in indignant silence the whole congregation rose and began to sing this hymn, till they fairly sang the priest out of church. Its tune is that known in England as Luther's Hymn, and tradition says that Luther noted it down from the singing of a travelling artisan. Luther's own title to it is—

A THANKSGIVING FOR THE HIGHEST BENEFITS WHICH GOD HAS SHOWN US IN CHRIST.

Dear Christian people, now rejoice !
　　Our hearts within us leap,
While we, as with one soul and voice,
　　With love and gladness deep,
Tell how our God beheld our need,
And sing that sweet and wondrous deed,
　　That hath so dearly cost Him.

Captive to Satan once I lay,
　　In inner death forlorn ;
My sins oppressed me night and day,
　　Therein I had been born,
And deeper fell howe'er I strove ;
My life had neither joy nor love,
　　So sore had sin possessed me.

My good works could avail me nought,
   For they with sin were stained ;
My will against God's justice fought,
   And dead to good remained ;
My anguish drove me to despair,
For Death I knew was waiting there,
    And what but Hell was left me ?

Then God in His eternity
   Looked on my boundless woe,
His deep compassions flowed toward me,
   True succour to bestow :
His Father's heart did yearn and melt
To heal the bitter pains I felt,
    Though it should cost His dearest.

He spake to His beloved Son:
   " Go Thou, my heart's bright Crown,
The time for pity is begun,
   Go Thou in mercy down
To break for men Sin's heavy chain,
To end for them Death's hopeless reign,
    And give them life eternal."

The Son delighteth to obey,
   And born of virgin mother,
Awhile on this low earth did stay,
   And thus became my Brother ;
His mighty power He hidden bore,
A servant's form like mine He wore,
    My foe for me to vanquish.

To me He spake: " Hold fast by Me,
   And thou shalt conquer now ;
Myself I wholly give for thee,
   For thee I wrestle now ;

For I am with thee, thou art Mine,
Henceforth My place is also thine,
The foe shall never part us.

" I know that he will shed My blood,
And take My life away ;
But I will bear it for thy good,
Only believe alway ;
Death swallows up this life of Mine,
My innocence all sins of thine,
And so art thou delivered.

" And when I rise to heaven above,
Where is my Father's home,
I still will be Thy Lord in love,
And bid my Spirit come
To solace thee in every woe,
To teach thee Me aright to know,
And into Truth to guide thee.

" And even as I have done and said,
So shalt thou say and do,
That so God's kingdom may be spread,
And He have honour due ;
And this last counsel give I thee,
From men's additions keep thou free
The treasure I have left thee."

We add Luther's version of the Song of Simeon :—

NUNC DIMITTIS.

In peace and joy I now depart,
According to God's will ;
For full of comfort is my heart,
So calm and still.
So doth God His promise keep,
And death to me is but a sleep.

Justus Jonas.—P. 115

'Tis Christ has wrought this work for me ;
 Thy dear and only Son,
Whom Thou hast suffered me to see,
 And made Him known
As our Help when woes are rife,
And e'en in death itself our Life.

For Thou in mercy unto all
 Hast set this Saviour forth,
And to His kingdom Thou dost call
 The whole sad earth,
Through Thy blessed, wholesome Word,
That now in every place is heard.

He is the Hope, the Saving Light,
 That heathen nations need,
And those who know Thee not aright
 Will teach and lead ;
While His Israel's joy He is,
His people's glory, praise, and bliss.

Among the friends enlisted by Luther as writers for
the new hymn-books, the principal were Justus Jonas,
who was for many years his colleague in the professorship of theology at Wittenberg ; and Paul Eber,
who stood in a similar relation to Melancthon.
Melancthon himself wrote no hymns, for the one or
two often attributed to him are really passages from his
writings versified by friends.   His work lay in the
scholarship which produced what was long the standard
edition in Germany of the Greek Testament, and in
the theology that gave shape to the Confession of
Augsburg.   Justus Jonas was the son of the burgomaster of Nordhausen, a clever young lawyer, who
very early became professor of jurisprudence at Erfurt

and a friend of Erasmus and Luther. So close was his intimacy with the latter, that he accompanied him to Worms, an act for which he was deprived of his salary as professor. Luther then induced him to study divinity and take orders, and for many years the two men lived in constant association at Wittenberg; Justus Jonas accompanied his friend on his last journey, stood by his death-bed, and with many tears preached his funeral sermon. Luther's death was followed, as he had himself foretold, by troubles and strife. For six years (from 1546 to 1552) Germany was distracted by a civil war, of which the object was to obtain toleration for the reformed doctrine, an end achieved at last by Maurice of Saxony, in the treaty of Passau. Nor was this the only struggle that was going on. Differences of opinion on intricate theological questions had already begun to divide the Reformers themselves. Various sects arose, but the chief division was that between the followers of Luther who adhered to the Confession of Augsburg, and those of Zwinglius who adopted the more Calvinistic views of the Swiss reformers, with a lower sacramental theory. These called themselves distinctively the Reformed Church, while the Lutherans adopted the name of the Evangelical Church; but the latter were by far the most numerous body, and occupied in most States the position of the National Protestant Church of Germany, while the Reformed Church took up that of an important and tolerated sect. Justus Jonas, who was not merely a good theologian, but a skilful jurist, naturally had to take part in all the many discussions and conferences in which the evangelical doctrine gradually assumed definite form and consistency, and the legal and political rights of its adherents were ascertained and asserted ; and of course he had to bear his share of the difficulties in which he was thus involved. On one occasion a Spanish officer quartered in his house received a large bribe to assassinate him, but was so much impressed by the piety, integrity, and kindness of his intended victim, that he confessed his purpose to him, and entreated forgiveness. Yet on his deathbed this well-proved servant of Christ suffered much from mental doubts and conflicts, until at last peace returned, and he fell asleep " as a tired soldier." What he did for hymnology was to help Luther in preparing metrical German versions of the Psalms, choosing by preference, as one can well understand, those which speak of David's sufferings from his enemies, and his trust in God's deliverance. Some of these are very celebrated, especially the one here given :—

PSALM CXXIV.

If God were not upon our side
 When foes around us rage,
Were not Himself our Help and Guide
 When bitter war they wage,
Were He not Israel's mighty Shield,
To whom their utmost crafts must yield,
 We surely must have perished.

But now no human wit or might
 Should make us quail for fear,
God sitteth in the highest height,
 And makes their counsels clear ;

When craftiest snares and nets they lay,
God goes to work another way,
    And makes a path before us.

In wrathful pride they rage and mock
    Against our souls in vain:
As billows meet with angry shock
    Out on the stormy main,
So they our lives with fury seek ;
But God hath pity on the weak,
    And Him they have forgotten.

They call us heretics, and lie
    In wait to spill our blood ;
Yet flaunt their Christian name on high,
    And boast they worship God.
Ah God ! that precious name of Thine
O'er many a wicked deed must shine,
    But Thou wilt once avenge it.

They open wide their ravenous jaws
    To swallow us indeed,
But thanks to God, who rules our cause,
    They shall not yet succeed :
Their snares He yet will bring to nought,
And overthrow what they have taught ;
    God is too mighty for them.

How richly He consoleth those
    Who have no other friend !
The door of grace doth never close ;
    Sense cannot comprehend
How this may be, and deems all lost,
When through this very cross a host
    Of champions God is raising.

Paul Eber.—P. 119.

Our foes, O God, are in Thy hand,
　Thou knowest every plot ;
But only give us strength to stand,
　And let us waver not,
Though Reason strive with Faith, and still
She fear to wholly trust Thy will,
　　And sees not Thy salvation.

But heaven and earth, O Lord, are Thine,
　By Thee alone were made,
Then let Thy light upon us shine,
　O Thou our only aid !
Kindle our hearts to love and faith
That shall be steadfast e'en to death,
　　Howe'er the world may murmur !

As Justus Jonas had somewhat of Luther's talents
and frank courage, so Paul Eber was not unlike his
great friend Melancthon. He was the son of a poor
tailor, a small delicate child, whose love of books
induced his father to stint himself even in food, in
order to send the boy to the Grammar School of
Nuremberg, one of the first schools into which the
reformed doctrine had penetrated. Paul Eber at
once imbibed its spirit, and as soon as he was old
enough, went to Wittenberg to sit at Luther's feet.
Attracted by his thoughtfulness and purity of manners,
Luther invited him to his table, where he met Melancthon, and as the lad wrote a remarkably clear and
delicate hand, while Melancthon wrote a particularly
bad one, the latter took him for his amanuensis.
From this time they lived on terms of the closest
intimacy, so that Luther used to call him " Philip's
familiar," and " Philip's treasury." He became pro-

fessor of Hebrew at Wittenberg, and married a wife whom Melancthon chose for him, with whom he lived most happily. But in the theological disputes of those days he, like many others of Melancthon's special followers, was accused of concealed Calvinism, and bitterly attacked ; and finally, at the conference of Altenburg, in 1569, he was named among those who were excluded on this ground from the Lord's Table and the privilege of becoming sponsors. He went home in cold March weather, wounded to the heart by this intolerance ; his health gave way, and the death of his wife, which occurred unexpectedly about this time, was his own deathblow. He died in 1569.

Eber's hymns have a tone of tenderness and pathos about them, which is much less characteristic of this period than the grave, manly trustfulness of Luther and Jonas. But they soon became very widely known, and in the following age, that of the Thirty Years' War, few hymns were more constantly used both in public and private, than one of his beginning :—

> " When in the hour of utmost need
>   We know not where to look for aid,
>   When days and nights of anxious thought
>   Nor help nor comfort yet have brought ;
>   Then this our comfort is alone,
>   That we may meet before Thy throne,
>   And cry, O faithful God, to Thee,
>   For rescue from our misery."

This hymn was composed in 1547, when the Imperial armies were besieging Wittenberg, and Eber with two others were the only professors who remained in the university. Two of his hymns for the dying have been always very commonly used at deathbeds and funerals in the Roman Catholic as well as the Evangelical parts of Germany. The one is,[1] "Lord Jesus Christ, true Man and God;" the other is the following childlike expression of perfect trust :—

DEATH IN THE LORD.

I fall asleep in Jesu's arms,[2]
Sin washed away, hushed all alarms,
For His dear blood, His righteousness,
My jewels are, my glorious dress,
Wherein before my God I stand
When I shall reach the heavenly land.

With peace and joy I now depart,
God's child I am with all my heart ;
I thank thee, Death, thou leadest me
To that true life where I would be.
So cleansed by Christ I fear not Death,
Lord Jesu, strengthen Thou my faith !

---

[1] "Herr Jesu Christ, wahr Mensch und Gott."

[2] Literally, "I fall asleep in Jesu's *wounds*." Similar expressions are common in the mediæval hymns, and in some of the later Roman Catholic ones. In the Evangelical hymns they occur much less frequently, and chiefly among the earlier Moravians.

CHAPTER VI.

A.D. 1520—1600.

LUTHER and his immediate friends were only the founders of the new German hymnology; it rapidly spread over a much wider field. The number of hymn-writers who suddenly sprang up at this time is indeed far too great to admit of any detailed account of them. It included not only clergymen and professors like those already mentioned, Erasmus Alber, whose secular writings especially his fables were also celebrated, and Nicholas Decius, a converted monk, whose German version of the "Gloria in excelsis,"

" All glory be to God on high,"

with its noble chorale, soon came into use all over Germany; it also included men of all ranks—princes, like the Margraves of Hesse and Brandenburg; soldiers and lawyers, like Reissner, who was at the siege of Rome, and Spengler, the town-clerk of Nuremberg; artisans, like Hans Sachs the shoemaker; and the unknown authors of those popular sacred songs which were on the lips of wandering craftsmen and maids at their work. But the ground-tones of this

religious poetry were everywhere the same—on the
doctrinal side a joyful assertion of God's free grace
and goodwill towards men, as shown in our Lord
Jesus Christ ; and on the experimental side an ardent
expression of hope in God for the future, and acceptance of His will in the present. These men felt
that He had suffered a great new light of Truth to
dawn on the world, and so though it might bring
much conflict it filled them also with a new life and
courage, and with a confident anticipation of a better
future, which found its expression even in the
services for the dying and the dead. Thus these
hymns have a certain manliness, breadth, and fervour
about them, which pre-eminently adapted them for
use in the church as the common voice of praise and
prayer. Even those which seem to us least adapted
for such a purpose, the doctrinal ones, were more
truly popular in those days, when this especial aspect
of religion was the thing men were thinking about
and fighting for, than we can well understand now.
So a hymn by Paul Speratus, the chaplain of the
Duke of Prussia, which begins—

> " Salvation hath come down to us
>   Of freest grace and love,
>   Works cannot stand before God's law,
>   A broken reed they prove ;
>   Faith looks to Jesus Christ alone,
>   He must for all our sins atone,
>   He is our one Redeemer "—

goes on through several verses with a statement of
the doctrine of justification by faith that sounds to
us like a bit out of the Augsburg Confession done

into rhyme. But in his own day it was as popular as Luther's hymns, and Luther himself is said to have given his last coin to a Prussian beggar from whom he heard it for the first time. Equally characteristic of the other class of hymns is such an one as that long attributed to the Elector John of Saxony, because he frequently used it during his imprisonment, but really written by Ambrosius Blaurer, a monk from the Black Forest who joined the Reformed Church.

> " What pleaseth God, that pleaseth me,
>   I will not fear nor tremble
> Though cares may fret, though I may see
>   My bitterest foes assemble;
> Though all things in confusion seem,
> I know God's will is still supreme:
> What must be, let it be—I rest
> Firmly on this, His will is best.

> " What pleaseth God I frankly take,
>   And only ask for patience ;
> He yet will help me, nor forsake
>   My soul amid temptations ;
> Though pain or death itself may threat,
> His power I know can save me yet:
> What must be, let it be—my trust
> The end will show was right and just."

*   *   *   *   *

Or take the following hymn, which surely embodies a noble conception of the duty and the aspirations of a Christian sovereign, and was composed by the prince whose name it bears.[1]

---

[1] In the original the verses form an acrostic on his name.

MARGRAVE GEORGE OF BRANDENBURG'S
SONG.

Grant me, Eternal God, such grace
   That no distress
May cause me e'er to flee from Thee ;
Let no false counsel me mislead,
   The heavenly Bread,
My soul's true food, be ne'er withdrawn from me ;
But late and early let me hear
   Thy teachings clear,
From teachers taught by Thee the faith ;
 And yield me still up to Thy will,
Until I yield my soul to Thee in death.

Teach me to make true order, Lord,
   That so Thy Word
The common man may understand ;
Convert my subjects to obey
   Thy gentle sway ;
Increase the Christian host within my land.
But stirreth now full many a sect
   That doth neglect
True Christian faith and foster strife,
 Save us from such, nor let them touch
Thy Word, our guide alike in death and life.

So grant us peace in these our days,
   Not strife that slays
The brother's love Thou dost commend ;
Thou mak'st the welfare of my State,
   Envy and hate
Keep far from me and all, till life shall end ;

Grant me Thy Spirit like a lamb,
    Thou know'st I am
But flesh and blood, and apt to take offence ;
    That mind of Thine be also mine,
For this I pray with all my diligence.

City and lands in every part,
    With earnest heart
To Thee who gav'st them I commend ;
They are a charge that I must bear
    With faithful care ;
Thou with good counsellors my throne befriend,
That all may see true justice done
    Clear as the sun,
To rich and poor impartially ;
    Not fraud and might, reason and right
Rule here,—for this, for this, I cry to Thee !

And let the nobles of our land
    Well understand
The faith, and find the one true Ground,
In all things earnest to fulfil
    Thy holy will ;
By all who seek Thee be Thou surely found ;
So every class within the State,
    Or small or great,
Or young or old, may praise Thy name most high,
    Give honour due and try to do
What Thou wouldst have, nor ever from Thee fly.

Nor be my own needs, Lord, forgot,
    Forsake me not,
But lead me ever in Thy way ;
Wisdom and judgment breathe in me,
    And ever be
Close at my side whate'er I do to-day ;

In my affairs act Thou, nor let the foe,
    Who well I know
With craft and wrath is working hour by hour,
  Me e'er deceive, or e'er bereave
Of Thy dear Presence that benumbs his power.

For burnt not once that heart of Thine
    With love divine
Thinking on all our pain and loss?
'Twas no light thing Thou didst for us,
    Accepting thus
So willingly the anguish of the cross,
Bearing the woes of death and sin
    For us to win
The life the Father had decreed
  For sinful man, e'er time began :—
Ah! let me reap the fruit of Thy sweet deed !

Lord, I have chosen the true gate,
    Narrow and strait,
And yet my footsteps often stray ;
Bid me of Thy sore sorrow think,
    Nor dare to shrink
Whate'er befall, but still press on Thy way.
Give me true faith to persevere
    Through doubt and fear,
Till soul and body part in death ;
  Then let the foe strike no last blow,
Grant me to yield to Thee in peace my breath.

O may a burgher's right in heaven
    To us be given
Of Thy free grace, we cannot purchase it.
And listen yet to one more prayer,
    Spare Thou, O spare
My brother's soul, which I to Thee commit ;

Thou know'st 'tis not in man to save,
    Wherefore I crave
Mercy and grace for all my brother men ;
    Thou, if Thou wilt, canst pardon guilt ;
Pardon and peace grant Thou, dear Lord.   Amen.

It is curious also to note that now, for the first
time, Northern Germany furnishes the largest proportion of singers ; hitherto the southern half of
Germany had claimed nearly all its literary and
poetical activity,—now on the contrary, the North
supplanted the Southern "Volkslied" on its own
ground. But the South could still boast of possessing at Nuremberg the best poet of his day, the one
who linked the times that were passing to the new
period that was coming in, for he characteristically
belonged to the Middle Ages, and yet was among
the earliest and warmest adherents of the Reformation. Nuremberg itself was one of the most splendid
results of those ages. It was a great free city, whose
social polity was the pride of its citizens and the
admiration of strangers, wealthy, and full of stirring
and successful commercial enterprise ; the home of
the great mechanical and scientific inventions of the
day ; and rich in treasures of Gothic art in its streets
and churches. Martin Schön was engraving, and
Albert Durer was painting there, where, according to
the old doggrel rhyme—

    "Hans Sachs, who was a shoe-
      Maker, and a poet too,"

was winding up with his own name the long roll of
her "Master-singers," and opening the way to the
new style of modern poetry. Hans Sachs was the
son of a tailor, and was born in 1494, during a fearful

epidemic of the plague. His parents were industrious, God-fearing people, who early sent him to the grammar-school ; but as his health was not strong, they thought it better he should be put to a trade than allowed to study as he wished. At fourteen accordingly he was apprenticed to a shoemaker, but about the same time he made the acquaintance of Leonard Nunnenbeck, who was a weaver and also the most celebrated " Master-singer " of the day. Nunnenbeck remarked the boy's talent, and at once received him among his pupils ; and when, at seventeen, Hans Sachs set out on his wanderings, his object was to perfect himself not only in the craft of shoemaking, but also in that of verse-making. He visited the great schools of his art in Mayence and Strasburg, and ere long made such progress that he himself acted as teacher in Frankfort and Munich. He was a favourite everywhere for his talent and his wit, but he led a singularly pure and abstemious life ; and at twenty-two returned to his native city, presented his master-piece as a shoemaker, and when admitted to the guild, married, and settled down in Nuremberg. Here he spent the rest of his long life,—for though he was a delicate child, he lived to be eighty-one,—working sometimes at his trade, sometimes giving instruction in the art of composition, more often engaged on his own compositions. These earned him in his own day great renown and a wide popularity, and he was the first author who lived to see a complete collected edition of his own works. It was published at Nuremberg in 1558, in five folio volumes. He was indeed a most prolific writer, surpassed only by Lopes de Vega, for he published more than six thousand poems, of course of very varying excellence. Almost every style of poetry, except the dramatic which he but slightly attempted, is largely represented among them,—lyrical, narrative, satirical, humorous and earnest. His highest merit, which won for him the admiration of Goethe, lay in his short tales, many of which are comic, though all have some moral point, and which are told with a spirit and humour, a freshness and pathos that both render them attractive in themselves and valuable as a vivid picture of the life of his times. The greater number of his more humorous poems belong to his later years ; most of his earlier ones are serious—first love-songs of a very pure and domestic character, then poems chiefly of the political and religious class. Such works, handling the most important topics of the day and circulated on broadsheets as fast as they were written, helped to form the public opinion of the times as powerfully as newspapers do now, and it was no slight gain to the cause of the Reformation that so ready and favourite a writer should from the first have taken that side. In 1523 he published a poem which soon spread all over Germany, called the "Nightingale of Wittenberg." It described the state of Christendom, by picturing the miseries of a poor flock of sheep which have fallen among wolves, and are especially exposed to the rapacity of a lion (Leo X.), who had craftily undertaken to defend them. Suddenly they hear the clear notes of a nightingale, foretelling the day-dawn, and the sheep who follow this voice are led out into a lovely sunny, safe meadow. His keen, shrewd rightmindedness made him appreciate how great an influence the new mode of thought would inevitably exercise on the domestic life, and also on the social and political condition of the nation ; and hence many of his poems take up the questions of the honourableness of marriage, the necessity of concession on the part of the rulers, and of love of the commonwealth and readiness to make sacrifices for it on the part of the people of Germany. He saw, too, the dangers of discord and quarrels among the Reformers ; and when Luther dies, he represents Theology as weeping over the coffin of the man of God, and mourning the treatment she receives at the hands of presumptuous sectaries. He comforts her by telling her that she has yet defenders left, and that Luther's doctrine has at least put an end for ever to all the monkey-tricks of relics and shrines, pretended miracles and indulgences. But he does not conceal his fears of the dissensions among Christians themselves, and exhorts them to hold fast by the pure Gospel : "Love God above all, and thy neighbour as thyself ; against that doctrine ban and edict, clergy and laity, school and preaching, monks and old women, will alike be powerless."

The most famous of his hymns is one that he wrote during the terrible siege of Nuremberg in 1561 :— "Why art thou thus cast down, my heart ?"[1] Of his others we give two ; the first is called

A FAIR MELODY: TO BE SUNG BY GOOD CHRISTIANS.

Awake, my heart's delight, awake
Thou Christian host, and hear
These tones that lovely music make,
God's Word most pure and clear,

---

[1] " Warum betrübst du dich mein Herz."

That now is sweetly sounding,
While dawn is piercing through the night
    Through God's dear love abounding.

The prophets' message now at last
    Our ears may hear again,
Locked up therewith in silence fast
    Long had the Gospel lain;
But now we hear their voices,
And many an anxious burdened soul
    In freedom now rejoices.

For conscience lay oppressed and bound
    By bans and men's commands,
Soul-traps and nets were all around;
    But now our German lands,
Behold the sun is risen,
And those foul shapes were ghosts and lies,
    And dare to burst their prison.

Christ sends us many messengers
    His gospel to proclaim,
And all the realm of darkness stirs
    To work them death or shame,
And quench the Truth in error;—
O Christendom, thou Bride of God,
    Fear not for all their terror!

Trust thou in flattering tongues no more,
    Though many they may be;
All human teachings dread thou sore,
    Though good they seem to thee;
But put thy whole affiance
In God's good-will and holy Word,
    There is our one reliance.

There yield thy heart and soul entire,
　　What it commands is good;
Where it forbids let no desire
　　E'er stir within thy blood;
Where it allows, maintain thou
Thy Christian freedom as Paul saith,
　　Yet from offence refrain thou.

The Word will save thee from the smart
　　Of sin and pains of hell,
If thou believe it with thy heart
　　No evil there can dwell;
'Twill make thee pure and holy,
And teach thee that in Jesus lies
　　Our hope and comfort solely.

Blest be the day and blest the hour
　　When thou didst see revealed
The Word of God in all its power,
　　The soul's true strength and shield;
Let nought to thee be dearer
In heaven or earth, no creature-love
　　E'er to thy heart be nearer.

O Christendom, here give thou heed,
　　By no false lore perplexed,
Here seek and find true life indeed
　　For this world and the next;
For he who dies believing
In Christ alone, shall live with Him,
　　His heavenly joys receiving.

As this poem makes us understand what many men
must have felt when the Gospel was once more made
accessible to them in their own language, and without

the intervention of "men's devices," so the next little song expresses that trust in Christ as the only Mediator and channel of salvation, which had been long obscured by teachings about the Virgin and the saints.

THE MEDIATOR.

O Christ, true Son of God most high,
    Thy name we praise for ever ;
Whoe'er to Thee for help doth cry
    Shall find Thee fail him never ;
        'Tis Thou wilt plead,
        Thou intercede
With God, for us who need Thy prayers so sore :
        Thy bitter strife
        Hath wrought us life,
And Thine be thanks and praise for evermore !

To Thee the Father giveth now
    All power in earth and heaven ;
Sin, Satan, Death to Thee must bow,
    All fetters Thou hast riven,
        Bade fear to cease,
        And made our peace,
That now to God we dare our hearts outpour :
        Thy bitter strife
        Hath wrought us life,
And Thine be thanks and praise for evermore !

Fulness of grace is in Thy Word ;
    The Life, the Truth, the Way
To life eternal art Thou, Lord ;
    To Thee alone we pray,
        Who didst appear
        A servant here

> To bear the sin that crushed the world before :
> Thy bitter strife
> Hath wrought us life,
> And Thine be thanks and praise for evermore !

Another link between the religious poetry of the Reformation and of that preceding age, was the hymnology of the Bohemian Brethren, which often reminds us in tone of the mediæval Latin hymns. These Brethren were the remains of an ancient Slavonic Christianity, which owed its origin to the teaching of two Greek monks in the ninth century, and was in existence before the papal authority and Roman liturgy found their way to Bohemia. Throughout the Middle Ages a tacit struggle existed between these two elements ; the Roman prevailed, but the earlier Greek still showed itself in the demand of the people for the possession of the Scriptures and the performance of worship in the vernacular ; and it was in a great measure due to his meeting this want that the doctrines of Huss were so readily received. At last the smouldering conflict burst into open warfare, which raged at intervals throughout the fifteenth century. It was a terrible war, embittered by the animosities alike of religion and race—a history of virulent and unrelenting persecution on one side, and of cruel retaliations on the other. At last a peace was made ; the Hussites withdrew to the borders of Bohemia and Moravia, and maintained a precarious existence, until the scanty remnants found a refuge in Saxony in 1725.

When the Reformation began, the Bohemian Brethren were among the first to hail it ; as early

as 1522 they sent messengers to Luther to wish him
success, and confer with him on questions of church
discipline. One of these was Michael Weiss, who
afterwards became the pastor of the German-speaking
congregations of Landskron and Fulnek, and for
their benefit translated into German the finest of the
Bohemian hymns, adding some of his own. Luther
greatly admired and highly recommended this hymn-
book ; it was republished with further additions by
their Bishop, John Horn, in 1540, and passed through
many editions both in Germany and Holland. Its
contents are of various kinds: some are entitled
" Hymns of Instruction," and were designed to put
the great truths of Christianity and the chief events
of the Gospel history, into a form in which they
might be easily understood and retained by unlettered
minds; others are liturgical, adapted to the festivals
of the Church, or morning and evening prayer,
and among these many are antiphons, often of very
elaborate structure, intended to be sung alternately
by priest and people ; others again are simply hymns
of Christian experience. The versification is fluent
and musical, reminding us that the Bohemian race
has always been distinguished by its musical gifts :
the tone has no fierceness, but much tenderness and
earnestness ; and the frequent references to persecution only implore steadfastness and protection, never
vengeance. The Christian sacrifice of entire self-
surrender to God, the union of the Church in Christ,
reliance on God in trouble,—these thoughts, which the
circumstances of their own career must have brought
very close to their hearts, meet us again and again
in their hymns. The following is

AN ANTIPHON ON THE PRAISE OF GOD.

Priest.

Praise, glory, thanks, be ever paid
To God the Father who hath all things made,
　　And to the Son,
Who hath atoned for all that we have done ;
And to the Holy Ghost be honour due,
Who the dead soul can with His gifts renew,
　　And doth impart
God's holy law to every chosen heart.

Response.

To this one God, the Lord of Sabaoth,
　　Be now and evermore
Glory and praise from all the hosts of heaven,
　　Resounding o'er and o'er ;
While all the realm of earth,
All tribes of human birth,
Sing of His greatness and His light,
His mercy, holiness, and might.

Priest.

Who, Lord, by searching e'er shall find out Thee,
Who fathom Thy dread Being's mystery ?
　　Resist Thy might,
Or hide from Thee and Thine all-piercing sight?
What is there that can live without Thy care,
Of all that swim the waves and fly in air,
　　Or man or beast?
For all 'tis Thou must spread the constant feast.

Response.

O God, Almighty Lord of Sabaoth !
　　'Tis Thou dost reign ;
And the whole world in shape and order due
　　Thou dost maintain ;
Beauty and fruitfulness are Thine,

'Tis Thou dost bid the heavens to shine,
Or sendest showers, or storm, or gloom ;
From Thee all life and motion come.

Priest.

Who, Lord, of us, with thought and tongue so weak,
Shall rightly of the wondrous kindness speak
      Which Thy dear Son
At Thy will doeth to us, and hath done?
For didst Thou not to us Thy dearest give,
And promise that in Him we all should live,
      From death set free,
And sin and Satan,—and at peace with Thee?

Response.

O God, how great to us, the sin-opprest,
      Hath been Thy love !
In Christ Thy Son Thou leadest us to rest,
      Bidding us prove
True conquerors o'er the world, the flesh,
The sin that ever tempts afresh ;
Clothed in faith's armour, called to be
Knights of a heavenly chivalry.

Priest.

Therefore, O Father, we Thy wisdom praise,
And ever thankful songs to Thee will raise,
      Who through Thy Son
For this Thy little flock so much hast done ;
O rule it by Thy Spirit from on high,
And if with much temptation Thou dost try,
      Grant it to shine
Here and hereafter as of gold most fine.

Response.

Rejoice, ye Christ-believing host, fear nought,
      Your cause is won !

For Christ, true Man and God, for you hath fought,
    And all is done.
His is the Name o'er every name ;
He can of right all honour claim ;
To Him be praise and thanks again,
Now and for evermore : Amen.

The next is a

HYMN FOR THE TRIED.

Lord, to Thy chosen ones apppear,
Gladden weak hearts weighed down by fear,
Let Thy Word's light, a guiding Star,
Arise on those who dwell afar.

Let none who seek Thee faint or tire,
But still press on with warm desire,
Shunning whate'er Thou dost condemn,
That Satan have no part in them.

Bid them Thy easy yoke to know,
Patient alike in joy and woe ;
In spirit, soul, and body still
Wholly surrendered to Thy will.

We yield, O Thou true Life, to Thee,
Wealth, honour, all things, utterly,
Fixing our hearts on Thee alone ;
O God Supreme, be Thou our own !

The last is one of a class of hymns for which they
are celebrated—morning and evening hymns.

AN EVENING HYMN.

Now God be with us, for the night is closing,
The light and darkness are of His disposing ;
And 'neath His shadow here to rest we yield us,
    For He will shield us.

Let evil thoughts and spirits flee before us ;
Till morning cometh, watch, O Master, o'er us ;
In soul and body Thou from harm defend us,
      Thine angels send us.

Let holy thoughts be ours when sleep o'ertakes us,
Our earliest thoughts be Thine when morning wakes us ;
All day serve Thee, in all that we are doing,
      Thy praise pursuing.

As Thy beloved, soothe the sick and weeping,
And bid the prisoner lose his griefs in sleeping ;
Widows and orphans we to Thee commend them,
      Do Thou befriend them.

We have no refuge, none on earth to aid us,
Save Thee, O Father, who Thine own hast made us ;
But Thy dear presence will not leave them lonely
      Who seek Thee only.

Father, Thy name be praised, Thy kingdom given,
Thy will be done on earth as 'tis in heaven ;
Keep us in life, forgive our sins, deliver
      Us now and ever.   Amen.

Two more singers of this period must be named
here, because they as distinctively connect this age
with the coming one, as Hans Sachs did with the
past. They were fast friends and fellow-helpers,—
the pastor and precentor of Joachimsthal, Johann
Matthesius and Nicolas Hermann. Joachimsthal was a
large village in the mountainous border-land between
Saxony and Bohemia ; mines had lately been discovered in its neighbourhood, and it was rapidly growing
into a prosperous little town ; it had embraced the
Reformed religion, and was distinguished by its

good schools. Here for many years Matthesius and Hermann led such a life as, happily for Germany, has been characteristic of many of her secluded districts since the Reformation,—quiet as to outward tenor amid those eventful times, hardworking in the cause of religion and education, homely in its circumstances, yet linked to the wider world and the best life of its time by its religious thought and its culture of poetry and music. The two friends were very unlike. Matthesius had been converted by reading accidentally some of Luther's tracts, and left the grammar-school of Joachimsthal of which he was rector, to become again a student at Wittenberg, and hear the lectures of Melancthon and Luther. Justus Jonas introduced him to Luther, who invited him to become one of the regular guests at his table, and ere long admitted him to his most intimate friendship. Luther very soon urged him to take orders, for which indeed he was well qualified, for he was a man of ability, of great piety, and had a gift of singularly persuasive eloquence; but he was so self-distrustful, that on his first attempt to preach he ascended the pulpit three times without being able to bring out a single word; and it was only Luther's almost vehement insistance that induced him to make one more effort, when he gave " a capital glorious sermon," as Luther says. He sympathised with Luther too in his love and practice of music, and after Luther's death wrote a biography of him, which is still a standard work. From Wittenberg he returned as pastor to Joachimsthal, where he laboured for the rest of his life, greatly cherished by its somewhat rough and mixed population, who were very proud of their pastor's eloquence and singularly pious and charitable life. Yet though outwardly smooth, life was no easy thing for him : he suffered much from the cares of a large family, especially after the death of his helpful wife ; and from mental and spiritual conflicts, which at times seriously affected his health. He died as he had often wished, in harness, being seized with a fit at the conclusion of a sermon. He wrote various devotional works, and some very good and sweet hymns ; of which several for the morning, for marriage, a cradle hymn, and for the miners, became very popular. But his influence on literature was not so great as that of his friend, who was precentor and organist of the church and master of the schools. The portrait of Nicolas Hermann in the library at Nuremberg shows a handsome, genial, yet shrewd-looking old man, and such he seems to have been —a man who threw himself wholly into the life of the people around him, and found interest and happiness in it. Few of his hymns and poems are intended or adapted for the Church ; they are meant for his school children ; for the girls and young men to sing, instead of profane songs ; for the occasions of domestic and daily life ; or for the perils and varying fortunes of a miner's hazardous calling. But he had a fatal facility of versification, and many of his poems are spoilt by their length, while others are but rhymed versions of some of Matthesius's sermons ; yet his best show that he had in good measure the real gift of song, and mark a new style in German hymnology, not the grave and lofty tone that had been caught from the Psalms of David, but the simple, earnest, picturesque manner of the popular songs. He was a passionate lover of music, and when old and infirm could picture heaven to himself no otherwise than as a place of delicious and joyful harmony. He writes once : " Every organist or lutanist in that life too will take some holy text, and strike upon his organ or his lute ; and every one will be able to sing at sight and by himself four or five different parts. There will be no more confusion and mistakes, which now often put many a good musician quite out of heart, especially when he has to begin again several times over." He died in 1561.

The hymns of these authors most frequently to be met with, are of course those adapted to Church use. A morning hymn by Matthesius—

> " My inmost heart now raises,
> In this fair morning hour,
> A hymn of thankful praises
> To God's almighty power "—

was the favourite morning hymn of Gustavus Adolphus. Many of Nicolas Hermann's hymns are to be found in all German hymn-books. One of these is the following

HYMN FOR THE DYING.

> When my last hour is close at hand,
> And I must hence betake me,
> Lord Jesu Christ beside me stand,
> Nor let Thy help forsake me.
> To Thee my soul I now commit,
> And safely wilt Thou cherish it
> Until again Thou wake me.

Conscience may sting my memory sore,
　And guilt my heart encumber;
But though as sands upon the shore
　My sins may be in number,
I will not quail, but think of Thee,
Thy death, Thy sorrows, borne for me,
　And sink in peace to slumber.

I have been grafted in the Vine,
　And hence my comfort borrow;
For surely Thou wilt keep me Thine
　Through utmost pain and sorrow;
Yea, though I die, I die in Thee,
Who through Thy death hast won for me
　Heaven's bright eternal morrow.

Since Thou from death didst rise again,
　In death Thou wilt not leave me;
Thy life declares my fears are vain,
　And doubts no more shall grieve me,
For Thou wilt have me where Thou art:
And so with joy I can depart,
　And know Thou wilt receive me.

And so I stretch mine arms to Thee,
　Now, O dear Jesu, take me!
Peaceful and calm my sleep shall be,
　No human voice shall wake me,
But Thou wilt ope the heavenly door
To life and joy for evermore,
　Thou, who dost ne'er forsake me!

And of Matthesius we give this

MINER'S SONG.

O Father, Son, and Holy Ghost,
Thou God, dost fix the miner's post,

Thy Word hath made the wondrous store
Of rock, and earth, and precious ore.

Good metal is a gift from Thee,
'Tis ours to use it honestly
For God and country, as 'tis fit,
Not give it our hearts and worship it.

Who sees God in the precious stone,
Works truly, prays to Him alone,
Believes in Christ with all his heart,
He doth the Christian miner's part.

God, who createdst quartz and sand,
Change them to ore in this our land ;
Thy blessing guide us where to find,
Thy Spirit give the wise clear mind.

Who hath Thee, knows Thy word and love
Better than much fine gold shall prove ;
Thy meanest gift is goods and gold,
Christ is the mine of wealth untold.

At Zarephath a smelter's wife
Maintained of old the prophet's life,
Believed his word, had peace and rest,
And God's dear blessing with her guest.

So we commend, Lord, to Thy grace
Thy little Church within this place ;
It hath received and keeps Thy Word,
Repay it with true prophets, Lord.

CHAPTER VII.

THE later years of the sixteenth and the opening of the seventeenth century are by no means so rich in hymn-writers as the era of the Reformation itself. Not that there was any diminution in the quantity of religious poetry, but the quality grew much poorer and thinner, and it fell chiefly into the hands of professional authors, instead of springing up all over the country out of the heart of the people. Still this period, too, has some very good and fine hymns, but a marked change of tone is perceptible in most of them; they are no longer filled with the joyful welcome of a new day, they more often lament the wickedness of the age, and anticipate coming evil times or the end of the world itself. And yet that age, so far from being at all particularly wicked or calamitous, was a time on the whole of peace and prosperity. Pestilences did indeed visit Germany at intervals, as in 1563 and 1597, but this was no new thing; such outbreaks occur periodically throughout the previous centuries. In other respects Germany was making rapid progress, both material and mental. In the course of a few

years after the peace of Passau, the Reformed religion
had spread over more than three-fourths of the country,
including all the most populous and active regions ;
while in literature so great a change had taken place,
that whereas a work of the fifteenth century seems far
away from us both in thought and language, a work
from the latter half of the sixteenth is written nearly
in the same German that is used now, and breathes
comparatively the spirit of modern life. The great
idea that every man is personally responsible for his
belief and his actions to God Himself, was making
itself felt in every field, breaking up old organizations
and the orderly but rigid routine of mediæval life,
prompting to new enterprises, inspiring men with
courage to bear imprisonment, exile, or death for their
faith. But it had brought its dangers and difficulties
too, not only in the actual persecutions and wars which,
though on a very limited scale, existed throughout this
period until they culminated in the great struggle of
the Thirty Years' War ; but still more in an excessive
individualism which rendered common action almost
impossible. For the new mode of thought gave
rise to mental conflicts and doubts and scruples
of conscience, for which there was no longer the
easy resolution of an authoritative decision of Church
or priest, and which saddened the lives of many
whom we should not now call specially religious
persons ; and it brought endless disputes on doctrinal
questions among the professors of the evangelical
faith themselves. Over the temporary compromise
between the Romanist and Protestant religions, known
as "the Interim;" over every shade of more or less
Calvinistic views of the Atonement and the Sacra-

ments, they quarrelled, not in words only but deeds: men were deprived of their offices or salaries, banished from one State to another, or excluded from the Lord's Supper and from the privilege of sponsorship. The political circumstances of the day bore the same impress of lack of unity. Germany was broken up into a multitude of little States, without a real centre of authority, and with no clearly defined relations between the princes and people within each State. Against all this division was ranged the growing power of the Order of the Jesuits on the religious side, and of the House of Hapsburg on the political; two powers that indeed represented unity, but unity springing from and leading back to despotism, and which soon formed a close and mighty alliance. It might well be that to thoughtful men the future looked dark.

Out of this time we choose Ambrose Lobwasser, Bartholomew Ringwaldt, Selnecker, and Helmboldt as the men who best represent its religious poetry.[1] Lobwasser was a professor of jurisprudence at Königsberg, and had strong leanings to the Calvinistic Church, though not actually belonging to it. He made a complete translation of the French Psalter of Marot and Beza, which was published with Goudimel's melodies in 1573, and went through many subsequent

---

[1] It should be remarked that it was during this period that two men wrote, whose prose works powerfully affected the religious life of Germany. One was the mystic, Jacob Böhme (died in 1624), whose influence becomes apparent in the literature of the period following the Thirty Years' War. The other was Johann Arndt (died 1621), whose works on the Christian Life—the "True Christianity," and "Garden of Paradise"—were the favourite devotional reading of all earnest Christians in Germany for more than a hundred years.

editions. It is noticeable chiefly because it long remained the recognised psalter, like Sternhold and Hopkins with us, and was the only hymn-book admitted to use in public worship by the Calvinistic churches. Otherwise its poetical merits are very small; it does not rise above the level of a sort of rhymed prose, and it furnished an unfortunate model for a flood of very prosaic rhymed paraphrases of doctrinal statements or passages of Scripture, which become wonderfully numerous at this time.

Ringwaldt was the author of the hymn so well known in England under the mistaken title of " Luther's Hymn,"—

> " Great God, what do I see and hear,
> The end of things created,"—

which is in fact a quotation rather freely handled from a celebrated hymn of his on the Second Advent to Judgment. He was a native of Frankfort-on-the-Oder; a man of cheerful, courageous, genial spirit, whose life was passed as the pastor of a little place called Langfeldt, where he died in 1598. But his many hymns and religious works strongly illustrate what has bee nsaid of the tone of feeling at that time, for they are generally penitential, or filled with warnings of the coming judgment. Among the best of the former is the following :—

PENITENCE.

> Lord Jesu Christ, my Highest Good,
> Thou Fountain of all grace,
> Behold how heavy is my mood,
> As I my past retrace,

How sore my conscience is beset
With keenest arrows of regret,
    That never cease to pierce me.

Alas ! when I remember all
    The life I once held dear,
A stone upon my heart doth fall,
    And I must quail for fear,
I know not where to take my flight ;
Ah Lord ! I must despair outright,
    But for Thy word of mercy.

But when I hear it sweetly sing
    Of peace for evermore,
My heart almost begins to spring,
    And laughs in me once more,
To know how merciful Thou art
To all who, with a contrite heart,
    Will come to Thee, O Jesus !

So I, too, dare to come to Thee,
    And at Thy feet I lay
My burden, while with bended knee
    And earnest heart I pray,
Forgive me, heal my conscience' strife,
For all the sins of all my life
    Forgive, dear Lord, forgive me !

Yea, O my God, forgive me now
    For Thy Name's blessed sake ;
The heavy yoke 'neath which I bow
    Do Thou in mercy break.
So shall my heart have peace at last,
And to Thy praise my years be passed
    In childlike, glad obedience.

Thy joyful Spirit give me strength,
  Thy wounds my healing be,
When my last hour must come at length,
  Wash Thou my soul for me ;
And take me when it seems Thee best,
In the true faith to heavenly rest
  For ever, Lord, with Thee.   Amen.

The career of Nicholas Selnecker, on the other hand, affords an example of that discord and persecution among the Protestants of which we have spoken. He was a cultivated, agreeable, and very able man, springing from one of the oldest families of Nuremberg, who prided themselves on their culture. As a boy, his remarkable musical gifts and personal beauty attracted the notice of Ferdinand, King of Rome, and his Italian confessor; and they laid a plan for having the boy kidnapped and carried to Spain. Fortunately his father discovered it in time to have him secretly conveyed to Wittenberg, where he was boarded in the house of Melancthon. As a man, the highest offices in the Lutheran Church were open to him, and he was distinguished by several of the Evangelical sovereigns. But he had an acute, and singularly just and candid mind, which inclined him to decided but moderate views, and hence he became a constant mark for attack to the extreme partisans on both sides. He was incessantly involved in controversy; he was seven times banished from Saxony—whenever, in fact, the ultra-Calvinistic party got the upper hand—and was seven times implored to return ; while he was turned out of Jena and Brunswick for being too lenient

to the Calvinists. So the life that might have been
rich in value and usefulness was almost wasted in
fruitless disputes and struggles, which were full of
suffering to a man who loved peace, and was keenly
alive to the dangers of disunion. He died in 1592, at
the age of sixty-two. Being a great lover of church-
music, he devoted much time and attention to the
improvement of the German liturgy, and himself
wrote several hymns, of which only two short ones
can be quoted here. The first is still commonly
used at the close of evening worship:—

EVENING-TIDE.

Lord Jesu Christ, with us abide,
For round us falls the evening-tide ;
Nor let Thy Word, our glorious light,
For us be ever quenched in night.

In these dark days that yet remain
May we Thy sacraments maintain,
And keep Thy Word, still true and pure,
And steadfast in the faith endure !

For his own daily prayer he wrote this:—

MORNING PRAYER.

Make me Thine own and keep me Thine,
Thou faithful God and Lord !
Let nought seduce this heart of mine
From Thee and Thy pure Word.

Let me ne'er waver nor grow cold,
But give me steadfastness ;
So shall I praise Thy grace untold
In heaven's eternal bliss.

Louis Helmboldt belongs in age to this date, but in the tone and power of his compositions he is more nearly akin to Luther and his contemporaries. He was, like Selnecker and Ringwaldt, a native of one of the great free cities, Mulhausen, where his father, a wealthy woollen manufacturer, was a senator and had married into one of the neighbouring noble families. At fifteen the young Louis already went to the university of Erfurt, and at eighteen his native city made him head-master of one of its schools—a position, however, which he found it best to resign in about eighteen months. He then returned to Erfurt, obtained a professorship, and for seventeen years was Dean of the Philosophical Faculty. At this university there was at that time both a Romanist and an Evangelical party ; and when the former from political circumstances for a while obtained the preponderance, Helmboldt, as a leader of the latter, was obliged to leave, to the great indignation of the town and the students. He went back to Mulhausen, and at the age of forty took orders, and was appointed by the town-council to one of their churches, and to the rectorship of a great school ; and was finally made general-superintendent, an office answering to that of a bishop with us. He was one of the principal poets of his day, and published a number of Latin odes and elegies, for which the Emperor Maximilian, at the Diet of Augsburg, awarded him the honours and emoluments of poet-laureate. Of his German writings the odes are said to be very poor, but he was a fertile song-writer both for the school and home, after the manner of Nicolas Hermann, and for the Church. One of his hymns is to be found in all

German hymn-books, and has rooted itself among the people. It was written in 1563, when a terrible pestilence attacked Erfurt, and in the course of a year destroyed 4,000 of its inhabitants, so that the university had to be broken up for some months. Helmboldt gave this hymn to the wife of one of his friends, as she was starting on a hasty flight from the city; and in most of the old hymn-books it is headed—

THE TRUE CHRISTIAN'S VADE-MECUM.

From God shall nought divide me,
  For He is true alway,
And on my path will guide me,
  Where else I oft should stray.
  His ever-bounteous hand
At morn and eve is heedful
To give me what is needful
  Where'er I go or stand.

If sorrow comes, He sent it,
  In Him I put my trust;
I never shall repent it,
  For He is true and just,
  And loves to bless us still.
My life and soul, I owe them
To Him who doth bestow them;
  Let Him do as He will.

Whate'er may be His pleasure
  Is surely best for me;
He gave His dearest treasure
  That our weak hearts might see

How good His will toward us,
And in His Son He gave us
Whate'er could bless and save us :
    Praise Him who loveth thus !

Yes, praise Him, for He never
    His needful help denies ;
Ah happy hour, whenever
    To Him our thoughts can rise !
    For all the time we spend
Without Him is but wasted,
Mere loss till we have tasted
    His joy that cannot end.

The world around is passing
    With all its pomp and pride ;
What men are here amassing
    Can never long abide ;
    We die—and it is gone.
But fear not, Christian sleeper,
God is our mighty Keeper,
    And we shall wake anon.

Then though on earth I suffer
    Much trial, well I know
I merit ways still rougher,
    And 'tis to heaven I go,
    For Christ I know and love ;
And every step leads thither,
Where, safe from blasts that wither,
    Joy dwells with Him above.

For 'tis our Father made us,
    And wills our good alone ;
The Son hath died to save us
    And make God's goodness known ;

The Spirit rules our ways,
And dwells through faith within us,
To God and Heaven to win us;
To Him be thanks and praise!

Several of the classical hymns of Germany belong
to this period, and resemble in spirit those of Ringwaldt and Helmboldt just quoted. The best are by
Schalling and Herberger, both pastors in Silesia, and
Pappus, a professor at Strasburg.

We give one of this style by Weingartner, the
pastor of Heilbronn, which became a great favourite
during the Thirty Years' War, and also a little poem
of a more personal character, which belongs to this
date, but is of unknown authorship :—

CONSOLATION.

In God my faithful God
I trust when dark my road ;
Though many woes o'ertake me,
Yet He will not forsake me;
His love it is doth send them,
And when 'tis best will end them.

My sins assail me sore,
But I despair no more :
I trust in Christ who loves me,
From this Rock nothing moves me,
Since I can all surrender
To Him, my soul's Defender.

If death my portion be,
Then death is gain to me,
And Christ my life for ever,
From whom no death can sever;
Come when it may, He'll shield me,
To Him I wholly yield me.

Ah Jesus Christ, my Lord !
So meek in deed and word,
Didst Thou not die to save us,
Because Thou fain wouldst have us,
After this life of sadness,
Heirs of Thy heavenly gladness?

" So be it " then I say
Heartily day by day !
Guide us while here we wander,
Till safely landed yonder,
We too, dear Lord, adore Thee,
And sing with joy before Thee !

A THANKSGIVING.

Thou burning Love, Thou holy Flame,
O Thou my God and Lord,
Thou hast preserved me by Thy Name,
When terrors were abroad ;
Thou helpest us in worst distress,
If we but cling to Thee,
Wherefore, my God, no bitterness
Shall ever make me flee.

Ah ! never can I praise enough
The mercy Thou hast shown !
When days were dark and storms were rough
Thou mad'st Thy kindness known,
Thy miracles of goodness then
Thou sufferedst me to see ;
O Bread of Life ! my heart again
Cries, let me cling to Thee !

Thee I desire, to Thee I cleave,
To Thee will I be true ;
As opes the floweret to receive
The May-time's quickening dew,

So in the time of grief and woe
Opens my heart to Thee,
And feels anew a living glow,
For Thou consolest me.

Ah! though I lived a thousand years,
And spake with thousand tongues,
I could not tell with words nor tears
What praise to Thee belongs.
Ah · o, it never can be told,
Not even, my God, to Thee,
How rich the gifts, how manifold,
That Thou hast showered on me!

This only, O my God, I pray,
Thy Spirit may abide
In me, and keep me in Thy way,
My Comfort and my Guide;
Let nothing evil reign within,
Thine angels send to me,
Let me escape all snares of sin,
And lead me home to Thee.

Hitherto the hymns of the Reformation had been
distinguished by their simplicity and appropriateness
to church use; their models had been found in the
earlier Latin hymns, or in the Psalms of the
Old Testament and the hymns handed down to
us by St. Luke. Now, however, for the first time
we encounter a new style, afterwards very prevalent, which reminds us of some of the later mediæval hymns addressed to the Virgin and saints,
and finds its scriptural ground in the Song of Solomon
and the Apocalypse. As yet most hymns were
addressed to God the Father through our Lord Jesus
Christ, or to the Holy Trinity, or in the case of

hymns of sorrow and penitence to the Saviour. But afterwards the mystical union of Christ with the soul became a favourite subject ; more secular allusions and similes were admitted, and a class of hymns begins to grow up, called in Germany " Hymns of the Love of Jesus." Some of these are extremely beautiful, and express most vividly that sense of fellowship with Christ, of His presence and tender sympathy, of personal love and gratitude to Him, which are among the deepest and truest experiences of the Christian life ; but it is a style which needs to be guarded, for it easily degenerates into sentimentality of a kind very injurious alike to true religion and poetical beauty.

The earliest examples of this style are two celebrated hymns written by Dr. Philip Nicolai in 1597, during a fearful pestilence in Westphalia, where he was pastor of the little town of Unna. More than 1,400 persons died in a very short time, and from his window he saw all the funerals pass to the graveyard close at hand. From these scenes of death he turned to the study of St. Augustine's " City of God " and the contemplation of the eternal life, and so absorbed himself in them that he remained cheerful and well amid the surrounding distress. In 1599 he published the fruit of his meditations in a treatise called " The Joyous Mirror of Life Eternal," a book of pious and devout reflection, to which he affixed two hymns that speedily attained a remarkable popularity, and are indeed admirable for their fervour of emotion and mastery over difficult but musical rhythms. One is—

> " Wake, awake, for night is flying,
> The watchmen on the heights are crying,
> Awake, Jerusalem, at last!"

which is well known in England from the use of its splendid chorale in Mendelssohn's " Elijah " to the words,

> " Sleepers, wake, a voice is calling."

The other hymn, " O Morning-Star," also possesses a very fine chorale ; and so popular did it soon become, that its tune was often chimed by city chimes, lines and verses from it were printed by way of ornament on the common earthenware of the country, and it was invariably used at weddings and certain festivals.   It is still to be found in all German hymn-books, but in a very modified form to suit more modern tastes. A translation of the original hymn is here attempted. Nicolai's title for it is—

A SPIRITUAL BRIDAL SONG OF THE BELIEV-
ING SOUL, CONCERNING HER HEAVENLY
BRIDEGROOM.

> O Morning-Star, how fair and bright
> Thou beamest forth in truth and light !
>   O Sovereign meek and lowly !
> Sweet Root of Jesse, David's Son,
> My King and Bridegroom, Thou hast won
>   My heart to love Thee solely !
> Lovely art Thou, fair and glorious,
>   All victorious,
>   Rich in blessing,
> Rule and might o'er all possessing.

> O King high-born, Pearl hardly won,
> True Son of God and Mary's Son,

Crown of exceeding glory !
My heart calls Thee a Lily, Lord,
Pure milk and honey is Thy Word,
   Thy sweetest Gospel-story.
Rose of Sharon, hail ! Hosanna !
      Heavenly Manna,
        Feed us ever ;
Lord, I can forget Thee never !

Clear Jasper, Ruby fervent red,
Deep deep within my heart now shed
   The glow of love's pure fire ;
Fill me with joy, grant me to be
Thy member closely joined to Thee,
   Whom all my thoughts desire ;
Toward Thee longing doth possess me,
      Turn and bless me,
        For Thy gladness
Eye and heart here pine in sadness.

But if Thou look on me in love,
There straightway falls from God above
   A ray of purest pleasure ;
Thy Word and Spirit, flesh and blood,
Refresh my soul with heavenly food.
   Thou art my hidden treasure.
Let Thy grace, Lord, warm and cheer me,
      O draw near me ;
        Thou hast taught us
Thee to seek, since Thou hast sought us.

Lord God, my Father, mighty Shield,
Thou in Thy Son art all revealed
   As Thou hast loved and known me ;
Thy Son hath me with Him betrothed,

In His own whitest raiment clothed,
He for His bride will own me.
Hallelujah!   Life in heaven
Hath He given,
With Him dwelling,
Still shall I His praise be telling.

Then touch the chords of harp and lute,
Let no sweet music now be mute,
But joyously resounding,
Tell of the Marriage-feast, the Bride,
The heavenly Bridegroom at her side,
'Mid love and joy abounding;
Shout for triumph, loudly sing ye,
Praises bring ye,
Fall before Him,
King of kings, let all adore Him!

Here my heart rests, and holds it fast,
The Lord I love is First and Last,
The End as the Beginning;
Here I can die, for I shall rise
Through Him, to His own Paradise
Above all tears and sinning.
Amen! Amen!   Come, Lord Jesus,
Soon release us,
With deep yearning,
Lord, we look for Thy returning!

It has been said that Nicolai's hymns owed some of
their popularity to the noble chorales he composed for
them; and it may be observed in general that the
rapid growth of sacred poetry in Germany at the era
of the Reformation was partly due to an equally
striking advance in church-music.   The song-loving

German people seized with avidity on this new opening for their art, and a very remarkable number of fine tunes were composed in this century, so that an old writer says, "Whensoever the Holy Ghost inspireth a new hymn, it is His wont to inspire some one with a good tune to fit it." Nearly all the collections of hymns also contained tunes, which were inseparably associated with certain hymns ; and it became the custom in most towns, for the city musicians to ascend the tower of the church or town-hall at certain hours of the day, and blow these sacred melodies from their horns, so that the people learnt them by heart from childhood. A great improvement took place in the organ about the same time, and Eccard, who lived at Mulhausen, and composed melodies for many of Helmboldt's hymns, introduced the practice of giving the air to the soprano instead of the tenor voice. Thus by the close of this century the chorale had assumed essentially its modern form, and the organ was universally used in Lutheran churches. The tune to Helmboldt's hymn above quoted has always been a peculiar favourite in Germany, and though harmonized by Eccard, was based on a secular air, as Helmboldt tells us—

> " Because so sweet in every part,
>   So tuneful is this air,
> That hearing it, a godly heart
>   Swims in delight most rare ;
> Therefore have I set words to it,
>   That every one may sing ;
> Whate'er his case, this song will fit,
>   And never harm can bring."

The chorales are distinguished by breadth and simplicity, and are peculiarly adapted for large masses of voices or for organ accompaniment; while compared with the Gregorian music which had preceded them, they formed a congregational rhythmical song. Great skill may be shown in the arrangement of the inner voices, and in such skill Luther took the keenest delight; he speaks of the wonderful wisdom of God as shown in music, "when the other parts play around the air, leading as it were a heavenly dance with it; meeting with pleasure, parting in pain, embracing and kissing each other again." "Whoever is not moved by such art as this, must of a truth be a coarse clod, not worthy to hear such lovely music, but only the waste wild bray of the old chanting, and the songs and music of the dogs and pigs."

CHAPTER VIII.

A.D. 1618—1650.

THE long peace of sixty years which had followed the treaty of Passau was drawing to an end ; and to understand the difference that was made by the Thirty Years' War that followed it, we must remember that Germany was already an old country, in the van of European civilization, with a social order, literature, and arts of many centuries' growth.

Some of the great cities, such as those of the Hanse League and Nuremberg for instance, were indeed beginning to lose a little of their pre-eminence, as the carrying trade of the world was finding new paths, and slipping into the hands of the English and the Netherlanders. But they were still the channel of communication between the east and west of Europe ; and the great development of the internal trade of Germany, its mines and its manufactures, was supplying to some extent the place of what was lost. It was also calling into existence all over the country smaller towns, which were centres of vigorous and active life ; while the country regions were thickly dotted with villages, and towns and villages alike had their local organization for self-government, their churches, and schools. The standard of comfort was substantially a high one, in food, in dress, and in furniture. Of course various articles of foreign production which are common now, and the lack of which we should sorely feel, were wholly unknown then ; but, on the other hand, there was far more artistic effort and beauty bestowed on the houses themselves, and on their internal ornamentation and furniture, than in later times. Many of the churches were beautiful specimens of Gothic architecture, and even in country places they were generally handsome stone buildings, often possessing rich altar furniture, painted windows, and a peal of bells—forms of decoration in which the Germans took great delight, and for which their skill was famous all over Europe. The quick-witted townspeople were accustomed greatly to despise their rural neighbours, and no doubt the difference of manners in those days of infrequent communication was far more marked than it is now; but the peasant had no reason to be ashamed of his lot. During the previous century a change had gradually taken place, which leaving certain feudal dues and rights to the lords, had in most parts of Germany practically transformed the peasant into the proprietor of his land. Agriculture was practised with great skill and care, the crops seem to have been large, the culture of wool and of the vine was carried to a greater extent even than now, and the number of animals of all kinds, but especially horses, proved by old parish records to have existed on the land, is very surprising. The houses were usually of clay, but were plentifully furnished with linen, bedding, pewter, and such wooden furniture as is now eagerly bought up by connoisseurs, while the warm and abundant clothing of the people was a common subject of remark among travellers. Mentally, too, the country was full of life ; education was carefully promoted, and just before the war broke out an association was formed, called " The Fruit-bearing Society," which aimed at fulfilling towards the German literature and language the functions of the Academy Della Crusca towards the Italian, and which counted among its members men of all ranks from the highest downward, and all the best writers of the day.

Over such a country swept to and fro the pitiless ever-recurring tempest of war, for the lifetime of a whole generation ; and when the great peace rejoicings took place at last in 1650,[1] it was a changed land which witnessed them. It is calculated by German writers who have been investigating recently the official records still left of the state of the country before and after the war, that over a considerable extent of it, four-fifths of the population and much more than four-fifths of the property were destroyed,[2] and taken as a whole, at least a half of both throughout Germany must have disappeared ; while it is only within the last thirty or forty years that Germany at large has attained the same point, either as to population, trade, or the productiveness of the soil, at which it stood early in the seventeenth century. Two hundred years have been necessary merely to recover lost ground !

1 The war began in 1618 and ended in 1648, but two years more were consumed in negotiations, during which time the armies, though not actually engaged in hostilities, were maintained, and pressed heavily the land.

2 See Freitag's " Bilder aus der deutschen Vergangenheit," the chapters on the Thirty Years' War.

Looked at broadly the conflict was a defensive war on the part of the Protestant against the Roman Catholic religion.   During its earlier years the advantage inclined on the whole to the Imperial side ; then came the " Lion of the North," Gustavus Adolphus, and swept back the tide of victory, and after his death it is hard to say which party had the advantage. Had either been strong enough to win a decided success, the war might have been sooner at an end ; but the opponents were nearly matched, and the Evangelical party, princes and people alike, felt that they could not yield—for them it was a struggle of life and death.   If the Imperialists had triumphed, despotism and Romanism under the Jesuits would have settled down over the whole land, as they did on the Austrian dominions.

Such a war brought with it many evils besides itself ; terrible disturbances of trade and currency, which perhaps most affected the cities ; bands of marauders who infested country regions where the use of locks and bolts had been almost forgotten.   Evangelical territories which fell into the hands of the Imperialists had to suffer a religious persecution, which cost many their lives, and drove hundreds of thousands into exile, so that the difficulties of the fortified cities of the north were much increased by the numbers of homeless fugitives who sought shelter there.   Towards the close of the war came scarcity of food, and pestilences, one of which, in 1637, was of frightful severity, such as had not been known for a hundred years.   But the worst was the actual devastation of the war itself. Gustavus Adolphus succeeded in introducing a higher discipline and tone into his army, and preventing the plundering and cruelties which were practised by the troops generally, but after his death no one else had the same power. As a rule, the soldiers plundered wherever they went, not only taking what they wanted, but often wantonly destroying what they could not carry off; the churches were robbed and battered down because they afforded a refuge to the poor villagers, and the bells were stolen to make guns; if a peasant was suspected of secreting any treasure, he was cruelly tortured ; girls and lads were constantly carried away by force. In many parts of Germany spots are still pointed out where the peasantry made hiding-places for themselves in the woods, while their few possessions were concealed in grave-yards, even in the very coffins of the dead. The towns suffered under forced contributions and the quartering of large bodies of troops, and sometimes had to endure the utmost horrors of siege and storm. Leipsic was besieged five, and Magdeburg six times. Towards the end of the war we are told of once flourishing towns reduced to forty inhabitants, who with their own hands unroofed their houses to avoid the taxation to which dwelling-houses were still liable, and dwelt in thatched hovels in the streets; and of villages wholly depopulated, or where a scanty remnant crept back to the familiar fields and covered in clay huts without windows, lest the firelight should serve as a beacon to attract their enemies.

When we read such a tale of disasters it seems wonderful that society should have survived, or the country recovered at all. We have to remember that after all there were intervals of rest, and some districts suffered less than others, were perhaps only once or twice visited by the armies. And certainly the immediate effect of the war on the mental activity of Germany was stimulating; it was not until the stillness of the peace had fully set in that the exhaustion which it had produced in this direction, as well as others, made itself felt. While the contest was going on, the call for exertion, the consciousness of fighting in a great cause, the enthusiasm excited all over evangelical Germany by the lofty character and splendid genius of Gustavus Adolphus, quickened men's love of their religion and their fatherland. This was especially true of the clergy at that time. Whether Romanist or Evangelical, the parish priests seem to have deserved well of their country by the way in which they stood by their flocks, comforting them in trouble, and encouraging the little community to re-organize itself and struggle on afresh after each new disaster. But the Evangelical clergy showed themselves particularly courageous in this way, for they were usually marked out for plunder and cruel ill-treatment by the Imperialist troops; yet when their churches were destroyed they assembled the people for prayer in the woods or on the hill-sides; when the school was broken up, they taught the children as long as it was possible to collect any; they obtained help for their people through the ecclesiastical organization from the more favoured regions; and they were the medium through which the higher intelligence of the country, and the sentiment of a common nationality and faith, penetrated to the mass of the people. Their influence is acknowledged to have been one of the most valuable in keeping society together, and preventing culture from dying out, even by those German

writers who lament the character of pedantry and
stiffness which they impressed on literature and
thought. And so it came about that this period of
suffering was one of literary and intellectual activity
in many ways ; and that once more especially a great
outburst of religious song took place, in which the
clergy bore the greatest share, but which was by no
means confined to them. A very large proportion of
the most famous hymns and hymn-writers of Germany
belong to this century, and the only difficulty is to
select from the number of its names.

Many of them were also members of the Fruit-
bearing Society, which from its motto and badge
—a palm-tree with the words "all for use"—is also
known as the Order of the Palm. It was founded
in 1617 by Ludwig, Prince of Anhalt-Cöthen, and,
though meant for serious work, had its fanciful side
in its imitation of an order of chivalry. Its head
was always to be a German prince ; no one was to
be admitted to membership except persons of some
distinction, either by birth or literary achievements or
both, and of unblemished character ; all its members
were bound to promote in every possible way the
purity and refinement of the German language and
the enrichment of its literature, and to cultivate
whatever was essentially national in language and
manners. A very large number of the noble classes,
among whom a high standard of cultivation was then
common, joined it, as well as the principal writers of
the time ; and it certainly did good service in furnish-
ing a centre for national feeling and for common
action, as well as in its own proper department. The
most eminent member of this society was Martin

Opitz, afterwards ennobled as Opitz von Bobersfeld. He was a native of Bunzlau, in Silesia, and with him begins what is termed the Silesian era of German poetry—a time when this country held the first rank in learning and literature among the German States as markedly as Swabia had done in the days of the Minne-singers. Opitz died of the plague at Dantzic in 1639, at the early age of forty-two; but his short life had been rich in mental labour. He had travelled much, and was well known at all the chief German courts; he had taken part in one military expedition, and had acquitted himself creditably of a more congenial employment—a diplomatic mission to Paris. His great work, however, lay in his "Treatise on German Poetry," and in the practical exemplification of its principles which he gave in his own poems. He was, in fact, the first to lay down the laws of German prosody, and he may be said to have given its form to German verse, as Luther did to German prose. This service has obtained him a higher place in his country's literature than the merits of his poems would intrinsically justify. They are easy, correct, and elegant, but have scarcely a spark of originality or force, yet in his own day they procured him the highest possible eulogies from princes and scholars, and not empty praise alone, but money, friends, and rank. Opitz was essentially a clever, industrious literary man of the world, with the art of making himself everywhere agreeable, and he was petted and caressed accordingly, more than was good for his work. Such a man would probably never have written religious poetry at all in ordinary times; but living as he did when grave thoughts and terrible struggles were in all men's

minds, he too was influenced by his age, and he wrote
a good deal of this kind—versions of all the epistles
for the Sundays of the year, of many of the Psalms,
and of the Song of Solomon. Among his sacred
poems, however, his hymns are by far the best, and
some are really fine. We give one, a

MORNING HYMN.

O Light, who out of Light wast born,
 O glorious Sun of Righteousness,
Thou sendest us anew the morn
 With pleasant light and cheerfulness ;
  Therefore it beseems us well
  Now with thankful lips to tell
   All we owe to Thee ;
  Let our hearts to Thee arise,
  Open Thou our inner eyes
   All Thy love to see.

O let Thy Spirit's clear-eyed day
 Break in upon our hearts' deep night,
And with its glowing radiance slay
 Our self-trust's cold deluding light ;
  See, we waver and are weak,
  Act and thought alike oft seek
   Paths that are not Thine !
  That our way may grow more clear,
  And our life more steadfast here,
   Bid Thy Sun to shine.

Unite, Lord, in the bonds of peace
 Our Church's scattered band ;
Bid wars and persecutions cease
 Through our sad fatherland ;

Grant us, Lord, O grant us rest !
That we, not too sore opprest,
    May our course fulfil
Through this fleeting Time, till Thou
Bring us where the angels now
    Praise Thy goodness still.

Next to Opitz, the chief poet of the time was
Paul Flemming, and in real poetical genius, in truth
and depth of feeling, he surpassed him ; yet Flemming was but little known during his lifetime, and
himself regarded Opitz with an almost idolatrous
reverence. He was a Saxon by birth, the son of
wealthy parents ; and though he adopted medicine as
his profession, he seems to have been independent of
its exercise. He had an energetic and fervid temperament, and an enthusiastic love for his country
and the cause of Evangelical religion, to which
he often gives expression in his verse. The love of
adventure, and the hope too of doing some good
service to his country, induced him to join an embassy
that was sent at first to Moscow, and afterwards by
way of Astrachan to Ispahan, an expedition that in
those days occupied seven years, and led him into
an incredible number of dangers and hardships. He
returned to Hamburg in 1639, and died the next year,
like so many of his contemporaries, in the prime of his
powers, for he was but thirty-one. Evidently he had
a keen eye for natural beauty, and he writes charming
descriptions of scenes that he beheld in his long
journey, as well as sweet and tender songs of love
and friendship ; but a shade of sadness is thrown over
them by his sorrow for his country, and the bitter
regret he felt at having left it in its trouble, for travels

which did not produce the expected results. One of his hymns, written on this journey, is a classical **one** in Germany. It is—

> " Where'er I go, whate'er my task,
> The counsel of my God I ask."

The following little poem is inscribed

TO MYSELF.

Let nothing make thee sad or fretful,
    Or too regretful,
      Be still ;
What God hath ordered must be right,
Then find in it thine own delight,
      My will.

Why shouldst thou fill to-day with sorrow
    About to-morrow,
      My heart ?
One watches all with care most true,
Doubt not that He will give thee too
      Thy part.

Only be steadfast, never waver,
    Nor seek earth's favour,
      But rest :
Thou knowest what God wills must be
For all His creatures, so for thee,
      The best.

SO HATH GOD LOVED THE WORLD.

Can it then be that hate should e'er be loved ?
    Yea, Love ! 'twas only on the world's cold heart,
    Cold, hard as iron, Thou couldst show Thine art,
There only all Thy strength and fire be proved.

'Tis on our ice Thy living radiance glows,
Makes day of night, for evil gives us good,
Riches for poverty, for hunger food,
   And heaven for earth.   True Friend of bitterest foes,
Thou Death of death, O Pain to nought but pain,
O Master who Thy work dost ne'er disdain,
   Serving Thy servants who can merit nought,
How can I fathom Thy abyss, O Love !
By so much deeper than our hearts can prove,
   As God is higher than man's highest thought.

Another of these men who were the leaders of the
secular literature of their age, and who also ranked
themselves among its religious poets, was Andreas
Gryphius, a Silesian like Opitz, and like him a
member of the Order of the Palm.   His great
achievement was the revival of the drama, to which
his tragedies gave its modern form in Germany,
as the poems of Opitz did to lyrical verse.   Thus
they too mark an epoch in German literature, and
they soon found imitators, but they have not kept
his name alive among the people as some of his
hymns have done.   He translated several of the
ancient Latin hymns very finely, and wrote many
of his own, which were published at first in a
small volume, under the title of " Tears for the
Passion of Jesus."   All his works are pervaded by
a deep tone of melancholy ; the *transitoriness* of all
things is the thought that meets us again and again,
and is rendered endurable only by a firm trust in
God.   " All flesh is grass . . . . but the Word of
the Lord abideth for ever ; "—this most ancient anti-
thesis of sorrow and consolation is the text of most

of his hymns and odes. His own life had been so darkened by sorrow that it was impossible his writings should not bear the same impress. Before the age of five-and-twenty he had lost his father by poison, his mother, brother, and sister by sickness; he had known poverty and hunger; he had been driven from one university by fire, from another by the plague; he and his brother had both suffered persecution for their religion, and the only gleam of sunshine in his life had been the kindness of the Count Palatine von Schönborn, to whose children he was tutor. Now his patron died, and he himself was brought to the very verge of the grave by a long and dangerous illness, from which indeed he at last recovered, but with broken health and spirits, and he died suddenly at the age of forty-seven, at a meeting of the Estates of the provinces of Glogau. Yet through all this he managed to become not only a distinguished poet and an earnest Christian, but an active man in public business, and a great scholar; he understood eleven languages; he travelled over a great part of Europe, lecturing on the most various scientific subjects, and receiving honours from the universities he visited; and after his return he was for many years the chief syndic of the principality of Glogau, and discharged the onerous duties of his post to the great satisfaction of the people. Of his " Spiritual Odes," the following is one of the most characteristic :—

PASSING AWAY.

All glories of this earth decay,
In smoke and ashes pass away,

Nor rock nor steel can last ;
What here gives pleasure to our eyes,
What we as most enduring prize,
    Is but an airy dream that fadeth fast.

What are the things whereof we boast ?
What are they worth we value most ?
    They are but simply naught.
What is the very life of man,
So brief, uncertain, void of plan ?
    Time's passing fancy with no substance fraught.

What is the fame we strive for sore,
And deem will last for evermore,
    But an illusion mere ?
So soon as hence the mind is fled,
The lips are pale, the man is dead,
    None asks what he achieved when dwelling here.

No wisest knowledge here avails,
O'er fools and wise men Death prevails,
    Nor lets them long abide.
Castles nor wealth can help at all ;
He who hath found the world too small,
    Now finds at last a narrow grave too wide.

There is no laughter here, no joy,
But some heart-sorrow, some annoy,
    Will poison it ere long :
Where wilt thou find unmixed delight,
Where honour that is always bright,
    Undimmed by scorn and hate, unvexed by wrong ?

    *   *   *   *   *

We reckon year to add to year,
And while we count, behold ! the bier
    Is standing at our door ;

With scarce the time to think or pray
We must be gone, and leave the day,
  And say good-night to Earth for evermore.

For even while Pleasure doth beguile,
And Strength looks forward with a smile,
  And Youth feels safe and free,
Death weaves his snares about our feet,
And Pleasure ceases to be sweet,
  And Youth and Strength and Courage fail and flee.

Up, heart, awake, as one who knows
Of all the gifts that Time bestows
  But one belongs to thee—
The Present ; for the Past doth fly
As a swift stream goes shooting by ;
  The Future—ah ! who knows whose that shall be ?

Laugh at the world, her honours vain,
Her fears and hopes, her love disdain,
  Find refuge with the One
Who is and ever shall be King,
To whom no Time a change can bring,
  From whom eternal life can come alone.

Ah well for him whose trust is here !
Built on the rock, he need not fear
  Time's changes and decay :
Though he may fall, he yet shall stand
For ever in the unchanging land,
  For very Strength itself shall be his stay.

SONNET.

In life's fair spring, its earliest tender bloom,
  Fell Death hath orphaned me ; and Sorrow's night
  Hath wrapped me round ; and the relentless might
Of Sickness bade my days in pain consume ;

My hours were shared with Want and Grief and Gloom.
  Supports, whereon as pillars firm I leant,
    Have all, alas ! but failed me, broke or bent ;
Alone I bear as best I may my doom.
Nay, not alone !   My God forsakes me not,
His Father-heart hath ne'er its truth forgot ;
  His eye and hand still for His child must care :
When man no help can find, then comes His hour,
When human strength is spent He shows His power,
When hid His presence seems ; behold ! our God is there !

Other Silesians distinguished themselves both as secular and sacred poets : among them were Buchner, professor of poetry at Wittenberg, who was the most intimate friend of Opitz ; Andreas Tscherning, a professor at Rostock, who wrote a little book of sacred poems called "The Spring-time of German Poetry," which had a very wide circulation in its own day ; and David von Schweinitz, an upright, God-fearing statesman, whose "Spiritual Harp of the Heart" was also very popular.   But from these minor poets, we must turn to the great hymn-writers of this period.   In general their hymns have a more reflective tone than those of the Reformation : they are never doctrinal, but always experimental or devotional ; more tender than the earlier hymns, they are not as yet deteriorated by exaggerated sentiment or self-introspection ; they are simple, sweet, fervent expressions of trust in God's goodness and self-surrender to Him.   Some of them breathe the very spirit of Christian courage, as that famous battle-song of Gustavus Adolphus,—

    "Fear not, O little flock, the foe,"—

which was long attributed to Altenburg, a pastor in Thuringia ; recent researches, however seem to have made it clear that he only composed the chorale, and that the hymn itself was written down roughly by Gustavus Adolphus after his victory at Leipsic, and reduced to regular verse by his chaplain, Dr. Fabricius, for the use of the army. Such again are the hymns of Apelles von Löwenstern, the saddler who rose to be a noble, a statesman, a poet, and a musician ; and such especially is the hymn which has become the popular " Te Deum " of Germany, and is always chosen on any great public occasion to express the united gratitude and praise of the people.

PRAISE.

Now thank we all our God
　With hearts and hands and voices,
Who wondrous things hath done,
　In whom His world rejoices ;
　　Who from our mother's arms
　　　Hath blessed us on our way
　　With countless gifts of love,
　　　And still is ours to-day.

Oh may this bounteous God
　Through all our life be near us,
With ever joyful hearts
　And blessed peace to cheer us,
　　And keep us in His grace,
　　　And guide us when perplexed,
　　And free us from all ills
　　　In this world and the next.

All praise and thanks to God
　The Father now be given,
The Son and Him who reigns
　With them in highest heaven,

> The one eternal God,
>   Whom earth and heaven adore ;
> For thus it was, is now,
>   And shall be evermore.

This simple but noble expression of trust and praise, with its fine chorale, was composed by Martin Rinkart, in 1644, when the hope of a general peace was dawning on the country. He was one of those provincial clergymen to whom Germany had so much reason to be grateful. The son of a poor coppersmith, he made his way at the University of Leipsic by dint of industry and his musical gifts, took orders, and was precentor of the church at Eisleben, and at the age of thirty-one was offered the place of Archdeacon at his native town of Eilenburg in Saxony. He went there as the war broke out, and died just after the peace, and throughout these thirty-one years he stood by his flock, and helped them to the utmost under every kind of distress. Of course he had to endure the quartering of soldiers in his house, and frequent plunderings of his little stock of grain and household goods. But these were small things. The plague of 1637 visited Eilenburg with extraordinary severity ; the town was overcrowded with fugitives from the country districts where the Swedes had been spreading devastation, and in this one year 8,000 persons died in it. The whole of the town council except three persons, a terrible number of school children, and the clergymen of the neighbouring parish, were all carried off; and Rinkart had to do the work of three men, and did it manfully at the beds of the sick and dying. He buried more than 4,000 persons, but through all his labours he himself remained perfectly well. The pestilence was followed by a famine so extreme that thirty or forty persons might be seen fighting in the streets for a dead cat or crow. Rinkart, with the burgomaster and one other citizen, did what could be done to organize assistance, and gave away everything but the barest rations for his own family, so that his door was surrounded by a crowd of poor starving wretches, who found it their only refuge. After all this suffering came the Swedes once more, and imposed upon the unhappy town a tribute of 30,000 dollars. Rinkart ventured to the camp to entreat the general for mercy, and when it was refused, turned to the citizens who followed him, saying, " Come, my children, we can find no hearing, no mercy with men, let us take refuge with God." He fell on his knees, and prayed with such touching earnestness that the Swedish general relented, and lowered his demand at last to 2,000 florins. So great were Rinkart's own losses and charities that he had the utmost difficulty in finding bread and clothes for his children, and was forced to mortgage his future income for several years. Yet how little his spirit was broken by all these calamities is shown by this hymn and others that he wrote ; some indeed speaking of his country's sorrows, but all breathing the same spirit of unbounded trust and readiness to give thanks.

Still more natural was it that at such a time the heavy sorrow, the ceaseless anxieties of earthly life, and the intense longing for the peace and joy of heaven, should find a voice in song; and of this

class is the lovely hymn of Meyfart, professor of
theology at Erfurt, who died in 1642,

" Jerusalem, thou city fair and high,"[1]

and so are several of the hymns of Simon Dach of
Königsberg.   At Königsberg in those stormy days
lived a little knot of friends who by no means escaped
their share of trouble, but found solace under it in
their religion, their mutual friendship, and the practice
of music and poetry.   The eldest of them was George
Weissel, pastor of one of the churches ; and next to
him was Robert Roberthin, a layman high in office
under the Elector of Brandenburg, and able from his
position occasionally to protect and assist his friends.
He was also a personal friend of Opitz, and was the
first to introduce the new Silesian style of verse
into the more barbarous Prussia.   Then came Simon
Dach professor of poetry, and Thilo professor of
rhetoric in the university, and Heinrich Albert the
organist of the cathedral.   All these men wrote hymns
or sacred poems, and Dach and Albert also composed
chorales.   Albert especially was a very distinguished
musician, and he was the author both of the words
and the flowing melody of that morning hymn,

" God, who madest earth and heaven,"[2]

which is still not infrequently played at early
morning in some of the quiet little German country
towns or baths.   He composed airs to many of
Dach's poems, and thus helped much in their rapid
diffusion among the people ; and the little band of
friends often assembled in a garden he had purchased

[1] " Jerusalem du hachgebante Stadt."
[2] " Gott des Himmels und der Erden."

outside Königsberg to hear some new poem or melody in the summer-house. Dach was however the most gifted of the group, and ranks high among German poets for the sweetness of form and depth of tender contemplative emotion to be found in his verse. A little love-song of his, written when courting the daughter of a neighbouring clergyman, has become one of the best known of the German popular songs, and is familiar to English readers in Mr. Longfellow's version of "Annie of Tharau."

Of his hymns, many of which are to be found in all German hymn-books, we give the following, written during the long and painful illness which preceded his death :—

HEAVEN.

O ye halls of Heaven,
Where the holy have their home,
They whose hearts were riven,
But through faith have overcome ;
They who here on earth
Knew not joy or mirth :

Thee I greet, fair Home,
Thee o'er all things else I seek ;
For o'er earth I roam
Desolate, and sad, and weak,
Never free below
From some cross or woe.

Only for thy sake
Have I strength not to despair,
But my heart's long ache
Willingly, nay gladly, bear ;
Sweet when I look up
Grows my bitter cup.

Did not my poor heart
Cherish yearning hope for thee,
   Long ago its smart
Had been all too sore for me ;
   Never can my breast
   Find elsewhere a rest.

God, Thou knowest well
What the pain that hurts me sore,
   Where my thoughts must dwell,
Grieving hourly o'er and o'er ;
   Thou and I alone
   Hear that inner moan.

But if I not yet
Bear a pilgrim's chastened soul,
   If I could forget,—
Let fresh trials o'er me roll ;
   Thou, my God, wilt bear
   More than half my care.

Let this life to me
Ever grow more waste and drear,
   If that so to Thee
I may cling more firm and near,
   And no dread of death
   Shake or chill my faith.

Ah ! in that fair place
Shall I not drink deep of joy,
   When I see Thy face,
When I meet Thy loving eye,
   When, like angels bright,
   I am clothed in light !

O ye halls of Heaven,
Where the holy have their home !
   Be the signal given,

End my griefs and bid me come ;
   All I long for is
   Soon to see thy bliss.

Of Roberthin we give a specimen of a different
style, earnest and sensible, but more commonplace in
expression and less fervent than Dach.

MAY-TIME IN WAR.

Worthy of praise the Master-hand
   That hath created all,
And Father-like, by sea and land,
   Where'er our eye can fall,
Preserves and feeds His creatures here,
   And sends us once again
The lovely flower-time of the year
   To gladden hill and plain.

'Tis May that brings to every sense
   A joy so keen and fit,
Her name can please when she is hence
   Whene'er we think of it.
The loveliest month of all the year
   Is round us everywhere ;
The winds blow soft, the sun is clear,
   And sweet and pure the air.

The plains are rich with many a hue,
   The forests with young shoots ;
Heaven's blessing seems to stream anew
   O'er earth and all her fruits.
The nightingale pours forth her lays
   From every little wood,
Doing her best to sing God's praise
   And tell us He is good.

The bees fly forth in busy swarm,
　　Their honey home to bring,
The swallow builds its nest so warm,
　　The lark begins to sing ;
No creature but can now be glad,
　　Its heart's desire can still ;
Man only is distraught and sad
　　Through his own darkened will :

Man who can ne'er with firmness wait,
　　Nor to one aim be true,
But must embitter his own fate,
　　And his own death pursue ;
Whose life at best so swiftly past,
　　A short, uncertain day,
Himself in deeper gloom must cast,
　　Shut from God's quickening ray.

How like a child his pride he feeds
　　With Reason ;—would he prove
His boasted Reason by his deeds
　　Of faith, and peace, and love !
Or learn from God, the Only Wise,
　　To rule his actions well ;
Then earth might be a Paradise,
　　Man makes it now a hell.

The two most famous hymn-writers of this time
were, however, Johann von Rist and Johann Heermann. Rist was born in 1607, the son of a pastor at
a village close to Hamburg, and was destined from the
first by his father to the study of theology. As a
youth he was distinguished by precocious and varied
talent ; he visited several universities, including
Leipsic, Utrecht, and Leyden, and studied mathe-

matics, chemistry, and medicine, as well as divinity. Still quite a young man, he returned to Hamburg with the reputation of a great traveller, scholar, and poet, and was at once appointed to a church just outside Hamburg, on the banks of the Elbe. Here he spent the remainder of his life, at first pleasantly enough, but in the later years of the war suffering like others severely under its scarcity, terror, and pestilence. He was an active pastor and a great preacher, and insisted much on a certain strictness of life ; for instance, he persuaded his people to abolish the customary merrymakings at Candlemas. Though he was a very strict Lutheran in doctrine, he was accused by some of the bigoted Lutherans of preaching too little against heresy and on controverted questions. His reply was " that he believed there were not above a couple of strangers in his congregation who held false doctrine, but plenty of people who led sinful lives ; and to accuse men of heresy never produced a living, fruitful faith in them, only pride and impulses of hatred." But if he wisely did not preach controversy, he had no objection to print it, and he became involved in many very acrimonious disputes, theological and literary. He was in correspondence with all the principal clergymen and authors of his time, " so that scarce a day passed on which he did not receive a letter," then a matter of great wonderment. But he was most celebrated for his religious poems and hymns, of which he published ten collections, containing between 600 and 700 pieces, intended to supply every possible requirement of public worship or private experience. That in such a mass of writings on a limited range of subjects there should be a great deal that is very watery and poor was inevitable; many of his poems are evidently manufactured to order; others in the attempt to attain a little individuality sink into depths of bombast and bad taste; the wonder is rather that so many are really good, and some belong to the first rank of hymns. In his own day they were all admired : he was the most fertile, and next to Opitz certainly the most favourite, poet of the time. Honours poured in upon him : he attained the highest titles in Church and State open to a clergyman, and received from the Emperor the crown of poet-laureate, and a patent of nobility. He founded a society of " Swans of the Elbe," of which he was the head, as a sort of offshoot of the great Fruit-bearing Society, and by the members of this order, and indeed by many others of his contemporaries, he is lauded as the Northern Apollo, the Cimbrian Swan, the God of the German Parnassus; a certain little hill near his residence, where he was accustomed to write his verses, being the Parnassus in question. His first volume of poems, " The Poetical Pleasure Garden," was partly secular, but his after-productions were almost exclusively sacred, they were caught up eagerly by the musicians of the day, and quickly found their way into congregational use in Evangelical Germany, while even among the Roman Catholics they were read with delight, and one Empress lamented, " that it were a great pity if the writer of such hymns should be sent to hell." He died at the age of sixty, in 1667.

In his youth Rist is said to have suffered much from mental conflicts, and one or two of his peniten-

tial hymns speak of such experience ; but his general
tone is rather one of unhesitating faith and courage,
and fervid love to the Saviour, such as breathe through
his hymns for Advent, and for the Holy Communion,
of which two,

"O Living Bread from heaven,"

and another,

"O Jesu, Sun of gladness,"

are still in constant use. Another hymn which,
partly from its noble and pathetic melody, has become a universal favourite, and the pattern on which
many others have been written, is the following one
on the Entombment. Rist himself says that he found
the first verse in a collection of religious popular
songs, and liked it so much that he wrote the others
to it.

EASTER EVE.

O darkest woe !
Ye tears, forth flow !
Has earth so sad a wonder ?
God the Father's only Son
Now lies buried yonder.

O son of man,
It was the ban
Of death on thee that brought Him
Down to suffer for thy sins,
And such woe hath wrought Him.

Behold thy Lord,
The Lamb of God,
Blood-sprinkled lies before thee,
Pouring out His life that He
May to life restore thee.

O Ground of faith,
Laid low in death ;
Sweet lips now silent sleeping !
Surely all that live must mourn
Here with bitter weeping.

Yea, blest is he
Whose heart shall be
Fixed here, who apprehendeth
Why the Lord of Glory thus
To the grave descendeth.

O Jesu blest,
My help and rest !
With tears I pray, Lord hear me,
Make me love Thee to the last,
And in death be near me.

As many hymns of Rist's are accessible to the
English reader, we choose one that is less known, but
that strongly illustrates his character.

THE TRUE JOY.

Now God be praised, and God alone !
The Source of Joy Thou art ;
Thy love no stint or bound hath known,
But loves a happy heart,
And sends full many a bright clear day
To cheer us on our mortal way,
Bids many a cloud depart.

Yea, Lord, I thank Thy gracious power
That hath bestowed on me
A mind that lives from hour to hour
From sad foreboding free ;

A mouth that Thou hast made so glad,
It smiles when other lips are sad,
   And fails the trembling knee.

But Thou so oft hast blessings shed,
   So oft bade sorrow cease,
That I with joy can eat my bread,
   And lay me down in peace ;
In Thy hands only lies my health,
'Tis Thou my honour and my wealth
   Canst lessen or increase.

And so with joy I drink my cup,
   And all this heart of mine,
O faithful God, to Thee looks up,
   And sings when Thou dost shine ;
With joy its daily task doth greet,
And doth its utmost, as is meet—
   But, Lord, success is Thine.

Then take not, Lord, this joy away,
   But let me cleave to Thee ;
Let pining melancholy stay
   For ever far from me,
Nor sadness make me slow to hear
When Thou, O Lord, art drawing near,
   And my heart's guest wouldst be.

Thy strength and solace let me prove,
   And bid my soul to know
Who loveth Thee with childlike love,
   No trial, fear, or woe,
Nor Satan's self can harm, nor death ;
A friend of God, a man of faith,
   Can conquer every foe.

Mere earthly pleasure cannot please,
   It were not to my mind
To live in proud, luxurious ease,
   And leave much gold behind ;
My highest aim, while here I dwell,
Is to live piously and well,
   To Thy will all resigned.

And ever do I take delight,
   My Maker, to behold
Thy flowery earth, Thy sun's dear light,
   All things Thy hand doth mould,
All living creatures that by field,
Or flood, or air, Thy praises yield,
   Who formed them from of old.

So grant me then in weal and woe
   Joyful and true to be ;
And when life's lamp is burning low
   And death at hand I see,
Then let this joy pierce through its pain,
And turn my very death to gain
   Of endless joys with Thee.

Born in 1585 at Rauten in Silesia, the youth and
early manhood of Johann Heermann fell in the comparatively quiet times that preceded the great war,
when people still had leisure for tranquil intellectual
enjoyments. Even at school the talent displayed in
young Heermann's Latin orations, and the grace of
his manner, attracted the notice of some of the great
noble families of Silesia ; and from one he received
the means of travel, from another, on his return, the
living of Köben. Here he had six peaceful years,
"the Sabbath of his life ;" happy in his work, his

marriage, his friendship with the family of Von Kottwitz, and his literary labours, which were already rendering him distinguished as a writer of Latin poems and epigrams. But in 1617 his troubles began : first came the death of his wife ; then the failure of his own health, which henceforward caused him great suffering throughout his life; and then the war.

No part of Germany suffered more in the war than Silesia. It was the constant battle-field of the contending parties, and its peculiar position entailed on it a fearful amount of religious persecution. The Hussite tendencies among its people, who were partly of Slavonic race, opened the way for the Reformation, which was very soon embraced by many of the great noble families, as well as generally by the towns. But Silesia belonged to the House of Austria, and hence its central government and higher ecclesiastics remained attached to Rome. For some time it was happy in princes and bishops who respected the toleration secured by the Peace of Passau ; but in 1609 a king succeeded who was the bitter foe of all Protestants, and was warmly supported by Bishop Charles of Breslau, a brother of the Emperor. Hence whenever in the course of the war a district fell into the hands of the Imperialists, the pastors were immediately turned out of their churches, mass was celebrated, and the people were forced by the greatest oppression to accept Jesuit priests. When the Swedes came, the Jesuits would be dispossessed and the Evangelical pastors restored, to be again banished at the next reverse of fortune. Finally, after the war was over and Silesia was left in the hands of Austria, the Evangelical religion was almost entirely suppressed, only three towns being permitted to erect *outside* their walls one small wooden building for the performance of evangelical worship. It was during the years 1623 to 1638—fifteen long years!—that the sufferings of Silesia were at their height. More than once it was devastated by regiments of wild Poles and Cossacks under General Dohna, who was commissioned to re-introduce the Romanist religion. He boasted that he performed greater miracles than St. Peter; for St. Peter converted thousands by a sermon, but he converted thousands without a sermon. His method of proselytism was to quarter his soldiers on the principal Evangelical inhabitants of the place, and allow them to exercise what licence they pleased, until the father of the household produced a certificate from the priest of having been to confession; then they would be removed to some other house, where the same process was repeated. So great was the terror inspired by these troops, that in some places the residents came out to meet them with protestations of their readiness to embrace Romanism; in others the population emigrated *en masse* at their approach. During this period Köben was plundered four times, on each of which occasions Heermann lost all his moveable possessions; he was frequently in danger of his life; was several times obliged to flee, and once had to remain a fugitive in concealment for seventeen weeks. But it was in the midst of all these troubles that he published, in 1630, his "Devoti Musica Cordis," a volume of original hymns which at once made a profound impression, and which was soon followed by two more. These hymns were the first in which the correct and elegant versification of Opitz was applied to religious subjects, but they possessed far higher merits than this ; they are distinguished by great depth and tenderness of feeling, by an intense love of the Saviour, and earnest but not self-conscious humility, while in form they are sweet and musical, though the thought sometimes is too much expanded. A remarkably large number have made for themselves a permanent place in the hymnology of the German Church, and several of the most beautiful among them are becoming known in England through translations, especially those on the Passion. We give here two that touchingly refer to the sorrows of his country and church :—

A SONG OF TEARS.

Ah ! Lord our God, let them not be confounded
Who, though by want, and woe, and pain surrounded,
Yet day and night still hope Thy help to see,
   And cry to Thee.

But put to shame Thy foes, who breathe defiance,
And make their own vain might their sole reliance,
And turn, oh turn to those who trust Thy Word :
   Have pity, Lord !

Against our foes some succour quickly send us ;
If Thou but speak the word they shall not end us,
But change to friends, lay down their useless arms,
   And cease all harms.

We stand bereft of help, and poor and lonely,
'Twere vain to trust in man ;—with Thee, Lord, only
We yet may dare great deeds whoe'er oppose,
   And quell our foes.

Thou art our Champion who canst overthrow them,
And save the little flock now crushed below them,
We trust in Thee ; Helper, Thy help we claim
      In Jesu's name !   Amen.

A SONG OF COMFORT.

Zion mourns in fear and anguish,
    Zion, city of our God :
" Ah," she saith, " how sore I languish,
    Bowed beneath how hard a load ;
God hath sure forsook me quite,
And forgot my evil plight ;"—
Nay, he chose thee, and thou art
Safely borne within His heart.

" Once," she mourns, " He promised plainly
    That His help should aye be near,
Yet I now must seek Him vainly
    In my days of woe and fear.
Will he then for evermore
Keep His anger, and no more
Look with pity on the poor,
And behold what they endure ?"

" Zion, surely I have loved thee,"
    Thus to her the Highest saith,
" True, that many woes have proved thee,
    And thy soul is sad to death,
Yet now cast thy griefs behind ;
Where wilt thou a mother find
For her babe will not provide,
Or can hate it, though she chide ?

" Nay, and couldst thou find a mother
    Who forgot her infant's claim,
Or whose wrath her love could smother,
    Yet would I be still the same ;

For my truth is pledged to thee,
Zion, thou art dear to me,
Thou within my heart art set,
And I never can forget.

" Let not Satan make thee craven,
    He can fright but cannot harm,
On My hands thy name is graven,
    And thy shield is still My arm.
How then could it other be
Than that I must think of thee,
And must build again thy walls,
And be true whate'er befalls?

" Thou before my eyes art ever,
    In my bosom thou art laid
As a nursing child, and never
    Shalt thou lack My timely aid.
Thee and Me no time nor stress,
War, nor danger, nor distress,
No, nor Satan's self can part,—
Only be thou strong of heart."

In 1638 Heermann's health became so much worse
that he was obliged to relinquish his charge at Köben
altogether, and the last nine years of his life were
spent in extreme distress from an affection resembling
incessant catarrh and low fever of a very severe
character. But he had a kind nurse in his second
wife ; whenever he rallied, study and writing were
his recreations, and he published successively a
number of devotional works. Another severe trial
befell him during this period of sickness : his eldest
son, a young man of much promise, fell under the
influence of the Jesuits at Breslau, and was on the
point of openly joining the Roman Catholic Church.

The remonstrances and arguments of his father, however, recalled him to the evangelical faith in which he
had been brought up; but his health gave way, and
he died in 1643 of a slow fever, which was commonly
supposed to be the effect of a powder given him by
the Jesuits when he quitted them.   At last, in 1647,
Heermann himself died, after many weeks of the
greatest prostration, which he bore with unwearied
patience.   It was in the course of this last illness
that he wrote a large number of verses and short
poems, from which we choose the following " Sighs "
and "Lament," as he himself calls them :—

IN DISTRESS OF MIND.

Jesu, Saviour, since that Thou
    Camest once from heaven,
Come, oh come to aid me now,
    For I long have striven.
Fear and pain assail me sore,
I can bear and do no more ;
Save me from this bitterness
Ere it slay me with distress.

" Thou loving Jesu Christ, who once as man wast born,
I too am but a man, ah ! leave me not forlorn ;
Fear hath overwhelmed my soul : O help me ! Saviour, save !
I sink, as sinks a ship beneath the engulphing wave."

IN BODILY PAIN.

Jesu, who didst stoop to prove
    Many a thousand pains for me,
When that heart so rich in love
    Bare our sins upon the tree,
Ah ! by all those woes of Thine,
Soothe, oh soothe these pains of mine !

Help, O Helper ! Thou alone,
　None but Thou, canst still this pain,
Hearken pitying to my moan,
　Look on me in love again ;
Praises from my lips shall flow
If Thou now Thy grace wilt show !

IN TEMPTATION.

Jesu, Victor over sin,
Help me now the fight to win.
Thou didst vanquish once, I know,
Him who seeks my overthrow ;
So to Thee my faith will cleave,
And her hold will never leave,
Till the weary battle's done
And the final triumph won ;
For I too through Thee may win,
Victor over death and sin.

AT THE APPROACH OF DEATH.

That Death is at my door, too well this anguish shows,
　Yet I will fear him not.　I bear Thee in my heart,
　Thou, O Lord Jesu Christ, with me, nay, *in* me, art,
And if I die, Thou wilt the gates of heaven unclose.

Why was Thy glorious form so marred, so sadly torn ?
　Only that I with Thee may know the depths of joy
　Throughout eternity.　Thou dying didst destroy
The sting of Death, and make our foe an empty scorn.

Ah then forsake me not !　Hast Thou not cleansed me
　From all the filth of sin wherewith I was defiled
　By th' arch-deceiver's arts ?　Then let me as a child
Now fall asleep in peace, and wake in joy with Thee.

CHAPTER IX.

As the seventeenth century passed on to its zenith, the promise of literary activity given by its earlier years was not fulfilled. Opitz, Flemming, and Gryphius were certainly not stars of the first magnitude, but at least they shone with a certain steady radiance as the brightest points among a luminous cloud of smaller writers; but as they one by one went out no others took their place. Yet it was just at this time that the religious song of Germany found its purest and sweetest expression in the hymns of Paul Gerhardt, who may be said to be the typical poet of the Lutheran Church, as Herbert is of the English. George Herbert's poems are meant to be read and meditated upon; they constantly remind us that the writer was a man of high breeding and culture, no less than an earnest Christian; Gerhardt's are intended to be set to music and sung in church, or learnt by heart by the children at home, and as constantly reveal the homeliness and simplicity, the deeply devout and quietly courageous spirit of the Lutheran pastor. Of his early life little is known. He was born in 1606, in a little town, Gräfinhainichen, in Saxony, where

his father was burgomaster. The whole of his youth
and early manhood fell in the time of war. That it
must have been a period full of disappointment and
hope deferred for him, is clear enough when we find a
man of his powers at the age of forty-five still only a
private tutor and candidate for holy orders. In 1651
he was living in this capacity in the family of an
advocate named Berthold, in Berlin. He had already
written many hymns, but was as yet unable to
publish them; and he was in love with Berthold's
daughter, but had no living to marry upon. About
the close of that year however, the living of a country
place called Mittenwalde was offered him: he was
ordained, and in 1655 he at last married Anna Maria
Berthold. At Mittenwalde he passed six quiet years,
during which he began to publish his hymns, which
immediately attracted great attention, and were
quickly adopted into the hymn-books of Brandenburg
and Saxony. His name thus became known, and in
1657 he was invited to the great church of St. Nicholas,
in Berlin, where his life was soon both a busy and
an honourable one. He worked most assiduously
and successfully in his pastoral duties; he brought out
many hymns, which were caught up by the people
much as Luther's had been of old; and he was
the favourite preacher of the city, whom crowds
flocked to hear. He is described to us as a man of
middle height, of quiet but firm and cheerful bearing;
while his preaching is said to have been very earnest
and persuasive, and full of Christian love and charity,
which he practised as well as preached by never
turning a beggar from his doors, and receiving widows
and orphans who needed help and shelter into his

own house. His religion and his temperament alike made him cheerful, and not all the many disappointments of his life seem ever to have embittered his mood; but he had a very tender and scrupulous conscience, and wherever a question of conscience seemed to him to be involved, he was liable to great mental conflict and an exaggerated estimate of trifles. In theology he was an ardent Lutheran, and ere long his zeal for his Church was put to the test.

Prussia was at that time governed by Frederick William I., "the Great Elector," whose memory is still revered in the country as the founder of its greatness. The mass of his people were Lutherans, but he himself belonged to the Reformed Church, to which his grandfather, the Elector Sigismund, had seceded from political motives. At the Peace of Westphalia, he was the one important German prince who acted as spokesman for the Calvinistic churches, and it was through his efforts they obtained the same legal recognition as the Lutherans. His next endeavour was to make peace between the two Churches within his own dominions. He saw clearly enough the waste of strength and the evil passions caused by their disunion and perpetual controversies, and he is not accused of any unjust bias or partiality towards his own Church, but the times were not then ripe for such an attempt, and he met with little success. In 1662 and 1663 he summoned the leading men of both Churches to a series of conferences on the points of dispute between them, in the hopes of thus arriving at some approximation of opinion, or at least at a declaration that the points of difference were "non-essential." But the result was the precise reverse of the Elector's hopes ; the more the doctors argued the farther apart they found themselves. The Calvinism of those days was not of the modified type to which we are accustomed, but advocated what would now be termed "extreme views," while the Lutherans, on the other hand, were very rigid in their own definitions of doctrine, and were in the habit of preaching against the Reformed Church with a scornful and bitter vehemence. Gerhardt, indeed, was not among those who did so ; his sermons, as well as his writings, were so free from controversy that many Calvinists attended his services, and his hymns had no greater admirer than the pious Electress Louisa, who herself belonged to the Reformed Church. But the whole cast of his thought was intrinsically anti-Calvinistic : that God is a loving Father over all His creatures, and that Christ died for all men, are the deepest, ever-recurring tones of his theology ; and hence he found it impossible to allow that the points of difference between himself and the Reformed Church were "non-essential." From the conferences he at first hoped a great deal ; he was diligent in attending them, and drew up most of the statements in explanation or defence of doctrine on the Lutheran side. But the Elector, wearied by the ill-success of these meetings, put a stop to them in 1664, and published an edict requiring the ministers of both communions to abstain from attacking each other's doctrines in the pulpit or elsewhere with harshness or want of charity ; and in 1665 he announced his intention of demanding from every beneficed Lutheran clergyman his subscription to a document pledging himself to observe the terms of this edict. This demand at once created the greatest excitement throughout the country, and in many places caused disturbances; for the stricter Lutherans, priests and people alike, regarded it as prohibiting the use of one of the recognised standards of the Lutheran faith, the "*Formula Concordiæ,*" in which the doctrines of the Reformed Church were condemned in strong terms, and considered it therefore to be an infringement on their legal rights, and an unwarrantable interference on the part of the civil power with the liberty of preaching. Accordingly a great number of the clergy refused to sign, and were deposed; and these were in general strongly supported by their flocks. Nearly the whole of the Berlin clergy took this part, and one of the most resolute among them was Paul Gerhardt, who being very ill at the time, assembled his brethren around his sick-bed, and entreated them to be steadfast in asserting their right to freedom of speech. Such a man's refusal could not be passed over, and early in 1666 he was deprived of his appointment; and when it appeared that many of his congregation were in the habit of resorting to his private house for religious counsel and worship, he was interdicted from performing any function of his office even in private. Of his deprivation he had said to some condoling friends "that it was but a small Berlin sort of martyrdom;" but this last prohibition wounded him deeply, and he had much private sorrow at the same time. Three of his five children had already died in infancy, and now he lost one of his two remaining sons, the child on whose death he wrote his touching hymn,

" Thou'rt mine, yes, still Thou art mine own,"

while his wife, worn out by sorrow and anxiety, fell into a long and slow decline. Many of his most beautiful hymns were written at this time, and among others,

" If God be on my side."

Meanwhile the city of Berlin did not take the loss of its favourite preacher quietly. Meetings were held and petitions addressed to the Elector—first by the burghers and guilds of trade, then by the Town Council, and finally by the Estates of Brandenburg, whose entreaty was said to have the support in private of the Electress herself. Then the Elector gave way, and declared that considering the tender conscience of the preacher Paul Gerhardt, and that he had never been guilty of bitterness and uncharitableness in the pulpit, an exception should be made in his case, and he should be permitted to resume his office without subscription. The whole city was rejoiced, but now a new difficulty arose. The Elector had sent word by one of his secretaries to Paul Gerhardt of his re-appointment, but had said also that he relied on Gerhardt's well-known moderation and loyalty, that even without subscription he would act in conformity with the spirit of the edict. This message perplexed Gerhardt's conscience once more ; an *implied* undertaking was, he said, to a Christian man as binding as any subscription could be, and he therefore felt himself still unable to accept office on these terms. A long period of fruitless negotiations ensued, and much mental distress on Gerhardt's part ; for these new scruples appeared even to many of his friends exaggerated. But how real they were to himself, is shown by his persistency, and his letters to the Town Council and Elector. "It was only the most urgent necessity," he writes to the latter, "which induced me to retire from my pastoral office, and should I now accept it again on these terms, I should do myself a great wrong ; and, so to speak, with my own hands inflict on my soul that wound which I had formerly, with such deep anguish of heart, striven to avert. I fear that God, in whose presence I walk on earth, and before whose judgment-seat I must one day appear ; and as my conscience hath spoken from my youth up, and yet speaks, I can see it no otherwise than that if I should accept my office I should draw on myself God's wrath and punishment." The Elector now commanded the Council to choose some one in Gerhardt's place ; and Gerhardt accepted the post of Archdeacon of Lübben, in Saxony. His removal there was, however, delayed by the long sickness and death of his wife ; and it was not till 1669 that he entered on his new duties. Here he spent the last seven years of his life ; but they were years of sadness, for his wife was gone, his only child had more than one dangerous illness, and he was living in a land of strangers. Lübben was a small place, and the Town Council was composed of rough and half-educated people, who subjected their clergyman to many annoyances. His refuge and refreshment was in his gift of song, "under circumstances which," says one of his contemporaries, "would have made most men cry rather than sing." He died in 1676, in his seventieth year, and his last words were a line from one of his own hymns—

" Us no death has power to kill."

Compared with most authors of his time, Paul Gerhardt wrote but little. He composed altogether one hundred and twenty-three hymns, which appeared at intervals from the year 1649 onwards, many of them for the first time in the "Praxis Pietatis Melica," a collection of hymns and tunes by Johann Crügen, the famous organist and composer of chorales. After Gerhardt's death they were republished separately, revised from his own MSS. by his son. As a poet he undoubtedly holds the highest place among the hymn-writers of Germany. His hymns seem to be the spontaneous outpouring of a heart that overflows with love, trust, and praise; his language is simple and pure; if it has sometimes a touch of homeliness, it has no vulgarism,[1] and at times it rises to a beauty and grace, which always give the impression of being unstudied, yet could hardly have been improved by art. His tenderness and fervour never degenerate into the sentimentality and petty conceits which were already becoming fashionable in his days; nor his penitence and sorrow into that morbid despondency which we find in Gryphius, and for which the disappointments of his own life might have furnished some excuse. If he is not altogether free from the long-windedness and repetition which are the besetting sins of so many German writers, and especially hymn-writers, he at least more rarely succumbs to them : and in his days they were not considered a blemish. One of his contemporaries, a certain Andreas Bucholz, who wrote a great deal of religious poetry which was then highly esteemed

---

The only hymn which does not deserve this commendation is a translation trom the Latin.

formally announces in his preface that he has spun out his poems as long as he could, for he observed that when people were reading sacred poems at home, they preferred long ones.   Gervinus, a severe judge of sacred poetry in general, says of Gerhardt : " If one man among the poets of the seventeenth century makes an attractive impression on us, it is Gerhardt. He recurred, as no one else had done, to Luther's genuine type of the popular religious song, only with such modifications as the altered circumstances demanded.   In Luther's time the old wrathful, implacable God of the Romanists had assumed the heavenly aspect of grace and compassion ; with Gerhardt the Merciful and Just One is a loving and benignant Man, whom he addresses with reverential intimacy. With Luther, it was the belief in free grace and the work of Atonement, in the Redemption which had burst the gates of hell, which inspired the Christian singer with his joyous confidence; with Gerhardt it is his faith in the love of God.   Like the old poets of the people, he is pious, *naïf*, earnest, without effort or affectation ; his style is as simple as refreshing, and attractive as his tone of thought."

Many of his hymns are already well known to English readers by translations from the time of Wesley downwards.   We give here three of those less frequently to be met with :[1]—

THE HOPE OF THE CONTRITE.

Hence, my heart, with such a thought
As that thou art cast away !

---

[1] Two verses which contain merely an expansion of the thought, are omitted from each of these hymns.

Is not God's Word promise-fraught?
  Heed not then what others say.
Art thou evil and unjust?
God is good, be He Thy trust.
Art thou death-struck, sin-defiled?
Faint not, God is reconciled.

Thou art sick, like other men,
  Of that sore disease within,
That began with Adam, when
  First he learned to yield to sin.
But despair not, God can cure,
Only make repentance sure;
Fear not that thy prayers and cries,
Even thine, He will despise.

His no bear's or lion's heart,
  Only thirsting after blood;
His compassions swiftly start,
  He but seeks thy highest good.
In thy Father's heart believe;
O'er our griefs He too doth grieve,
Is afflicted in our woe,
Sorrow for our death doth know.

" As I live," He surely saith,
  " I would have the sinner turn,
Never do I will his death,
  But that he should yield, and learn
'Tis my joy whene'er a child
Back is won from wanderings wild,
Of My flock I would not spare
E'en the least and lowest there."

Ah! no shepherd e'er, as He,
  Watched for every sheep that errs!
If His heart thou couldst but see,
  How with sorrowing love it stirs,

How it thirsts and aches and yearns
Over one who heedless turns,
And from God and good doth rove,—
Thou must weep for very love.

For God loves not only those
    Who are safe within His fold ;
Nay, He loves His very foes,
    Whom that Enemy of old
Hath seduced with lies too well,
Till weak man hath dared rebel
Against Him, whose lightest word
Through the universe is heard.

Yet God seeks them by His care,
    And through all the hosts of heaven
Joy grows brighter even there,
    When the bonds of sin are riven ;
Then God's pardon covers o'er
All the evil done before,
Every dark and sinful spot,
All is buried and forgot.

For no ocean's mighty force,
    And no fathomless abyss,
And no stream's resistless course,
    Match a love so vast as His ;
Nought are they to what He pours
Daily through this life of ours,
That with sin we daily fill
Striving with His perfect will.

Rest, O heart, then, be content !
    Why shouldst thou go mourning on ?
Why thy strength in toil be spent ?
    More than thou canst need is won.

Though thy guilt may seem to thee
Deep and mighty as the sea,
'Tis to God and to His love
What a finger's strength might move.

Open, O my God, the gates
  Whence such tender mercies flow ;
Here my heart with longing waits,
  Let me all Thy sweetness know,
Everywhere and every hour
Own Thy love's constraining power ;
And this one thing I implore,
Never let me grieve Thee more !

THE TRUST OF THE TRIED.

To God's all-gracious heart and mind
  My heart and mind I yield ;
In seeming loss my gain I find,
  In death, life stands revealed.
I am His own whose glorious throne
  In highest heaven is set ;
Beneath His stroke or sorrow's yoke
  His heart upholds me yet.

There is but one thing cannot fail,
  That is my Father's love ;
A sea of troubles may assail
  My soul,—'tis but to prove
And train my mind, by warnings kind,
  To love the Good through pain ;
When firm I stand, full soon His hand
  Can raise me up again.

Yet oft we think, is aught withdrawn
  That flesh and blood desire,
Our joy is lost, o'ercast our dawn,
  And faith and courage tire ;

With toil and care our hearts we wear,
    O'er our lost hope we brood ;
Nor think that all that doth befall
    Is meant to work our good.

But where God rules it must be so,
    It must bring joy again ;
What now we deem but cross and woe
    Shall turn to comfort then.
Have patience still, His gracious will
    Through thickest clouds shall gleam ;
Then torturing fears, and hopeless tears,
    Shall vanish like a dream.

The field can never bear its fruits,
    Save winter storm and freeze ;
Man's goodness withers at its roots
    In days of constant ease ;
The bitter draught of aloes quaffed,
    Health tints the cheeks once more ;
So to our heart can sorrow's smart
    New energy restore.

Then, O my God, with joy I cast
    My load of care on Thee ;
Take me, and while this life shall last
    Do as Thou wilt with me.
Send weal or woe, as Thou shalt know
    Will teach me their true worth,
And fit me best to stand their test,
    And show Thy glory forth.

If happy sunshine be Thy gift,
    With joy I take it, Lord ;
If o'er dark stormy seas I drift,
    I hear Thy guiding word ;

If lengthened life, with blessings rife,
 Before my feet be spread,
So Thou my Guide wilt still abide,
 With joy that path I tread.

But must I walk the vale of death
 Through sad and sunless ways,
I pass along in quiet faith,
 Thy glance my fear allays ;
Through the dark land my Shepherd's hand
 Leads to an end so bright,
That I shall there with praise declare
 That all God's ways are right !

THE MARRIAGE OF CHRISTIAN HEARTS.

Full of wonder, full of art,
 Full of wisdom, full of power,
Full of grace to charm the heart,
 Full of solace hour by hour,
Full of wonders, ye shall prove
Is the bond of wedded love.

Two who ne'er upon this earth
 Have each other's faces seen,
Never from their hour of birth
 In each other's thoughts have been,
Find their hearts and hands shall meet
In a bond God maketh sweet.

Here a father trains his child,
 There another watches his :
Driven by winds uncertain, wild,
 Sure their paths through life must miss ;
Nay, but when the time is there,
See a well-consorted pair.

Here a prudent son has grown,
    There a maid in virtue drest ;
Each one is the other's crown,
    Each the other's sweetest rest,
Each the other's joy and light,
But they know it not aright ;

Till it pleaseth Him who holds
    All the world within His hand,
Then the fated hour unfolds
    All the joy that He hath planned,
And in act and deed we see
The long-hidden mystery.

Each one finds and each one takes
    What the Highest for him chose ;
For where Heaven the union makes
    Vainly Earth would interpose ;
And what Heaven hath bid befall
Wisely is ordained for all.

" This or that were otherwise
    Better ordered," oft we say ;
But as darkness fondly tries
    E'er to match the glorious day,
So must fail our human sense
Scanning God's omnipotence.

Where He joins, Man, place no bar !
    Well He knows who best should meet ;
All our schemes blind errors mar,
    His thought only is complete ;
Only His work standeth fast,
When nought else endures the blast.

See the children of His love
    Who in holy marriage dwell,
In what tranquil joy they move,

How their Father prospers well
All their work to happy ends,
And His blessing daily sends :

How their love ne'er fades away,
　But in freshest beauty blooms,
When all other loves decay,
　Other light is lost in glooms,
Other truth no more is true,
Still their constancy is new.

For that love hath hidden springs,
　Where its youth is aye renewed ;
Through their daily talk it sings,
　Sweetens all their daily food,
Gives their hearts a quiet rest,
E'en when toil and care-opprest.

Comes there aught of pain and loss,
　Yet this love is calm and still,
Cheerfully accepts the cross,
　Thinks it is our Father's will,
Trusts the future time will bring
Brighter days upon its wing.

Thus through all their lifetime rolls
　God's rich blessing like a stream,
Feeds their bodies, heals their souls,
　Strengthens every prop and beam,
Makes the house once poor and small,
Rich and great and loved by all.

And at last, when all fulfilled
　Are His purposes of love
Here on earth, He yet doth build
　Fairer homes in heaven above,
Where enwrapt in His embrace
They shall know His depths of grace.

> Full of grace to charm the heart,
>   Full of solace hour by hour,
> Full of wonder, full of art,
>   Full of wisdom, full of power,
> Full of wonders, ye shall prove,
> Is the bond of wedded love.

Among the admirers of Paul Gerhardt we have named the wife of the Great Elector, Louisa Henrietta of Brandenburg. This princess, who was herself a hymn-writer of no mean ability, shines out upon us from among the confused and tragic scenes of that seventeenth century, as almost the ideal of a noble Christian lady. She was the daughter of the Prince of Orange, and grand-daughter on her mother's side of the Admiral Coligny who fell in the Massacre of St. Bartholomew's Day. Her mother, herself a woman of unusual intelligence and piety, educated her with the greatest care ; at her wish the princess was instructed in graver studies than were common with the women of those days, and also in practical household management, and all kinds of feminine handicrafts. She grew up tall, fair-haired, and graceful, and at nineteen was married, at the Hague, to the Elector of Brandenburg. As her father was then very ill with a protracted and fatal malady, she did not however at once leave home, but nursed her father till his death, and then awaited the birth of her first child. In 1649 she set out on her way to Berlin in late autumn weather, and through a country devastated by war and famine. Under the hardships of the journey her own health suffered, and her little son sickened ; and when she arrived in Berlin, it was not to bring her husband and people an heir to the throne, but with empty arms and an aching heart, for the poor infant had died by the way. But she found consolation in the devoted attachment of her husband; he could not bear to be separated from her, and it soon became her custom to accompany him in all the numerous journeys he was constantly making, even in more than one winter campaign against the Swedes and Poles. He consulted her on all affairs of state, and she entered warmly into his plans for restoring prosperity to the land which had suffered so much from war. She sent to Holland for skilful agriculturists, and established model farms in various parts of Prussia; she introduced the culture of the potato, which was before unknown there; and she founded primary schools all over the country, where they had been almost entirely swept away. So deep was the gratitude she won from the common people that the name "Louisa" became the favourite name for girls, and as lately as thirty or forty years ago her portrait was still to be found on cottage walls. When at home her favourite residence was her country house Oranienburg, near Berlin. She had neither inclination nor time for gaiety, beyond what her position required; for, besides all these serious occupations, she took part in works of charity, and was strict in the performance of her religious duties. She was always present at divine service, where she appeared in a very simple dress, and made it a rule never to look in her mirror before going to church. In religion she belonged to the Reformed Church, but she was in the habit of friendly intercourse with Lutherans, and earnestly desired to see peace between the two communions. But one source of sorrow weighed secretly on the princess's heart:

she had no second child; and if the Elector had no son, his race became extinct, and at his death a war of succession might be apprehended. Long she brooded over this grief; at last she resolved to make the greatest sacrifice in her power, and to demand a divorce for the sake of the country. She acknowledged afterwards that she found it very hard to come to this resolution, and it cost her many hours of tears and prayers, but it was done; she appeared before the Elector, and formally announced to him her intention of applying for a divorce, that might enable him for the sake of his people to marry again. But the Elector refused to listen to her proposal; had she forgotten the command that man should not sever what God had joined? If it pleased God to punish them and their country by childlessness, let them submit; but never would he consent to break an oath he had sworn in God's sight. No doubt it was with a lightened heart that she went back to Oranienburg, where a few months of tranquillity so far restored her health, that at length her wishes were fulfilled, and she bore another son. He was born on a Tuesday; and in memory of this great blessing she kept every Tuesday with its own religious observances for the rest of her life, and also founded an orphan-house at Oranienburg for fatherless children. Two more sons followed in due time, one of whom became afterwards the first king of Prussia. The last of the three was born in 1666 at Cleves, and then her health failed, worn out by the great exertions which her life had demanded, and she died, after many months of slow decline, in 1667, at the age of thirty-nine.

One of her last acts is said to have been to induce

the Elector to give up his demand on the Lutheran clergy, and to grant them freedom from the obnoxious subscription, an act[1] which put an end to the discontent and resistance to the government then so widely spread. Among her favourite recreations, especially in times of toil and anxiety, was the reading and singing of hymns, and at her request Otto von Schwerin, the great friend of herself and her husband, made a collection of them which was afterwards published and widely circulated. To this he contributed one or two, and the Electress four hymns, two of which have become classical in Germany ; one is the celebrated Easter hymn,

"Jesus, my Redeemer lives,"[2]

which, with its beautiful chorale, is now in various versions becoming familiar to us in England. It is probable that the Electress composed both the words and the melody of this hymn, but that Schwerin polished the former and Crüger harmonized the latter for her. To this day it ranks among the most popular of German hymns. We give another as being less known, which contains an affecting expression of the consciousness of sin and ingratitude in a life, in which those around her could scarce discern a failing.

PENITENCE.

I will return unto the Lord
From all my evil ways ;
O God, do Thou Thy help afford,
Teach me to seek Thy face,

---

[1] It was not formally published till early in 1668, when Gerhardt had already accepted the archdeaconry of Lübben.

[2] "Jesus meine Zuversicht."

Thy Holy Spirit's strength impart
Who can anew create my heart,
  Deny me not this grace.

For man sees not his wretched plight
  Till Thy touch make him see ;
Without Thy Spirit's inner light
  All blind and dead is he,
Biassed in sense and will and deed ;
O Father, let me now be freed
  From this great misery !

Lord, knock in mercy at my door,
  And all that I have done
Against Thee, do Thou set before
  This heart, till it is won
To mourn that it was e'er so weak,
And in my grief adown this cheek
  Hot tears of sorrow run.

For of thy gifts, ah ! what a wealth
  Hast Thou on me bestowed ;
To Thee I owe my life and health,
  My cup hath overflowed ;
Than food and raiment Thou dost grant
So much besides, that no real want
  Hath darkened my abode.

And Thou in Christ hast rescued me
  From out of death's dark flood,
Thou dost not leave my soul to be
  In lack of any good ;
And lest I dwell in careless ease,
Forgetting Him who gave me these,
  Betimes I feel Thy rod.

Have I then striven as sure I ought,
　To love Thee and obey?
Ah no! this heart and conscience fraught
　With grief, full truly say
I have forgot Thee, and they mourn
With deep remorse and anguish torn
　For Sin's long easy sway.

Till now in false security
　My conscience slept, and said,
" There yet is time enough for thee ;
　God is not stern," it said ;
" So strict account He doth not keep,
The Shepherd's patience with His sheep
　Not soon is spent and fled."

But suddenly that sleep was broke,
　And now my heart will break ;
Thy voice in mighty thunders spoke,
　Thy lightnings made me quake ;
I see the realms of death and hell
Advance in power I cannot quell
　My soul their prey to make.

Ah Jesu Christ! our mighty Rock,
　I flee alone to Thee,
Within Thy clefts from every shock
　O hide and shelter me !
O Lamb of God, didst Thou not bear
All sins of men and e'en my share
　Upon the fatal tree ?

Then with Thy Father intercede,
　That He no more should think
Of all my sins, each evil deed
　That makes me quail and shrink.

Ah let the burden of my guilt,
For which such precious blood was spilt,
    Beneath the ocean sink !

And henceforth will I day by day,
    With strenuous ceaseless care,
From all false pleasures turn away,
    And rather all things bear
Than willingly to sin give place:
Dear Lord, give Thou Thy strength and grace
    To do as I declare !

The Court of Prussia was not the only one at which religious poetry was cultivated. At that of Weimar, the duke who had been a famous general in the Thirty Years' War was a good hymn-writer, and so was his librarian, George Neumarck, the author of one of the best known and finest of the German hymns, "Leave God to order all thy ways."[1] At that of Brunswick not only the Duke, Anton Ulrich, but nearly all the members of his family cultivated both poetry and music with considerable success. Anton Ulrich himself was a very learned man, pupil of two of the most distinguished scholars of the day, and a good and pious sovereign. The stain on his career is that in extreme old age he embraced the Roman Catholic religion avowedly from political motives, and then again reverted to Lutheranism on his death-bed ; but except for this inconsistency he deserved and enjoyed the esteem of his people. His hymns are extremely good, graceful in form, and deep in feeling, and have become very well known. The following little song is among those less commonly to be met with :—

[1] " Wer nur den lieben Gott lässt walten."

PATIENCE AND HUMILITY.

Patience and Humility !
Where these two companions be,
On their lover they bestow
Quiet calm through weal and woe.

He unmoved meets Fortune's frown,
Sees her wheel go up and down,
Ready stands to face alike
Or her smiles or her dislike.

If she frown like blackest night,
Threatening to o'erwhelm him quite,
Patience still will stand his friend,
Bidding him await the end.

If she smile and all restore,
And he grow elate once more,
Safe through snares of wealth and pride
Soft Humility can glide.

If his plans and wishes fail,
Nor his best-laid schemes avail,
Patience helps him still to hope,
And with disappointment cope.

If his efforts all succeed,
And he earn the hero's meed,
Still Humility will say,
" This shall also pass away."

If unkind the world shall prove,
And no heart give love for love,
Patience comforts, "Sad thy lot,
But thou hast deserved it not."

If he sit in highest state,
Friends around him, rich and great,
From all cares and burdens free ;
Safe is still Humility.

Patience is for days of gloom,
Pining grief to overcome ;
But Humility for joy,
Lest it cheat us and destroy.

So until my journey ends
These I choose for daily friends,
For Humility is blest,
And sweet Patience giveth rest.

Only two more names can be mentioned from this circle of writers. The first is that of Albinus, a clergyman of Naumberg, and member of the Order of the Palm, who wrote several very sweet and popular hymns on the joys of heaven, something in the style of Simon Dach. The other is that of Johann Frank (1618—1677), who ranks only second to Gerhardt as a hymn-writer, and with him marks the transition from the earlier to the later school of German religious poetry. In the former, the congregational hymn—"the church-song" as Germans call it—had furnished the type for all compositions of this class, even for those, like the "Ode" of Gryphius given above, which were not meant for church use. Hence it was required that the poem should be capable of being set to music, and should embody such phases of feeling and experience as might fairly be attributed to any large gathering of sincere Christians. These conditions necessitated a certain compression and finish in form, and a certain breadth and vigour in thought; but they also excluded much both in rhythm and sentiment which might legitimately claim a place in Christian poetry. From this time onwards a more personal and individual tone is to be remarked even in congregational hymns, and with it a tendency to reproduce special forms of Christian experience, often of a mystical character. Gerhardt stands precisely on the culminating point between the two schools. His whole tone and style of thought belong to the elder school, but the distinct individuality and expression of personal sentiment which are impressed on his poems already point to the newer. Frank stands near him, but on the side of the newer school; his leading thought is the union of the soul with its Redeemer; "that Christ be *in* you the hope of glory" is the keynote of his hymns. The style both of his religious and secular poetry is curiously unlike what we should have anticipated from the little we know of his life. He was the son of an advocate in the little town of Güben in Saxony. Having lost his father early, he was brought up by relations, who sent him to the university of Königsberg when Simon Dach and his friends were living there; he travelled a little, and then settled down as an advocate in Güben, and became successively councillor, burgomaster of the town, and representative of the province. It sounds like the career of a diligent, sensible, quiet German citizen, but he was also one of the principal poets of the day, and a very voluminous one. His secular poems, like those of his contemporary George Neumarck, belong to the pastoral school, and are long-winded and affected to an extraordinary degree. His religious songs, on the other hand, published in 1674 under the title of the " Spiritual Zion," are remarkably fine; condensed, and polished in style, with a fervid and impassioned movement of thought. The following is one of his most celebrated hymns, but from its peculiar metre it loses much in translation :—

TO THE SAVIOUR.

Jesu, priceless treasure,
Source of purest pleasure,
 Truest friend to me!
Long my heart hath panted,
Till it well-nigh fainted,
 Thirsting after Thee!
Thine I am, O spotless Lamb!
I will suffer nought to hide Thee,
 Ask for nought beside Thee.

In Thine arm I rest me,
Foes who would molest me
 Cannot reach me here;
Though the earth be shaking,
Every heart be quaking,
 Jesus calms my fear;
Sin and hell in conflict fell
With their heaviest storms assail me,
 Jesus will not fail me.

Satan, I defy thee;
Death, I need not fly thee;
 Fear, I bid thee cease!
Rage, O world, thy noises
Cannot drown our voices
 Singing still of peace;

For God's power guards every hour,
Earth and all the depths adore Him,
   Silent bow before Him.

Wealth, I will not heed thee,
Wherefore should I need thee,
   Jesus is my joy !
Honours, ye may glisten,
But I will not listen,
   Ye the soul destroy !
Want or loss or shame or cross
Ne'er to leave my Lord shall move me,
   Since He deigns to love me.

Farewell, thou who choosest
Earth, and heaven refusest,
   Thou wilt tempt in vain ;
Farewell, sins, nor blind me,
Get ye far behind me,
   Come not forth again ;
Past your hour, O pomp and power ;
Godless life, thy bonds I sever,
   Farewell now for ever !

Hence all thoughts of sadness,
For the Lord of gladness,
   Jesus, enters in !
Those who love the Father,
Though the storms may gather,
   Still have peace within ;
Yea, whate'er I here must bear
Still in Thee lies purest pleasure,
   Jesu, priceless treasure !

CHAPTER X.

THOUGH the middle of the seventeenth century marks an epoch in the literature of Germany, different tendencies of thought are never really parted by so sharp a line of demarcation : the new school first grows up by the side of the old one; and so in this instance too we must go back to the days of the great war for the men who first introduce the new style. In an unpoetical age like the one that was now approaching— empty of the great interests and vivid sentiment of a common life that furnish the soil on which true poetry springs—the art is apt to degenerate into an artificial sort of composition of either a didactic or a sentimental kind, which here and there rises a little above the dead level of mere verse-making, where some real gift of song has been bestowed. But it also often happens that the originators of even these styles are very superior to their successors. Certainly Friedrich von Logau, who may be regarded as the beginner of the epigrammatic and didactic poetry, which continued to be so popular in Germany for the next hundred years, has far more thought and vigour of expression than most who followed in his footsteps.

He was born in 1604, of one of the most ancient and noble families in Silesia; his estates lay in that province; he was privy councillor to the Duke of Brieg and Liegnitz; he was a member of the Fruit-bearing Society, and died in 1655. Few as these facts are, they at least make us understand how closely all the tumults of the war must have touched him, and how he nevertheless found time and thought for literary work. And his poems give the same picture,—of a man of strong and original genius, honest and downright, deeply interested in the questions of the day; loving his country, hating foreigners, and the war which benefited none but the foreign mercenaries; longing for a domestic country-life, and mourning over the desolation of his own paternal inheritance. He is distinguished in satire and epigram, and his principal work is a collection of more than three thousand epigrams and aphorisms in verse which were published first in 1639, and afterwards in 1654 under the title of " Three Thousand German Proverbs and Poems, by Solomon of Golaw." Some of these are rough and unpolished in form, but most have force and clear strong sense, and his influence on the writers of his own time was marked. In the next century Lessing again drew attention to his works, and he has ever since ranked among the most important writers of this period.

Logau's poems are chiefly secular, but he also composed a number of religious aphorisms, which were printed in a separate volume in 1704, and all his writings are imbued with a spirit of unaffected manly piety. It is to him we owe those sayings which Mr. Longfellow has made familiar to us, especially that profound one:

RETRIBUTION.

Though the mills of God grind slowly, yet they grind exceeding small;
Though with patience He stands waiting, with exactness
grinds He all.

SIN.

Manlike is it to fall into sin;
Fiendlike is it to dwell therein;
Christlike is it for sin to grieve;
Godlike is it all sin to leave.[1]

THE HIGHEST GOOD.

In this world every man will deem
What pleases him, is good supreme;
But he who gains by his good hap
These four things, sits in Fortune's lap:
A gracious God, a loving wife,
Calm death to end a healthful life.

TOLERANCE.

What force is there on earth can faith compel?
Force can produce denial, not faith as well.

DARKNESS.

Whene'er between the human heart and God's love from on
high
Earth's shadow falls,—our day grows dark, eclipse o'erspreads
our sky;
The sun of God's dear solace gone, whence true delight we
gain,
Only the world is left the heart—that meaneth only pain.

[1] These two versions are quoted from Mr. Longfellow's poems.

EPITAPH ON HIS WIFE.

Reader, dost thou seek to know
What it is that lies below?
Ah! a gift, Mortality
Left too short a time with me.
'Twas a pearl of virtue true,
And a rose of freshest hue,
Gold of faultless purity,
Crimson of shy modesty,
Crystal clear of self-control,
Emerald of the chastest soul,
Ruby of a wedded heart,
Opal of sweet household art,
Sun among all women bright,
To one man his heart's delight,
To her home a fence secure,
In distress its pillar sure,
Busy hand in daily toil,
Cooling breeze in life's turmoil,
Sugar in the bitter day,
Medicine charming pain away,
Friendship in the hour of need,
Truth till death in very deed.

Gentle reader, ah! how much,
More than art of mine can touch,
Have I here resigned to fill
This deep grave: so God doth will!
Stand and ponder o'er in thought
What sore mischief Death has wrought;
Then if one that marks thee say,
Why dost linger by the way?
Answer, that there lieth near
Virtue's self encoffined here!

Another celebrated writer of this period, whose works belong to the newer school, is Johann Valentin Andrea. He was born in 1586, of a family already eminent for learning; he distinguished himself at the universities, and then for some years travelled all over Europe as tutor to various pupils of noble families. Returning to Wurtemberg he came under the influence of the pious and venerable Arndt, became an earnestly religious man and took orders. For many years he was the chief clergyman at Calw, where during the earlier period of the war, when Wurtemberg was as yet untouched, he organized a system of relief and succour to the sufferers elsewhere, which was so energetically carried out, that within five years 11,000 persons had received from it essential assistance. But Calw's own turn came ere long: in 1634 it was stormed and given up to plunder, and Andrea, who was particularly obnoxious to the Imperialists for the part he had taken, fled into the forests with some of his friends. They were hunted for days with bloodhounds, but finally, after undergoing fearful hardships, escaped by the aid of friendly country-people. As soon as the way was open he returned to his charge, where he was received with tears of joy; but in the next two years there followed the usual list of disasters which marked the course of the war,— famine, pestilence, and the passage of troops, until more than two-thirds of the inhabitants had perished, and the small remainder owed to the eloquent exertions of Andrea the scanty support which reached them from other cities. When the storm rolled away from that region of Germany, Andrea consented to leave Calw and accept the post of court preacher at

Stuttgardt. Here he had to cope with difficulties of another and less congenial type. He was a man of fervid and strict piety, with high ideas of church discipline, and the court of Wurtemberg was given up to luxury and amusement as if the country were not bleeding at every pore. He did contrive to make his own house a refuge for the poor, especially those of his own order, to found a theological college, and to inspire new life and better order into the churches more immediately under his influence. But the court disliked him and he had many annoyances and failures to endure, and at last his weakened health furnished a good excuse for getting rid of him by an honourable promotion. He died in 1654 as prelate of Adelberg. His greatest influence was as a Church reformer and a prose writer; he wrote many theological, controversial, and satirical works, both in Latin and German, which earned for him an important place in the prose literature of his day, and admission into the Fruit-bearing Society. But he also published in 1619 a volume of sacred poems called "Spiritual Pastime" (*Geistliche Kurzweil*), which have the merit of deep, pregnant thought in trenchant but often harsh and abrupt expression. We give one called

FORGOTTEN LOVE.

Generous Love! why art thou hidden so on earth
That scarce a heart now knows the truth of thy exalted birth?
  In God Himself there lies thy spring,
   Whence thou in grace dost flow,
  To make all creatures, everything,
   Work man's true good below.

Loveliest Love ! why art thou now so all-concealed,
We cannot taste thy sweetness, nor see thy power revealed ?
   Yet thou the bitter world canst fill
    With honey sweet and pure,
   The sorest pain thy touch can still,
    The heaviest sorrow cure.

Heart-uniting Love ! why art thou shut from us so close,
We fail to find thy constancy, we cannot bless our foes?
   Yet thou in one canst all men bind
    Now scattered far apart,
   In thee may all their solace find,
    And peace and joy of heart.

Constant, true Love ! why art thou lost to us, alas !
That never doth thy steadfastness before our vision pass ?
   Thou dost all covenants uphold,
    Thy promise all may trust,
   For Love can nevermore grow old,
    And Truth can never rust.

Candid, bright Love ! why art thou now so covered o'er with
  lies,   [prize ?
That we thy light and righteousness can neither see nor
   Yet thou dost teach us what is true,
    And dost command the right ;
   In honour giving earth its due,
    While heavenward guides thy light.

Humble, sweet Love ! ah why so far from thee we drift,
No more we seek or value thy fair and costly gift ?
   To seek our neighbour's welfare most
    Thou teachest, as Christ says,
   Nor sufferest us of aught to boast
    Since all is Jesu's grace.

Glowing, warm Love ! why do we scorn thee and disown,
Till o'er the land, in field or town, thy fervour is unknown ?

Thou teachest us with all our powers
To hold the Gospel fast,
That so Christ's kingdom may be ours
In spite of fiercest blast.

Comforting Love ! why art thou chased away so far,
Thy courage cannot strengthen us, who dwell in strife and war?
Thou takest from the cross its weight,
And from the cup its gall,
So Christian men can face their fate,
For they are brethren all.

Holiest Love ! how we forget thy very name,
So that thy heavenly nature on earth wins only blame !
While lip-religion fills the land,
Nay, worldly talk is heard
Till Christian souls in peril stand
To lose the living Word.

God-fearing Love ! why do thy foes, alas ! prevail ?
For many boast the Christian name, yet at thy service quail.
They bear nought, shun nought, love their pelf,
Fast not and run no race,
Nor pray, nor rest, nor die to self,
Yet trust they shall find grace.

Among the leaders of this didactic school may
be mentioned a whole family of the name of Olea-
rius, who throughout this century were clergymen
and hymn-writers, and the last of whom published, in 1707, one of the earliest works on German
hymnology. In the next century it included Hiller
and Rambach, two of the chief hymn-writers of that
time, and a more famous author in Gellert, whose
hymns and odes mark at once its zenith and its close.

The founders of the sentimental school were Harsdörffer and Sigismund von Birken, both belonging to

Southern Germany, where this school flourished more than in the north. Harsdörffer (born in 1607) was a wealthy magistrate and merchant of Nuremberg, belonging to one of the oldest families of its ancient mercantile aristocracy, and in spite of wars and hard times he lived an easy, prosperous life. His prudence in affairs was so highly esteemed that princes and private persons alike applied to him for advice, while in literature he was an active member of the Fruit-bearing Society, and wrote a great deal of poetry both sacred and secular, with some prose works ; among the latter is one which he avers would enable any man who followed its rules to master the whole art of poetry in six hours. In 1644 we find this respected magistrate, then thirty-seven years of age, engaged in a poetical contest, like those of the old troubadours, with a rival poet named Klai, in which the prize was to be a garland of flowers. The judges could not decide which of the two was entitled to the wreath, and so a flower from it was given to each, and they agreed in memory of the occasion to found a new order, that of the " Flowers," and send the remaining blossoms to those friendly poets whom they invited to join them. This order has maintained its existence up to the present day, and celebrated its two hundredth anniversary in 1844. Its members especially devoted themselves to pastoral poetry; and as their usual place of meeting was Pegnitz, near Nuremberg, they were christened by the public "the shepherds and shepherdesses of Pegnitz." Among themselves each was designated by some pastoral name, and in their religious poetry they glorified the pastoral life as peculiarly pleasing to God. Were not all the patriarchs shepherds? Did not our Lord use the same title for Himself and His ministers? Was not the Song of Solomon a pastoral idyll? And thus, as this style became fashionable, it coloured even the hymns of the day, and brought about a change in the whole tone of its religious poetry. It was at this time that the hymn of Nicolai's, quoted above, became so popular, that not only were hundreds of imitations of it composed, but in a secularised form it was widely circulated as a popular love-song. Harsdörffer died in 1658, and was succeeded as head of the order by Sigismund von Birken, a more famous poet than himself, and at one time tutor of the Duke Anton Ulrich. It was under Von Birken that a work was published in 1673, which with his own poems forms a repertory of the productions of this school. It consists of poetical versions of the " Meditations " of a celebrated divine, Dr. Müller of Rostock, thrown into a pastoral form by twenty-nine of these Pegnitz shepherds and shepherdesses. This is now unreadable, but a few of Birken's own poems have found their way into recent collections, and so have some by his friend and follower, Erasmus Finx of Nuremberg. The last great representative of this school was Gessner,[1] who lived in the middle of the next century (1730—1787), and whose " Death of Abel " is said to have been translated into more languages than any other German work, and to have been the first that attracted the attention of Europe to modern German literature. In these days, however, it is difficult to understand what was the charm of those high-flown and wordy

[1] Gessner, and some others of this school, wrote their so-called poems chiefly in prose.

compositions, of which the "Death of Abel" is by far the best.

But the earliest poet of this school deserves notice both for his own sake, and because he is the first Roman Catholic poet of any note since the Reformation. Hitherto the intellectual activity of Germany had been all on the side of the Reformed doctrine; it was so still to a great degree, but the order of the Jesuits was beginning in Southern Germany to push back the advancing tide of Lutheranism, and it is among them that we meet with the first Roman Catholic writers who made a mark on the literature of their time. These were Johann Jacob Balde and Friedrich von Spee. Balde (1603–1668) wrote almost exclusively in Latin, but his " *Carmina Lyrica* " are said to possess remarkable power and fire, and were very much read and imitated in his own day. Friedrich von Spee, on the contrary, wrote in German, expressly as he says, because "it is not only in the Latin tongue, but in the German no less, that men can speak and compose good poetry; if this have been wanting, 'tis the fault not of the tongue, but of the persons who use it." He himself belonged to a noble family of Bavaria, and was born either in 1591 or 1595, at Kaiserswerth. He entered the order of Jesuits as a youth, and taught moral philosophy at Cologne until 1627, when he was transferred to Wurzburg. Here it was part of his duty to act as confessor to the poor creatures who were victims of the popular mania about witchcraft, and he is said to have witnessed the last hours of no fewer than two hundred of these unfortunate persons. The distress of mind thus caused him injured his health, and prematurely whitened his hair, but he did not merely pity, he acted ; to him belongs the great distinction of being the first man in Europe to write openly against trials for witchcraft. It was no slight effort of courage to do so then, but he had the reward of making at once at least one convert, the Count of Schönborn, who afterwards as Archbishop of Mayence was the first prince who prohibited such trials within his dominions. Spee's work, "*De processu contra sagas liber*" (Treatise concerning the Trial of Witches), attracted much attention, and was translated into several languages. He died in 1635 at Trèves, of a fever caught while attending on sick and wounded soldiers—an honourable end to so honourable a life. His principal work, " The Nightingale's Rival " (" *Trutz-Nachtigall*"), was not published till 1649, and in 1666 his " Golden Book of Virtue." Selections from them, somewhat abridged and modified, have appeared from time to time ever since; one, edited in 1849 by W. Smets, a canon of Cologne cathedral, has now a wide circulation.

As a poet, Spee reminds us not a little of the Minne-singers ; he has all their love of nature, their delight in spring-time and the song of birds, and much of their fluency and mastery over rhyme and metre. There is great beauty and grace in his poems, though many of them are too much spun out, and overloaded with quaint conceits. But their chief defect to us is that the pastoral tone, which he had caught from the Italians, seems unbefitting such serious themes as those to which it is here often applied. In one poem, for instance, the moon as the shepherd of the stars gathers her flock around her, and bids them look down with pity and wonder on the sorrows of Daphnis, which are then described through several stanzas, and prove to be the Agony of our Lord in the Garden. Or again, the poet wanders into the woods: near a waterfall he utters the name of Jesus; it is repeated; at first he thinks it is some kindred heart responding to his own, then that it may be Jesus Himself condescending thus to sport with him, then he finds it is the echo, and from that time his delight is to play at ball with the echo, tossing the name of the Beloved to and fro, till all the woods ring with the sweet sound. All this is told in flowing verses, in which the answers of the echo are introduced with great skill; and were the subject an earthly love, it would be a charming little poem. The following is one of his best-known poems, and very characteristic of his style:—

A LOVE-SONG OF THE BRIDE OF CHRIST, IN EARLY SUMMERTIDE.

The gloomy winter now is o'er,
    The storks are back again,
The song of birds is heard once more,
    And nests are built amain.
        The leaves so fair
        Steal forth to air,
    The flowers give promise good;
        The brooks awake,
        And like a snake
    Wind glittering through the wood.

The streams are smiling in the light,
    And all the tiny rills,
The little daughters silver-white
    Of mighty rocks and hills,
        In rapid throng
        Now shoot along

Like arrows on their way ;
 Nor lack they voice
 That can rejoice
As with the stones they play.

Diana, huntress pure and proud,
 And wave and wood-nymphs all,
Now laugh and sport, a merry crowd,
 Where greenwood shadows fall ;
  The sun shines down
  To gild her crown
 And fills with darts her quiver ;
  Her swiftest steed
  Runs loose with speed
 By smoothest road and river.

The summer winds, those youths so fair
 On whispering wings who glide,
Sport with the nymphs in ambient air
 As on light clouds they ride.
  Each tree and bough
  Its utmost now
 Of wealth has all displayed,
  That bird and beast
  When heat-oppressed
 May hide in cooling shade.

The birds' sweet minstrelsy anew
 Its " tirra-lirra " sings,
And many a branch makes music too
 As on the breeze it swings ;
  Each slender spray
  Doth bend and sway
 In time to that sweet tune,
  And many a lute
  And warbling flute
 Is heard beneath the moon.

Where'er one gazes, far and near,
　The world is gay and bright,
All hearts are filled with gladsome cheer,
　With hope and quick delight;
　　'Tis I alone
　　Still grieve and moan,
　No end my sorrow finds,
　　Since Thee to me,
　　And me to Thee,
　Thy troth, O Jesu, binds.

O Jesu, it is only I
　In constant grief must be,
'Tis I alone must mourn and sigh,
　For I am not with Thee !
　　Ah constant grief
　　Without relief
　If we must dwell apart !
　　O bitter lot
　　To see Thee not,
　How sore it wounds my heart !

Nought in the world can give me joy
　But only Jesu's love,
All sport and pleasure but annoy
　Till He the veil remove :
　　With many a cry
　　I call Him nigh
　For many a weary hour,
　　Yet never hear
　　His step draw near ;
　Ah well these tears may shower !

For what avails the lovely spring,
　The sunshine and the light,
The silver brooklet's joyous ring,
　The trees so fair bedight,

The balmy wind
With breath so kind,
The soft meandering stream,
The birds' clear song,
The May-day long,
The meadow's emerald gleam?

What all the joy, the sport, the play,
The happy earth can show?
Without Him grief is mine alway,
And pain and pining woe.
So sore this smart
It breaks my heart,
If Him I may not find;
For Him I weep,
And reft of sleep
Breathe sighs on every wind.

Farewell, O spring-time, rosy dawns,
Fields, forests decked anew,
Foliage and flowers and grassy lawns
All wet with sweetest dew,
Streams flowing by,
Clear azure sky,
Darts of the golden sun!
Full well I know
That grief and woe
O'er me have triumph won.

O Jesu, Jesu, faithful Lord,
Why grieve this heart so sore?
Wilt Thou not now Thy help afford?
Look on me, I implore,
For penitence
And pain would hence

In one swift moment flee,
    If but these eyes
    With sweet surprise
Might rest, dear Lord, on Thee !

A far greater poet than Spee, and one who curiously combines the characteristics of all the various tendencies of thought just mentioned, is Angelus Silesius. Like Spee he employs pastoral titles and imagery to express the love of the soul for her heavenly Bridegroom, and he delights in the beauty of the natural world ; like Logau, he gives us a book full of aphorisms ; and, like Johann Frank, he is imbued with a certain profound and ardent mysticism. His real name was Johann Scheffler, and he was born at Breslau in 1624 of Lutheran parents, and educated at the university of his native place for the profession of medicinè. From very early years he showed a strong predilection for metaphysical and theological researches, and was greatly attracted by the writings of Jacob Böhme. When he grew up he visited the universities of Holland, then famous as medical schools, and sought the acquaintance of men who were remarkable for piety, especially the members of a certain society which had been formed in Amsterdam by the disciples of Böhme. On his return to Silesia he was made private physician to the Duke of Wurtemberg-Ols, and here again was brought into contact with the same kind of thought, for his most intimate friend at Ols was Abraham von Frankenberg, a personal disciple of Böhme, who had written a life of his master. Frankenberg introduced him to the works of many other mystics, especially those of Tauler, Ruysbroeck, and Schwenkfeld, and at his death bequeathed to Scheffler a large library of such works, including many important manuscripts. The tone of piety thus nourished in Scheffler found no congenial air in his native church at Ols. To him the all-important thing was union with Christ, the life of God in the soul ; to the Lutheran clergy of Ols this sounded unmeaning, or even a little heretical ; what they cared for were certain definitions of dogma and external rules of conduct. They began to attack Scheffler; he replied, and they succeeded only too well in driving him out of the Lutheran and into the Roman Catholic Church. He was received into the latter in 1653, when he was twenty-eight years old ; and from this time devoted himself to its service with all the zeal of a proselyte. He was now made private physician to the Emperor Ferdinand III. ; but ere long he renounced his profession entirely, took orders, and returned to Breslau, where he died in the Jesuit convent in 1677. By his exertions the Roman Catholics of Breslau obtained permission to celebrate the festival of Corpus Christi by a public procession through the streets, which had been prohibited since the Reformation. The first time that the practice was resumed was in 1662, on which occasion Scheffler (who had now adopted the name of Angelus) bore the monstrance containing the consecrated Host.

Throughout these years Angelus was constantly engaged in fierce controversy with the church he had left, especially with his old enemy Herr Freitag, the court preacher at Ols ; but it is not by his polemical writings that he is remembered. They do not display any extraordinary ability, and they are marked by a bitterness and vehemence which is in strange contrast with the tone of his poems. So strong is this contrast that, coupled with the absence of any peculiarly Romanist doctrine (except in nine hymns addressed to the Virgin and the saints, which are appended to one of the later editions), it has led to the assumption that his hymns were written before his conversion ; at any rate they were quickly adopted into the hymn-books of the Evangelical Church, and are always counted among the precious treasures of its devotional poetry. The principal work in which they appeared was published first in 1657, and afterwards went through many editions. Its title and preface show the influence of the taste of the times ; it is called, " Sacred Joys of the Soul, or the Enamoured Psyche," and was followed by another collection entitled " The Mourning Psyche." [1] In the preface the " Enamoured Psyche" is admonished to forsake all earthly affections and love the Redeemer alone ; for in Christ is the kindest grace, the most graceful loveliness, the loveliest attractiveness, the most attractive beauty ; He is the charming Daphnis, the careful Corydon, the faithful Damon, the crown of all virtuous shepherds and shepherdesses ; with Him are the beneficent Galathea (kindness), the noble Sophia (wisdom), the fair Callisto (beauty), &c. Some of the hymns of Angelus bear traces of the same style, and have a strong likeness to the one of Spee's already quoted. But a large proportion of them are in quite a different tone, earnest, grave and noble, with a peculiar intensity both of feeling and expression. Such are his well-known hymns : " O

[1] " Heilige Seelenlust oder die verliebte Psyche," and " Die betrübte Psyche."

Love, who formedst me to wear;" "Thee will I love,
my Strength, my Tower;" "O holiest Love, whom
most I love," and many others, which breathe a
profound love to God in Christ, as the Source and
Manifestation of an inexpressible Beauty and Love,
with an ardent longing for entire self-surrender to
Him. The two following little poems are chosen
from those less commonly quoted.

THE HIGHEST SEEKS THE LOWEST.

O Good beyond compare!
 Who would not worship Thee?
What heart that would not long to bear
 Some grief or smart for Thee?
Who would not that his soul and mind
Were wholly unto Thee inclined?

Thou art that Radiance keen,
 For angel-eyes too pure,
Which mortal man hath never seen;
 Yet in this land obscure,
More common than the light of day
Thou shinest round our path alway.

Thou art the Majesty
 Whom nature bows before,
From whom not hell itself can flee,
 Whom earth and heaven adore;
And yet Thou bendest down to show
How Thou canst care for one so low!

Reason's deep primal Source,
 Pure Wisdom art Thou still,
Whose sway with mild resistless force
 Works everywhere its will;
And yet so great Thy grace to me
That Thou wouldst have me reign with Thee.

Thou art the Good Supreme,
  No good canst Thou receive,
The Joy whence only joy can stream,
  To Thee we nought can give;
And yet Thou askest for my heart,
That in Thy joy it may have part.

All Beauty is Thine own,
  Nought fairer canst Thou find,
'Tis Thy own loveliness alone
  Can please Thy Perfect Mind;
And yet Thy love hath chosen me
The shadow, to be sought by Thee.

Thy Throne is fixed on high,
  The depths before it quake,
Vainly would earth's poor kingdoms try
  Th' eternal rule to shake;
And yet a sinning child to save
Thou stoopest to the cross and grave.

O Good beyond compare!
  Who would not worship Thee?
What heart so cold it would not bear
  Some pain and smart for Thee?
Oh would that all my soul and mind
Longed but for this, my God to find!

A SONG AT DAY-BREAK.

Morning Star in darksome night,
Who the sad earth makest bright,
      I am Thine!
      In me shine,
Fill me with Thy light divine!

Lo, Thy heaven is in me here,
Longs to see its Star appear ;
    Break of Day,
    No more delay,
Come and chase these mists away !

For Thy brightness, O my Star,
Earth's poor sun surpasseth far ;
    From Thy sight,
    Lovely Light,
Other suns must hide in night.

All things stand revealed by Thee,
Past and Present and To-Be,
    And Thy smile
    Can erewhile
Night itself of gloom beguile.

Where Thy joyous splendours dart
Faith soon follows in the heart,
    Star most clear,
    Far and near
Thou as Lord art worshipped here !

Come then, Golden Light of souls,
Ere fresh darkness o'er me rolls,
    Be Thou mine,
    In me shine,
Fill me with Thy Light divine !

His other most important work was a collection of spiritual aphorisms, after the manner of Logau, published in 1674 under the title of "The Cherubinical Wanderer" (" *Der cherubinische Wandersmann* "). After having fallen into oblivion, this work was brought forward and re-edited by Friedrich von Schlegel, and has since then been several times republished.

It consists of a series of short sayings, generally comprised in a single couplet, at most in two or three, on the deepest relations of the human soul to God. Many of these sayings are pearls of wisdom, lustrous with a wealth of meaning which grows upon the reader the more he ponders them; but it is no less true that others pass the bounds of deep but sober thought into a mystical pantheism, of which the expression is often extremely and even wilfully jarring. Angelus defends himself against the charge of pantheism by an appeal to the writings of other mystics, especially Tauler; but Tauler, if at times he seems to merge the personality of the human soul in the abyss of the Divine Nature, is practically guarded by his clear, unflinching recognition of duty, and at least he never loses the Divine in the human. It is this last tendency which strikes at times an insoluble discord in these aphorisms. We can only give a very few of them :—

"Th' Unspeakable, that men use God to call,
Utters and shows itself in the One Word to all.

God is all virtue's aim, its impulse and its prize,
In Him its sole reward, its only 'wherefore' lies.

The nobler aught, the commoner 'twill be,
God and His sunshine to the world are free.

My God, how oft do I Thy gifts implore,
Yet know I crave Thyself, oh, how much more!
Give what Thou wilt, eternal life or aught,
If Thou withhold Thyself, Thou giv'st me nought.

All goodness flows from God, therefore 'tis His alone;
Evil springs up in thee, that may'st thou call thy own.

Is aught of good in thee?   Give God the praise of all
To claim it for thine own, is ever man's true Fall.

The noblest prayer is, when one evermore
Grows inly liker that he kneels before.

Faith by itself is dead, it cannot live and move
Till into it is breathed the living soul of Love.

The rose demands no reasons, she blooms and scents the air,
Nor asks if any see her, nor knows that she is fair.

How fairly shines the snow, whene'er the sun's bright
      beams
Illume and colour it with heavenly gleams;
So shines thy soul, white, dazzling as the snow,
When o'er it plays the Day-spring's radiant glow."

Angelus was the founder of what is termed the
second Silesian school of poetry, as that founded by
Opitz is called the first.   The secular productions of
this school are singularly trivial in thought, and trite
and bombastic in expression; but its religious poems,
though not free from grave defects, never fell quite
so low, and some among them were really good.
These had a strong influence on the pietistic hymn-
writers of the next period; and where their ardent
mysticism was tempered with a scriptural and
practical tone of piety, as in Tersteegen, Arnold,
Schmolke, &c., the results are often very beautiful.
Among the best of the school were Knorr von
Rosenroth, author of the lovely little hymn, "Day-
spring of Eternity," and some others—a friend of
Henry More and Lightfoot, and a student of alchemy
and the Talmud, who knew almost the entire Bible

by heart; Christian Scriver, a clergyman at Magdeburg; Homburg, a lawyer of Naumburg; and two
countesses of Schwarzburg-Rudolstadt, who wrote
very sweet and graceful verses.

Although the Roman Catholic Church had produced only two or three original poets, it had not
been unaffected by the great spread of vernacular
hymns since the Reformation. Their use was still
prohibited in church at the ordinary services, but they
were commonly employed at certain festivals, and
collections of them were placed in the hands of the
people. These consisted partly of translations from
the Latin, partly of modified versions of the Lutheran
hymns, partly of the old popular religious songs. It is
indeed to the activity of the priests during the seventeenth century that we owe most of the collections of
these ancient songs. Only a few were actually composed in this century, and the eighteenth was utterly
barren of any good ones. Their great flowering time
was in the fifteenth and sixteenth centuries, and
again in the early part of the present century. But
of those found in collections of this period, though
themselves probably of earlier date, we give two :—

AGAINST THE LUST OF THE WORLD.

> Jesu be ne'er forgot,
> That the World harm us not!
> False is she, proud and cold,
> False are her gifts and gold.
>
> Jesu be ne'er forgot,
> That Honour harm us not!
> Brittle as glass her throne,
> Worthless as straws her crown.

Jesu be ne'er forgot,
That her Pomp hurt us not!
Pomp and the praise of men
Vanish in mist again.

Jesu be ne'er forgot,
That the Flesh hurt us not!
Dust all and merest show,
What doth so fairly glow.

O Flesh, O fading grass,
Passing as bubbles pass,
Fresh to-day and rosy red,
Sick to-morrow, pale and dead!

WHY MY SOUL IS GLAD.

Why is it that life is no longer sad,
And my soul within me is now so glad?
Because with repentance earnest and meet
I cast me at Christ my Saviour's feet.

The light of my eyes had waxen dim
Because my heart had forsaken Him,
My heart was aching and pined away,
Long and weary seemed night and day:

Then to make me love Him still more and more
He forgave the sin I had done before,
And this is the reason, and only this,
That this soul of mine hath found her bliss.

Dear soul, then keep thee now pure and free,
That nought of error be found in thee,
And so prepare thee, through gladness here,
For a heaven of joy without a tear.

CHAPTER XI.

A.D. 1660—1750.

A HUNDRED years elapsed between the close of the great struggle which determined the boundaries and relations of Romanism and Protestantism in Germany, and the opening of that Seven Years' War in which Prussia first asserted her rivalry with Austria for the leadership of their common race. It was a dreary period in German story. Politically the empire had fallen asunder into a number of separate despotic little states ; and the sentiment of national unity had become so nearly extinct, that the loss of the fertile and beautiful Alsace to France seems to have been viewed with wonderful indifference, and the achievements of a general like Prince Eugene only roused a little personal admiration for himself. Socially the life of the people had greatly deteriorated. The rural population was terribly diminished in numbers and wealth ; their means of communication were restricted by the destruction of their horses and the neglect of the roads ; their schools had disappeared, and were but very slowly replaced ; their new houses and churches were bare and barn-like compared to the old ones ; their periodical gatherings for certain purposes of local self-government or for festivities had fallen into disuse. It was a vegetating sort of existence, and the writers of the following age bear testimony to the illiterateness and coarseness of manners which prevailed towards the end of the seventeenth century, even among the gentry of the country districts. In the towns things were but little better. The commerce of Germany had received a serious check; her merchant princes had sunk to the level of petty traders, and adopted the manners and culture of the latter class. Her old free cities were decaying; only a few of the newer ones were growing, and what intellectual life then existed, centred in them, as at Hamburg or Berlin, or at the court of any sovereign who specially protected letters, or still more at the universities. But throughout this period Germany contributes only one really great name to literature —that of Leibnitz; while in France it was the age of Louis XIV. and XV., of military glory and social brilliancy, of Racine and Molière, of Fénélon and Bossuet, of Bayle and Voltaire. And so German men and women found their own life mean and tiresome, and were carried away by admiration of their splendid neighbour, till it became the fashion to imitate whatever was French in manners, dress, or tone of thought, and the very language was wretchedly corrupted by the intermixture of French phrases. Frederick the Great was the first hero to the German people at large who roused in them anew a pride in their own country, yet he himself ostentatiously despised it, and preferred France. Of course there was another class, of which his father may be taken as the type, who hated foreign ways and upheld whatever was most antiquated and unrefined as peculiarly German; but in general the tide set in favour of the foreigners. The pastoral school was an imitation of the Italians; the French were now the great models, and very unfortunate ones for a people whose natural genius was so totally different. German literature reached its lowest ebb under these influences, and one of the earliest signs of its revival was a rebellion against French classicism, and an admiration for our Shakespeare and Milton.

Religion suffered under the same depression. On the one hand was a rigid Lutheranism, which had petrified what had once been living convictions into dead dogmas, and which gave its whole attention to controversies about definitions of doctrines in which the people had ceased to feel a genuine interest. On the other was a genteel indifference, which idolized "enlightenment" (the favourite watchword of the eighteenth century), and indemnified itself for its compliance with certain outward observances by laughing at the whole affair in private. Rabener, a satirist of this period, when characterising the earlier part of the eighteenth century, says, "There was a time in Germany when no satire could be witty at the expense of anything but the Bible, and there were lively heads which had, so to speak, a complete satirical concordance in readiness, that their wit might never run dry. . . . If a groom is conscious of possessing a more cultivated mind than the dairymaid, he startles her by a jest on some text or hymn. All the servants scream with laughter, all admire him, down to the very cowboy, and the poor dairymaid, who is not so witty, stands there abashed."

It was against all this formalism and indifference that the reaction towards a more spiritual and living faith took place, which is known by the name of Pietism. In many points this movement resembled that of Methodism in England, but it preceded it by seventy years. Like Methodism, it laid great stress on the necessity of the new birth ; it prohibited certain amusements and modes of life which had been hitherto considered as at least harmless; and it encouraged private assemblies of Christian persons for purposes of edification, such as the study of the Scriptures or the interchange of spiritual experiences. Like Methodism, too, it encountered at first no little ridicule, and even persecution. It was accused of being an attempt to found a new sect, and vehemently opposed on this ground ; but, unlike Methodism, though it might here and there give rise to some insignificant bodies of separatists, it never did break off from the national church of the country, but remained as a whole a movement within, not outside of it. For nearly a hundred years Pietism exerted a most powerful influence both on the religious and social life of Germany, then it almost entirely disappeared in the new world of thought that opened on that country towards the close of the eighteenth century, and it is only in recent times that traces of its characteristic style of piety are again to be discovered there.

The type of character that we meet with in its earlier followers has something peculiarly attractive about it,—a cordial, active, sincere piety, marked at once by deep and earnest emotion, and by a certain simplicity and sobriety. Ernst Moritz Arndt says of such men: "I can still remember having seen in my early boyhood old men of Spener and Franke's school in pulpits and in houses ; and the blessedness of their strong and strengthening faith, the serene, quiet cheerfulness of a life which no sorrows, no storms of the world without, no unreasonableness of men, could disturb or lay waste, still floats like a lovely flower before the eye of memory." Spener, and through him his immediate disciples, had been led to see a truth which might well produce this result. For what their favourite theme of the insufficiency of a dead faith, and the necessity of a change in the heart and life, really meant was this: that no mere intellectual acceptance of certain doctrines, however true, would save a man, but only a heart and will set right towards God and his neighbour, which must manifest themselves in a life of prayer and charity. Thus they had learnt that Christianity was not primarily a system of doctrine, but a life ; for them religion had been brought back from the sphere of mere reasoning and controversy to that of affection and practical conduct. In after years the negations and limitations of Pietism also bore their appropriate fruit, and of a very different kind ; but as yet we have to do only with its true and nobler side.

Its founder was Philip Jacob Spener, who was born in 1635 in a little village of Alsace. His parents were pious persons, who dedicated their little son from his birth to the ministry, and rejoiced to see that even as a child he showed signs of unusual seriousness. He seems indeed through life to have possessed one of those sweet and harmonious characters which, when strengthened and ennobled by an earnest religion, pass untouched through temptation, and attract affection and admiration from all sides. As a child, it is said those who had charge of him could not remember that he ever committed any actual fault ; once, at the age of thirteen, he joined in a dance, but remorse for what he thought a worldly compliance made him rush away from it in tears of bitter sorrow. He went through school and more than one university with distinction, and blameless as to the ordinary errors of youth ; travelled for some years ; was tutor to two princes of the Palatinate ; then took orders, married, and was appointed, at the age of thirty-one, first preacher and pastor of Frankfort-on-the-Maine. Here his sermons, so unlike the dry controversial disquisitions stuffed with Greek and Latin quotations which the people were accustomed to hear, soon drew crowds to his church, and many persons came to him in private for further counsel. Thus grew up certain meetings for conversation on religious subjects, which afterwards became celebrated under the name of "*collegia pietatis.*" They were held at first in his house, and when the numbers became too great, in his church ; both men and women were present, but as a rule the men only spoke. He also wrote a book on the necessity of a complete reformation in the Church, which excited great attention ; and he took up warmly the cause of education, especially of the very lowest classes. For twenty years he laboured in Frankfort, doing much good, but virulently attacked by the old orthodox party, who saw no use in these new lights, and wished to expel him from the Church ; and not a little embarrassed at times by the zeal of some of his own converts, who began to declare that the Lutheran Church was Babylon, and it was a duty to come out of her. About this time, in 1686, the Elector of Saxony, who in passing through Frankfort had heard him preach, invited him to accept the post of first preacher to the Court at Dresden, a place which was then considered to be the highest dignity in the whole Lutheran Church, and carried with it great influence on ecclesiastical affairs in general. Spener accepted it, and at once began to enlarge his sphere of labour. Besides his directly pastoral duties, he now received into his house a number of young men who wished to become clergymen, one of whom, August Herrmann Franke, was in after years his own chief coadjutor and successor in the new movement. He also carried through various reforms in the Church and education which he had much at heart, among others, that the study of the Scriptures in the original languages should be made an imperative part of the theological course at the University of Leipsic. Of course all this energy raised up enemies as well as friends, but for some time the Elector and the mass of the people were in his favour, and nothing could be done against him. Ere long, however, he himself destroyed his favour with the Elector by addressing to him a private but very earnest remonstrance against one of his personal vices, that of intoxication. The Elector was enraged ; Spener's enemies of course represented that he was wanting in loyalty and proper respect, and he was obliged to resign. He was next, in 1689, invited to occupy the church at Berlin where Paul Gerhardt had preached, and the remainder of his life was spent in that city. The Elector (son of the great Elector and afterwards King of Prussia) was his friend, and when in 1694 he founded a new university at Halle, he appointed to its faculty of theology the pupils and friends whom Spener recommended to him. Spener's influence had now spread over a wide extent of Germany. He had raised up a whole school of energetic men, who were carrying out his ideas in the pulpit, in the new university, and in schemes of active benevolence such as had been hitherto unknown. In Halle, Franke was establishing the first Orphan-house; in Berlin, Baron von Canstein was setting on foot the first Bible Society. Throughout Germany people applied to him for advice or assistance, so that he received more than six hundred letters in a year asking for spiritual counsel, besides all the personal visits for a similar purpose which were of daily occurrence. Acute, gentle, dignified, quick in reading character, and ready in sympathy, he seems to have been remarkably fitted for this position of a sort of universal confessor, and numbers of persons whom he had never seen were earnest in their expressions of gratitude to him for his aid. He had a gentle, clever wife and eleven children, and his house was then considered to be the model of an orderly, cheerful, Christian household. It was not till he was close on seventy that his strength gave way, and after a short illness he died in 1705.

Of his immediate disciples, the most noted were Franke, Joachim Lange, and Breithaupt : the first as a spiritual teacher and leader; the second as the most learned representative of the order, and its champion in the controversies of the day ; the third as a hardworking professor of theology among the students of Halle. Franke was a man of the same type of piety as Spener, but more ardent and passionate in temperament. He belonged to a respectable family of Lubeck, where his father was Syndic; and in 1684, at the age of twenty-one, was sent to the university of Leipsic. The fame of Spener soon attracted him over to Dresden, and the young Franke speedily enrolled himself among the master's most attached disciples. At Spener's instigation in 1686, as a private tutor, he opened classes for the study of the Bible, and though when he began them not a single Bible or New Testament was to be found in any bookseller's shop in Leipsic, within a few months he had from 300 to 400 pupils, many of whom were converted to the new mode of life. It was at this time that the name of Pietists was given to this party in contempt, and in 1690 their opponents in the university succeeded in having these lectures prohibited. On this Franke joined Spener at Dresden, who procured him an appointment with Breithaupt to a church at Erfurt. There his private meetings, the great number of books that were sent to him, and above all the startling effect produced by his sermons, awakened the envy and hostility of the old orthodox and the Romanist parties, who united in accusing him to the Roman Catholic prince as "one of the men who are turning the world upside down." One of his packets of books was seized, and he was summoned before the council, but when, on opening it, it was found to contain nothing but Bibles, the council was fain to let him go again. Presently, however, a decree from the prince deprived him of his post, and commanded him to leave Erfurt

within two days, and it was on his journey to Gotha
on this occasion that he wrote his celebrated hymn,
"Thank God that towards eternity." A few months
later, through Spener's recommendation, he received
the incumbency of one of the suburban churches of
Halle, with a promise of the professorship of Greek
and Oriental languages in the university about to
be founded there. He accordingly went to Halle in
December 1691, and it remained his residence for
thirty-five years, until his death in 1727. Shortly after
his own removal there, Breithaupt, Lange, Anton,
and other friends of the same way of thinking, also
received professorships and pulpits in Halle, and for
many years Halle continued to be the head-quarters
of the Pietistic movement. Spener had given to it
its first spiritual impulse, Franke gave it its practical
organization and utility. Numbers of students flocked
to the new university; nothing like the concourse had
been seen since the days of Luther at Wittenberg.
Within thirty years it had sent out more than 6,000
graduates in theology, besides some thousands who
had been trained in the theological schools founded
by Franke. These men spread themselves all over
evangelical Germany; early in the eighteenth century
they had made their way into other universities than
Halle, and occupied the majority of the pulpits in all
the States, while even the old orthodox party had
been gradually modified by their example, and had
adopted many of their innovations. But Franke's
great work, for which his name must always be held
in grateful remembrance, was that he first in his times
set on foot schemes of organized Christian benevolence,
and recalled Christian people to the duty of personal

effort for the most degraded classes of society. The suburb of Glaucha, where his church was situated, was one of the worst parts of Halle, in which all the low beer-houses and dancing saloons were to be found. Its population was excessively poor and totally uncared for; he laboured as their pastor, gave relief to the poor in a systematic manner, sought out employment for them, founded free schools, and finally his famous Orphan-house. In these undertakings he obtained personal help from his students; money was another matter. He began his schools with four dollars and sixteen groschen, his Orphan-house with seven dollars; it was, as he himself says, "founded in faith and prayer;" he had no lists of subscribers, and he was more than once reduced to his last shilling. But help always came at the right moment; the work grew and prospered as more people came to know of it, and at last he had the happiness of seeing his great schools built on what had been the site of the very worst houses in Glaucha. At the time of his death the establishment contained 145 orphans who were entirely provided for there, 2,200 scholars who were receiving a free education, and it gave daily dinners to nearly 400 poor students at the university, while it also included a printing and publishing house, and a dispensary. Similar institutions were founded in imitation of it in many other German towns, and it is not too much to say that Germany owes to the Pietists the resuscitation of her educational system after the war, the introduction of systematic provision for the poor, and the revival of a purer and more refined domestic life.

During all this period the hymnology of Germany

was almost entirely in their hands. Their chief singer was Anastasius Freylinghausen, who was married to Franke's only daughter, and was his father-in-law's successor in the pulpit and the management of the Orphan-house. He was a man of gentle, retiring disposition, liable to severe attacks of nervous pain, but of unwearied activity and a most loving and disinterested spirit. Franke used to say that his own sermons were like a waterspout, which drenched the land but soon ran off again, Freylinghausen's like a gentle steady shower, which penetrated to the depths of the soil. He wrote forty-four hymns of his own, and in 1704 published a hymn-book containing both old and new hymns, which remained for some generations the favourite collection for private reading among pious persons in Germany. It went through numberless editions, and was frequently enriched by new additions. One of Freylinghausen's best known hymns is the following. Several others have been already translated into English, and one or two have found their way into our hymn-books:—

JESUS IS ALL IN ALL.

Thou art First and Best,
Jesu, sweetest Rest!
Life of those who else were dying,
Light of those in darkness lying,
Ever be Thou blest,
Jesu, sweetest Rest.

Life, that stooped to be
Slain for such as me,
Who to save us death hast tasted,
Pardon life and blessings wasted,

Take away our load,
Lead us back to God !

Brightness of His Face !|
To redeem our race,
Ere time was, Thou wast appointed,
Thou didst veil Thee, God's Anointed,
In our human race :
Brightness of His Face !

Conqueror, Thou alone
Hast the powers o'erthrown
Of the world, the flesh, the devil ;
Souls that once were slaves to evil,
Thou hast made Thine own,
Conqueror, Thou alone !

Highest Majesty !
King and Prophet ! see
To Thy gentle rule submitting,
At Thy feet like Mary sitting,
I would learn from Thee,
Highest Majesty !

O Thou Light Divine !
Make me wholly Thine.
Wisdom by Thy Spirit knowing,
With Thy love and ardour glowing,
Thou within me shine,
O Thou Light Divine !

Thy humility
And Thy kindness be
In my heart for ever dwelling,
Pride and anger thence dispelling,
Till Thyself Thou see
Mirrored, Lord, in me.

Is my foolish mind
To the world inclined?
Strengthen it no more to waver,
But to seek alone Thy favour,
Wealth in Thee to find ;
Grant me, Lord, Thy mind.

In the darksome night,
When the billows' might
Roars around my little vessel,
And with bitter fears I wrestle,
Let Thy arm of might
Save me in the night.

Let my soul be strong,
Bold to suffer wrong
For Thy sake though I should perish ;
Life nor earthly wealth to cherish,
All to Thee belong ;
Only make me strong.

And when I must die
Let me feel Thee nigh ;
Through the valley walk beside me,
To the heavenly glory guide me,
Till I find me nigh
To Thy throne on high.

Almost all the leading men of this school occasionally composed hymns, but there were many among them who did not write more than two or three. Franke himself wrote only three hymns, which were all good : the one already named, " What within me and without," and a third, better known in Bogatzky's version, " Awake, thou Spirit, who of

old." Spener wrote eleven, from which we choose
the following :—

QUIETNESS OF HEART.

Shall I o'er the future fret,
And the past for aye regret?
Shall I ne'er at evening close
Smiling eyes in calm repose?
Shall the thought be ne'er forgot,
What may be my future lot?
Since these torturing cares are vain,
And their end can ne'er attain.

God hath kept me hitherto ;
Can He cease, then, to be true?
Why should I just now despair,
Can He weary of His care?
Hence, tormenting terrors, hence !
God shall be my confidence ;
Let Him lead me as He will,
O my soul, and be thou still.

Whatsoe'er my heart hath planned,
He alone can understand
What is good and well for me,
What will really hurtful be ;
If I will but let Him choose,
No true good I e'er shall lose,
But self-will and busy thought
Oft mistaken paths have sought.

If obscure my place and low,
I will bid my proud heart know
'Tis the safer from a fall,
Free from cares that vex and thrall ;

Or if God would have me great,
I accept my high estate,
He the needful powers will give
Worthily to Him to live.

If He send within my door
Worldly wealth unknown before,
May He also let me find
Wealth of soul and heart and mind ;
Or if poverty be sent,
I can still be well content,
For a rich eternity
Well I know is waiting me.

If my God should health bestow,
Zealously I strive to show
How I thank Him, how my aim
Is to spread His glorious Name ;
And when sickness comes again,
May His Spirit 'mid my pain
Whisper, " There is blessing true
In this bitter medicine too."

If I number many a year
In life's ever-vexed career,
Oft my heart will find a day
When awhile it may be gay;
Or if soon the end shall come,
I am but the sooner home,
Freed from all my sorrows' load,
Happy with my Lord and God.

So to God I leave it all ;
Whatsoe'er may here befall,
Joy or trial, life or death,
I receive it all in faith,

And this anxious heart of mine
Learns to trust its Guide Divine,
Since it well hath understood
All things work the Christian good.

The number of hymn-writers among the Pietists is thus very large: among the principal of the older school are Lange; Winkler and Schade, two of Spener's curates in Berlin; the Freiherr von Canitz, one of his earliest noble converts, and an author of merit in general literature; Richter, the physician of the Orphan-house at Halle; and Laurentius Laurenti, precentor of the cathedral at Bremen. Two of the best hymns of this period were written by men who, as far as we know, never wrote any others. One is "All praise and thanks to God Most High," which was composed in 1673 by Johann Schutz, a man of high standing in the Town Council of Frankfort, who was Spener's most intimate friend during his residence in that city: the other is, "Whate'er my God ordains is right," of which the author was Samuel Rodigast, head-master of the principal gymnasium of Berlin, and also a friend of Spener's. He wrote it in 1675 for a sick friend.

Of the younger Pietists who had grown up under the influence rather of Franke and Freylinghausen than of Spener, the chief hymn-writers are Allen-dorf, pastor of St. Ulrich's Church in Halle, Woltersdorf, Rambach, and Bogatzky, whose name is still known among us as the author of the "Golden Treasury," a work which has been translated into most European languages, and from fifty to a hundred years ago was the favourite book for daily devotional reading of pious people in England. Bogatzky belonged to a worldly and ambitious family; he began life as a page at court, and his father was bent on his entering the army. He himself was even then more inclined to study; and a certain friend of his family, an old Count Reuss, a religious and clever man, induced his father to let him go to Halle and see Franke. The result was his determination to study theology, and to cast in his lot with the Pietists. His delicate health prevented him from ever taking the regular charge of a church, and he devoted himself through life to authorship, assistance in charitable undertakings, and speaking in private assemblies. His noble birth procured him admittance to the higher circles of society, and he counted many converts among the nobility of Silesia, Bohemia, and Saxony. Freylinghausen, and afterwards Franke's son Gottlieb Franke, were his most intimate friends; and the latter invited him, after his wife's death, to occupy apartments in the Orphanhouse, where the last twenty-eight years of his life were spent, until his death in 1774, at the age of eighty-four. He lived long enough to see the tide of feeling in Halle turned against the Pietists who had so long swayed it, and in favour of the scepticism which was then spreading from France into Germany; and this experience darkened his later years, for in place of the veneration with which he had been once regarded, he was frequently the subject of ridicule and of attacks from the younger students. Bogatzky, with the other writers just named, were the chief authors of a certain collection of hymns, called from its place of publication the "Cöthen Hymns." Both in character, and in the position it occupied in the religious history of the time, this book strongly resembled the " Olney Hymns " of Newton and Cowper; but comparatively few of its original productions are now ranked among the classical hymns of Germany. Those of Bogatzky are among the best; he composed about four hundred hymns in all for this and other collections, some of which have great thoughtfulness and dignity, but not the simplicity or melody which would adapt them for congregational use. The following was composed after witnessing a storm among the mountains of the Riesengebirge :—

THE ALMIGHTY GOD.

Jehovah, God of boundless strength and might,
    How great Thy glory, Lord, in all the earth !
How wondrously Thy wisdom guides aright
    The creatures all to whom Thy Word gave birth !
Thou only art the Lord for evermore,
    Perfection absolute alone art Thou,
    Worthy alone that heaven and earth should bow
Before Thy throne, and awe-struck Thee adore.

The hosts of heaven proclaim Thee wise and just,
    And every flower that blooms beside our ways,
Each tiny worm that creeps along the dust,
    Or murmuring forest-bough, declares Thy praise !
Alas ! that man for whom these all were made,
    Himself his Maker's master-piece,—that he
    So slow to praise and gratitude should be,
So apt to rest in what must pass and fade !

Ah who would dare rebel against Thee here?
  Who pride himself on gifts that are not his?
Who fail to worship Thee in lowly fear?
  Nor trust the care that cannot guide amiss?
Hath man once owned Thy great Omnipotence,
  Mistrust and doubt he then can cast aside
  And in humility and hope abide,
Though clouds may veil Thy ways from sight and sense.

Before Thy power the hills and valleys shake,
  The winds and waves are silent at Thy word;
The devils hear it, and with fear they quake,
  While all the heavens to quicker joy are stirred.
O'er countless worlds Thou, mighty King, dost reign!
  And yet in me dost condescend to dwell;
  Must not Thy presence every fear dispel,
Or could I trust Thy power, my God, in vain?

Eternal Being! Perfect Purity!
  Exalted evermore, Thou triune God!
What am I, Lord of Hosts, compared to Thee?
  How canst Thou choose my heart for Thine abode?
I cast me down before Thee in the dust,
  Low at Thy feet a withered leaf I lie,
  Yet Thou dost bid me with Thy hosts on high
Sing of Thy praise, look up to Thee and trust.

Would I could praise Thee with an angel's tongue!
  By all that lives and breathes below, above,
In earth and heaven, O be Thy praises sung,
  And teach my heart Thee, only Thee, to love!
O Lord of Hosts, fill Thou my every thought,
  In all things let me seek Thy glory first,
  All idol-worship be to me accurst,
For Thou art God alone, and I am nought.

By the end of the century, the influence of Pietism was perceptible in many quarters where it was not formally accepted. The old orthodox party, as it was called, changed its character, and the best of its hymns are henceforward scarcely to be distinguished from those of the Pietists. Little of real merit was produced at this time, though two of the writers of this school, Neumeister, a pastor in Hamburg (died 1756), and Schmolke, wrote an enormous quantity. The latter (1672-1737) was called in his own day the "Silesian Rist," and had really much in common with Rist—his extraordinary facility, his tendency to wordiness, and his occasional excellence. Schmolke composed altogether 1188 poems and hymns of a religious character, and it may well be imagined that a large number of them are poor enough; yet a few are really very good, with an easy flow, a heartiness, and a simplicity that are rarely found among the hymns of this period. He was for many years the pastor of Schweidnitz, in Silesia, and was a man of great personal piety, which was proved by the patience and cheerfulness with which he bore seven years of illness following a paralytic stroke.

A good many of Schmolke's best hymns have been translated into English already; we therefore give one from another writer of the so-called "orthodox party," whose hymns are among the most thoughtful and poetical of this period. This is Wolfgang Dessler (1660-1722), a pupil of Erasmus Finx of Nuremberg, and head-master of the grammar-school of that city.

A SONG OF THE CROSS.

Courage, my heart, press cheerly on
  Along the thorny way,
For joy shall come with victory won,
  Though pain be ours to-day:
    Nor shrink the load to take
    Which love shall easy make ;
Can these light transient woes compare
With glory that awaits us there ?

'Twas by a path of sorrows drear
  Christ entered into rest ;
And shall I look for roses here
  Or think that earth is blest ?
    Heaven's whitest lilies blow
    From earth's sharp crown of woe,
Who here his cross can meekly bear
Shall wear the kingly purple there.

Where would the garden's splendour be
  If north and south winds slept ?
Its spices flow most fragrantly
  When long the clouds have wept.
    Only do Thou remain
    My Rest in every pain,
My Sun that cheers me still with light,'
When storms of grief would else affright.

For Thou, my God, art Sun and Shield
  To every faithful heart,
That to be made like Thee would yield
  To trial's fiercest smart,
    Would bear earth's darkest woe
    If Heaven may but bestow
On patient love the martyr's palm,
For vanquished grief, Thy perfect calm.

And yet, dear Lord, this shrinking heart
Still trembles as of yore :
Come, Cross beloved, nor e'er depart
Till I have learnt Thy lore !
Here, scorned with Him I love,
There, crowned with Him above ;
Here to the cross with Jesus pressed,
There comforted with Him and blest.

Then I will meekly yield me up
To suffer all Thy will ;
I know the seeming bitter cup
O'erflows with mercy still ;
In every cross I'll see
The crown that waits for me,
Thy patience shines and beckons on
Until the starry heights are won.

In Southern Germany Pietism found its most congenial soil in Wurtemberg, where the ground had
already been prepared by the labours of Andrea.
At first it showed itself in small fanatical sects, which
drew down on themselves not a little contempt
and even persecution, and a prohibition of all private
meetings for any religious purpose whatever.   But it
soon found an excellent leader in Albert Bengel (1687–
1732), one of the brightest examples of this school.
He was a man of earnest piety, and of a remarkably powerful and sagacious mind, whose position as
head of the important theological seminary of Den-
kendorf, and afterwards as prelate and member of the
consistory, gave him great influence over the whole
development of religious thought in Wurtemberg, and
enabled him among other things to procure the repeal

of the law against religious meetings. He was the author of many prose works on theology, of which those on Biblical criticism, especially his "Gnomon," held a high place in the estimation of theologians; and he also wrote a few good hymns.[1] But the chief poet of this part of Germany was Philip Frederick Hiller. He was the son of a pastor in Wurtemberg (1699-1769), a pupil and afterwards a friend of Bengel's, and himself a pastor in two or three villages of his native country, and finally for many years at a small place called Steinheim. In his early manhood he was a small, fair, active man, cheerful and alert, with a fine resonant voice, and great skill in music, and he was happily married. But life brought him many depressing trials; he had a large family, and an extremely small income; the part of the country where he lived was one in which the sectarian spirit was strongest, and the principal families in his parish were infected by it, and either rejected his ministrations or received them in an unfriendly and critical spirit. He fell into ill health, and after a long struggle with it he was obliged to succumb in his fifty-second year, and give up preaching. With rest he recovered to some extent, but he entirely lost his voice, so that for the rest of his life he could only speak in a husky whisper. Still he continued to hold the living of Steinheim; he had a curate to preach for him, and he was able after a time to resume most of his pastoral duties, while the enforced leisure which

---

[1] He was a student of prophecy, and fixed on the year 1836 as the close of the present dispensation, candidly adding, however, "Should that year pass over without some wonderful change, there must be a fundamental error in my system."

his illness brought him was occupied with writing religious works. Among them was a collection of short poems in alexandrines called "Sacred Morning Hours," and a "Life of Jesus" in the same metre; but his best known were two volumes of hymns: one, called the "Little Paradise," consisted chiefly of poetical versions of prayers from Arndt's "Garden of Paradise;" the other, "The Casket of Spiritual Songs," was entirely original. This last soon obtained a very wide popularity throughout Southern Germany; it is still the commonest book in Wurtemberg next to the Bible itself; and German emigrants, of whom a very large proportion belong to these regions, have carried it to the backwoods of America and the mountains of the Caucasus. We are told that some thirty years ago a German colony in the latter country was attacked by a hostile tribe of Circassians, and the sons and daughters carried into slavery. As they were torn from their parents' arms, some of the latter hastily cut up two copies of Hiller's "Casket," and distributed the leaves among their children that they might not forget their religion among the barbarians.

Hiller's model was Paul Gerhardt; he has indeed less poetical power than Gerhardt, and his style is more purely didactic, but his hymns are never in bad taste, never irreverent or extravagant; they are written in modest scriptural language, and their predominant tones are those experiences of penitence, of gratitude to the Saviour, of trust in the compassionate love of God, which are common to all Christians. Many too are appropriate to special conditions of life, such as health or sickness, marriage, childhood or old age, and thus his "Casket" forms a useful manual of daily devotion. Well is it for any people that hymns of such deep, thoughtful, practical piety should be their daily spiritual food. We give two of the best known: the first is more reflective and less simply popular than many of Hiller's; the latter is a very favourite hymn in sickness.

THE GROUND OF ALL THINGS.

Thou fathomless Abyss of Love,
　O God, Eternal highest Good!
Whom doth some wondrous impulse move
　To pour Thy mercies like a flood
Around our life; Thou Sea of Grace,
　Fountain of comfort ever nigh,
　Healer of souls that wounded lie;
Hearken, my spirit cries to Thee,
O very Love, canst Thou love me?

O bounteous Being! let me praise
　And thank Thee from my spirit's ground;
Thy wisdom far transcends our gaze,
　Thy loving-kindness hath no bound;
How tender to the sin-defiled,
　How great to us who are so small,
　How fatherly and true to all,
Deigning to count the least thy child:
　Hearken, my spirit cries to Thee,
　O mighty Love, wilt Thou love me?

My prayers, my longings Thou dost hear,
　And for my wants dost Thou provide,
Thou countest every sigh and tear,
　No sorrow from Thine eye can hide,

Thou sendest it, and know'st it well ;
　From Thee comes pain and its relief,
　Thou triest me with care and grief,
That faith and love may in me dwell ;
　And so my spirit cries to Thee,
　O tender Love, now love Thou me !

And Thou dost all our sins forgive,
　Thy Word hath promised grace and aid,
Solace and light, that we should live
　Of death and sin no more afraid ;
Thou givest us Thy dearest Son,
　Made of our race, through love supreme,
　To bear our burden and redeem
The souls that so much ill had done ;
　And so my spirit cries to Thee,
　O wondrous Love, canst Thou love me ?

The love of Christ shall bid me feel
　That He hath made me all His own ;
I hear that pleading love's appeal
　Whene'er His gospel is made known ;
And His example here on earth
　Shall be my rule in all I do,
　In utmost pain my pattern true,
My Guide in time of wealth or dearth ;
　Hearken, my spirit cries to Thee,
　O holy Love, dwell Thou in me !

That Love hath suffered and was slain
　To make my death a thing of nought ;
And rose to glorious life again,
　That I might rise in heart and thought
And hath ascended up on high,

To make for me an open way
To heaven itself, where day by day
Our faith and hope may upwards fly;
    Hearken, my spirit cries to Thee,
    O Son of Love, now love Thou me!

And Thou Thy Spirit dost bestow
    To hallow all our life to Thee,
To pour clear light on all below,
    And give the blinded power to see;
Thou Comforter from age to age
    Of all the weary, all who weep;
    Whose peace within us true and deep
Is earnest of our heritage:
    Hearken, my spirit cries to Thee,
    Spirit of Love, O love Thou me!

*   *   *   *   *   *

So doth Thy boundless Love embrace
    My life, my death, and life to come;
O let me know it in that place
    Where only is our proper home!
Thy Love is life and endless rest:
    There is no good to add to this,
    In earth or heaven our only bliss
Is by Thy Love to be possest:
    Therefore my spirit cries to Thee,
    O Blessed Love, dwell Thou in me!

HE MAKETH ALL OUR BED IN OUR SICKNESS.

Bed of sickness! thou art sweet,
If I lie at Jesu's feet;
Only there true health I find,
Health of body and of mind;

Only there is living life,
When His voice ends fear and strife,
" Lo thy sins are all forgot ;"
Then can Death affright me not.

Lord, I thank Thy ceaseless care ;
All my suffering Thou dost share,
Thou true penitence hast sent
Whereof needs not to repent ;
Breathest longing through my pain,
Thy salvation to attain,
Breathest faith within my breast,
On Thy grace alone to rest.

Great Physician of the soul,
Thou canst fear and pain control,
Thine the power is to forgive,
Thine to make faith truly live ;
Is this sickness for me meet ?
Lay me only at Thy feet,
I shall live there on Thy grace,
Live to thank Thee and to praise.

It was under the impulse received from the Pietists
that the Reformed Church first produced any hymn-
writers of mark ; but from this time onwards it can
show a succession of such authors, though it was
never nearly so rich in them as the Lutheran. Its
first poet too was, with the exception of Tersteegen,
by far its best, Joachim Neander. He belonged to a
family of Bremen in easy circumstances, and in his
youth was a wild and careless student. One day he
and two of his comrades went into St. Martin's Church
at Bremen, with the intention of making a jest of
the whole affair. But the sermon touched him so

deeply that he determined to visit the preacher in private; and from this time he began to draw back from many of the coarser pleasures in which he had formerly indulged. But he was still a passionate lover of the chase, and once followed his game on foot so far that night came on, and he utterly lost his way among rocky and wooded hills, where the climbing was difficult even in daylight. He wandered about for some time, and then suddenly discovered that he was in a most dangerous position, and that one step forward, which he had been on the point of making, would have thrown him over a precipice. A horror came over him that almost deprived him of the power of motion, and in this extremity he prayed earnestly to God for help, vowing an entire devotion of himself to His service in the future. All at once his courage returned; he felt as though a hand were leading him, and following the path thus indicated, he at length reached his home in safety. From this day he kept his vow, and a complete change took place in his mode of life. After completing his university course he accompanied some rich merchants' sons to Frankfort, and here he made the acquaintance of Spener, Schütz, and the little clique of religious persons, of whom Spener was the centre in that city, and a warm friendship grew up between them which lasted through life.

In 1674 he was made head-master of the grammar-school at Dusseldorf, belonging to the Reformed Church. It flourished exceedingly under his rule; but he also set on foot private religious meetings after the pattern of Spener's, and these gave great offence. He was accused of heresy; and one day the elders of the church made their way into the school, and before the pupils charged him in an abusive manner with various errors of doctrine, ending with the announcement that he was deposed from his mastership, forbidden to preach, and banished from the town. His pupils would have liked to fight for him, but he forbade them, and submitted. It was summertime, and feeling himself utterly friendless there, he wandered out to a deep and beautiful glen near Mettmann on the Rhine, where for some months he lived in a cavern, which is still known by the name of "Neander's Cave." In this retreat he composed many hymns, and among them the following :—

SONG OF SUMMER.

O Thou true God alone,
Thou Good no creature-soul can comprehend,
Thou great and Holy One,
The Lord of Hosts most strong,
To Thee I raise my song,
Thou art the Lord, whose wonders never end!

A deep and holy awe
Put Thou, my God, within my inmost soul,
While near Thy feet I draw,
And my heart sings in me,
And my voice praises Thee;
Do Thou all wandering sense and thought control.

Let all things join with me
To tell Thy praises and Thy fame abroad;
Let earth and sky and sea,
With voices pure and clear,
Resounding far and near,
Proclaim how great the glory of the Lord!

O God, the crystal light
Of Thy most stainless sunshine here is mine,
It floods my outer sight;
Ah let me well discern
Thyself where'er I turn,
And see Thy power through all Thy creatures shine.

Lo, how the cloudless dome
Like to a clear and dazzling mirror gleams,
Of light the very home;
O Thou, transform my heart,
Till pure in every part
It mirrors back undimmed Thy golden beams.

Hark, how the air is sweet
With music from a thousand warbling throats,
Which Echo doth repeat;
To Thee I also sing,
Keep me beneath Thy wing,
Disdain not Thou to list my harsher notes.

Ah! Lord, the universe
Is bright and laughing, full of pomp and mirth;
Each summer doth rehearse
A tale for ever new,
Of wonders Thou canst do
In sunny skies and on the fruitful earth.

Thee all the mountains praise,
The rocks and glens are full of song to Thee;
They bid me join my lays
And laud the Almighty Rock,
Who safe from every shock
Beneath Thy shadow here dost shelter me.

I hear the waters rush
Far down beneath me in the hidden glen,
They break the quiet hush,
And quicken all my mind
With keen desire to find
The Fountain whence all gladness flows to men.

How various and how fair
I find Thy works where'er I turn my sight;
Beauty is everywhere
Without or stint or bound,
And Wonder all around;
Would that all hearts would ponder this aright!

Wisdom hath made them all,
Its order reigns through all these wondrous things!
Earth's brightness doth recall
Thy brighter Love to mind,
So endless and so kind;
Sing, O my soul, as now all nature sings.

In 1679 he was called to the very church in Bremen
which he had once entered in mockery, but he only
preached there one year; he died at Easter, 1680, not
quite forty years old. Neander's style is unequal;
occasional harshnesses contrast with very musical
lines, but there is a glow, a sweetness, and a depth
about his hymns which have made many of them
justly and lastingly popular among the German
people.

CHAPTER XII.

THE impulse given to religious life by the Pietistic movement coincided, to a certain extent, with that received from the study of Böhme and similar writers, and under the combined action of the two a number of preachers and writers, and even of small sects, sprang up in various parts of Germany, who seceded from the national Church, and claimed a greater strictness both of life and doctrine. The general characteristic of these, as is frequently the case, was an exaggerated individualism ; because religion is an inward life in the individual soul, therefore to them it was nothing else. The outward aids, the guiding principles and defined sphere of action presented by the written Word and the Church, were valueless, or positive stumbling-blocks if they interfered with the movements of the inspired soul. Some of these men lost themselves in wild vagaries of belief and even of morals ; as the followers of a man named Eller and a woman named Eva Butler, who made many converts in Southern Germany : others of purer life still believed themselves to enjoy immediate revelations, like a certain Fraülein von Asseburg, whose

visions were widely talked of and believed in by
many good and educated persons ; indeed a whole
sect grew up, which asserted the continuance of direct
revelation and miraculous gifts in the believers, and
was known by the name of Inspirationists. To this
belonged an iron-master's apprentice named Rosen-
bach, and a wig-maker of Nuremberg named Tennhart,
who roamed all over Germany calling themselves the
prophet and chancellor of God, and made many
proselytes. In Silesia there was a community of
inspired children, who built a little church for themselves, preached and prayed in it, and whose prayers
were supposed to have a wonder-working power.
But there were not wanting among these Separatists
men of a far higher type, of unmistakeable piety and
no little ability, much of whose conduct and teachings awaken admiration, though marred by want of
breadth and judgment. Such men were Petersen,
a leader of the Chiliasts, or those who were looking
for a speedy advent of the Lord ; Dippel, a controversial writer and great preacher,—he was the chemist
who discovered Prussian blue and an oil that bears
his name ; and Hochmann, a friend of Tersteegen, who
used to travel about the country attacking the luke-
warmness of the established clergy, and would rise
up in church when the sermon was over and preach
another from his own point of view. The influence
of these Separatists on hymnology was for the most
part simply mischievous, and their hymn-books contain
about the worst specimens to be found, poor as poetry,
fiercely intolerant towards their fellow-Christians, and
full of a fantastic and irreverent adoration of the
Redeemer. On the other hand, two of the nobler

minds among them produced some of the very best hymns which the newer school has to show, and which were at once adopted with delight by the whole Evangelical church of Germany. These were Gottfried Arnold and Gerhard Tersteegen, men in whom we see two well-marked and differing types of the mystic. Arnold, of a passionate impetuous temperament, has a soul with the dusky glow of a repressed fire, that at times breaks forth into a clear, ardent flame; Tersteegen's mind, naturally humble and peace-loving, is like a profound crystal lake, that cares only to reflect the heavens above and nothing of the earth around. It must be observed, however, that both these men, though they held much intercourse with the Separatists, and were frequently in antagonism with preachers and members of the established churches, yet never actually joined any sect.

Gottfried Arnold, born in 1666 at a small village in Saxony, was the son of a poor schoolmaster, and lost his mother while he was yet quite a child. Thus his early years were marked by struggle and hardship, and an absence of that home-tenderness which might have softened his naturally rugged and overbearing disposition. In 1689 he came to Dresden, at the age of two-and-twenty, as tutor in a noble family. Here he met with Spener, was strongly attracted by him, and considered that he owed his conversion to Spener's meetings for religious conversation. Their friendship continued through life. Spener had a great admiration for Arnold's genius and entire conscientiousness, and frequently employed his influence with success on his behalf. Arnold was deeply attached to Spener, but he thought him too gentle, too much inclined to balance between the opposite sides of a question, and not unfrequently censured his practical conduct. At Dresden, as soon as he was converted, he at once began to express in the most open and severe manner, his disapprobation of the life that was going on around him, a proceeding which of course led to an abrupt dismissal from his situation. For the next sixteen years he led an unsettled life. He received various appointments, among them a professorship at Giessen, and wherever he went, his energy, earnestness, and eloquence were sure to produce an effect and to win him followers. But he always made enemies too by his fierce attacks on whatever seemed to him wrong, especially on the old orthodox party; and as he was in the habit of familiar intercourse with sectarians such as Dippel, and of abstaining from divine service and the Holy Communion where he was not satisfied with the minister, it was easy to find charges against him which generally ensured his removal after a time. In his earlier years he strongly advocated an ascetic life, and spoke much in praise of celibacy, but at the age of thirty-four he married; and though he himself testified that this marriage, which was in every respect a suitable one, had been of great assistance to him in the spiritual life, it gave offence to many of the more zealous of his admirers. Yet amid all these distractions he was a man of truly German industry in the way of authorship, his greatest work being "An Impartial History of the Church and all Heresies," which earned him from his adversaries the reproach of being the arch-heretic himself. But he is now best remembered by his hymns, of which he wrote 130, and among them several of very great beauty. Many are rather poems than hymns, and he also composed a number of religious madrigals and poetical aphorisms, but these are somewhat sentimental and exaggerated in style, and have not maintained their place like the hymns. The latter first appeared in 1697, under the title "Sparks of Divine Love," and the volume was frequently reprinted with additions.

In 1707 Arnold was appointed pastor of Perleberg in Brandenburg, and here he spent the last seven years of his life in unwearied activity, but in peace, for his congregation were of his own way of thinking, and he was protected by the King. In 1713 his health began to fail, and at Easter 1714, while he was celebrating the Holy Communion, a Prussian recruiting party burst into the church and dragged away a number of young men from the very steps of the altar. This outrage and his unavailing efforts to save the members of his flock, so affected him that he took to his bed two days afterwards and died within a few weeks.

Perhaps the best of Arnold's hymns is his deeply thoughtful

"How blest to all Thy followers, Lord, the road;"

but many others are very fine. We give the following :—

THE KINGDOM OF GOD.

Anoint us with Thy blessed love,
O Wisdom, through and through,
Till Thy sweet impulses remove
All dread and fear undue,

And we behold ourselves in Thee
A purified Humanity,
              And live Thy risen life.

O Perfect Manhood, once again
    Descend Thou in our race,
Be all its lower nature slain,
    Transform us of Thy grace,
Till pure and holy as Thou art
Thine image shine from every heart,
              And Thou within us live.

Prepare the Church, O Lord, Thy Bride,
    With glory and with strength,
Let life flow from her far and wide,
    Till she may see at length
New members given her day by day,
That shall not wither nor decay,
              Wherein Thyself hast joy.

Redeemer, Thine the power alone,
    Ah yield Thee to us, Lord !
Let God's fair temple once o'erthrown
    Be in our race restored ;
Thou, Man of men, didst take our flesh
Only to give us life afresh,
              And render all things new.

Then all the glory shall return
    That we had lost of yore,
Long severed souls shall homewards yearn
    And cleave to Thee once more ;
Then shall the Father and the Son
Through their one Spirit make us one ;
              Christ's prayer at last fulfilled !

LIFE'S VOYAGE.

Full many a way, full many a path,
The all-encircling Ocean hath,
Let each man only see to this,
That his own course he do not miss.

Or long or devious be thy way,
What matter, if thou do not stray?
Or lead it thee by east or west,
What matter, if thou reach thy rest?

The ways are countless, none the same,
Yet each one hath its proper aim,
Only forget not aye to heed
If to the haven thine will lead.

For there are currents undiscerned,
As many a ship too late hath learned,
That deemed itself full safe to be,
Yet sank upon the open sea.

Another's course may not be thine,
But Christ on all alike will shine;
Leave thou thy brother where he is,
Pursue thy way in quietness.

One is the haven;—let there be
In us who seek it, unity;
Vast is the ocean, surely there
Is room for all men and to spare.

Then heedfully go on thy way,
Care only that on that great Day,
Whether thy course be long or short,
Thy vessel may be found in port.

TRUTH.

I leave Him not, who came to save
   When I had trifled hope away;
He must be mine until the grave
   Since once He deigned to be my stay;
O world, I put thy offers by,
My loyal love hath one reply,
     I leave Him not.

I leave Him not;—for since He chose
   Me for His own, I choose Him too;
Since He for me faced all my foes,
   In death itself will I be true;
Why tempt me, Earth, with false delight?
Why seek, O Hell, my soul t' affright?
     I leave Him not.

I leave Him not; He leaves not me,
   The Saviour evermore the same,
Who since He suffered on the tree,
   Beareth that high and glorious Name;
Whate'er the storms that on me fall,
His Godhead's glory streams through all:
     I leave Him not.

I leave Him not; Earth I can leave,
   With all her glory and her power,
But He, to whom my soul must cleave,
   Is caring for me every hour,
Leading me through the tedious night,
Up to the very Source of Light:
     I leave Him not.

I leave Him not; what wouldst thou, Sin?
Thou hast been buried in the sea.
What would ye, depths of Hell, begin?
Ye have no part or power in me!
Thy sting, O Death, I shall not feel,
Christ will His life in me reveal:
I leave Him not.

Gerhard Tersteegen, born at Mors in Westphalia in 1697, was the son of a respectable tradesman; he was educated at the grammar-school of his native place, and then bound apprentice to an elder brother, a shop-keeper at Mülheim. From his childhood he was delicate in health, thoughtful, and of scrupulous conscience. At Mülheim he became acquainted with a tradesman, a very religious man, who took much notice of him, and under his influence he was con-verted, and resolved to devote himself entirely to the service of God. His days were busy, but he used to pass whole nights in prayer and fasting, and as soon as his time was out he declared his intention of leaving his brother, and choosing some more retired and less disturbing mode of life. He accordingly removed to a little cottage near Mülheim, where for some years he supported himself by weaving silk ribbons, and lived quite alone, except for the presence during the day of a little girl who wound his silk for him. His habits were very simple; he usually took nothing but milk, water, and meal, never touching tea or coffee, and giving away in charity to the poor the money thus saved. His relations, who seem to have been a thriving and money-getting set of people, were so ashamed of this poor and peculiar member of the family, that they refused even to hear his name mentioned, and when he was sick he suffered great privations for want of proper care. Yet he was very happy in his solitude, with its opportunities for uninterrupted meditation and communion with God, until that searching trial of spiritual deadness fell upon him, which so many of God's saints have had to endure for a time. For five years he was in a " state of darkness ;" he had no sensible impression of the love of God, nay, there were hours when he began to doubt whether there was a God at all. It was at this time he sang—

> " Lost in darkness, girt with dangers,
>   Round me strangers,
>   Through an alien land I roam ;
>   Outward trials, bitter losses,
>   Inward crosses,
>   Lord, Thou know'st have sought me home.
>
> Sin of courage hath bereft me,
>   And hath left me
>   Scarce a spark of faith or hope ;
>   Bitter tears my heart oft sheddeth,
>   As it dreadeth
>   I am past Thy mercy's scope.
>
> Peace I cannot find ; O take me,
>   Lord, and make me
>   From this yoke of evil free ;
>   Calm this longing never sleeping,
>   Still my weeping,
>   Give me hope once more in Thee."

He could obtain no help from outside ; but at last one day, when he was on a journey to a neighbouring city, he received such an internal manifestation of the goodness of God and the sufficiency of the Saviour, that all doubts and troubles vanished in a moment.[1] Henceforward he had peace and joy, and an intense power of realizing the unseen which, combined with the experience he had lately gone through, gave him a wonderful faculty of touching and strengthening other hearts. He now (in 1725) admitted a young friend, named Heinrich Sommer, to live with him. The two worked ten hours daily at the loom, two hours Tersteegen devoted to private prayer, and the rest of his time to writing devotional works, and addressing private meetings of friends on religion. This last occupation, which he had begun reluctantly and in the quietest manner, soon became his principal one. So many persons were impressed by him, so many more urgently sought the opportunity of hearing him, that he was at last induced to give up his weaving altogether, and devote himself to this informal but real kind of ministry. Considerable sums of money had been already offered him by friends, which he had invariably declined; now he accepted a small regular income, but in order that he might not be entirely without manual occupation, he set up a dispensary for the poor in his house, and compounded the medicines himself, employing an assistant as the work increased. The thirty years of his life, from thirty to sixty years of age, were spent in the most incessant exertion for the good of others, though his own health was always

---

[1] It is supposed to have been on this occasion that he wrote with his own blood a form of self-dedication to Jesus Christ which is found in the preface to his works.

delicate, and from time to time he had severe attacks of illness and of neuralgic pain. From morning to night he never had a moment to himself; the number of those who flocked to him for counsel was so great that there were frequently twenty or thirty persons waiting in his outer room for a chance of speaking to him, while his meetings were always attended by as many as could crowd into the rooms on the ground-floor of his little house, about four hundred persons. People came to him from England, Holland, Sweden, and Switzerland; sick persons would send for him, and he would pass hours or whole nights by their bedside; if he went into the neighbouring country for rest, people would watch for him by the roadside, and carry him off to the nearest barn, where a congregation would immediately assemble. He had an immense correspondence, and new editions of his hymns and other religious works were constantly demanded. To his quiet temperament this incessant labour and absence of solitude was most uncongenial, but he accepted it willingly as his appointed task. "I love most to be with the Father, but I am glad to be with the children," he said. His intercourse with those who came to him seems to have been marked by a most searching insight into character, yet by a gentleness and affectionateness, an anxiety to cherish even the faintest sparks of spiritual life, which nothing could tire out. Some attempts were made to hinder his irregular ministerial activity, but he demanded an interview with the superior clergy of his native place, and so entirely justified himself in their eyes that they never allowed him to be interfered with. Nor did he ever join any sect, though many, especially the Moravians, made advances to him. When he was sixty-one, the exertion of so much speaking brought on an internal injury which was almost fatal; he recovered and lived to the age of seventy-four, but he is said to have looked like a corpse, and he was obliged to give up all travelling, and addressing large assemblies. But he toiled as assiduously as ever in private conversation and correspondence, and was able to revise his various books, of which the principal were "The Spiritual Flower Garden," a volume of hymns and poems; and "Spiritual Crumbs," a collection of sermons and addresses which had been taken down in short-hand. He died in 1769.

Tersteegen was a mystic of the purest type. In his earlier days, as he himself tells us, he laid too much stress on bodily exercises and violent emotions, but in later life he was singularly free from extravagance or intolerance. "My religion is this," he says: "that as one reconciled to God by the blood of Christ, I suffer myself to be led by the Spirit of Jesus, through daily dying, suffering, and prayer, out of myself and all created things, that I may live alone to God in Christ; and clinging to this my God by faith and love, I hope to become one spirit with Him, and through His free mercy in Christ to attain eternal salvation. And I feel myself to be of the same faith with every one who believes thus, of whatever class or nation or creed he may be." Again, in the preface to his poems, he says: "In that sweet name of Jesus, Immanuel, *God with us*, the tender and overflowing love of God has made for itself a new way into the very depths of our hearts, and has come unspeakably close to us poor fallen children of Adam.   Since then the kingdom of God is so near at hand, nay, has come within us, we need make no wide circuit through much knowledge and laborious effort to get thither ; but we may enter at once by this new, open, and living Way into the sanctuary of inward and eternal communion with God.   We have but to let this deep, mysterious, intimate Divine Love lead us out from the cheating pleasures of this world and the tormenting life of egotism ; and for this end to give our heart and will captive to this inward Love, that it may become our All in all, and guide us of its free pleasure.   Behold this is the whole kernel of the matter."

Many of Tersteegen's hymns have already been rendered into English, and two of them, translated by Wesley, are to be found in nearly all our hymn-books. These are, " Lo, God is here, let us adore," and " Thou hidden Love of God."   The following little poems are taken from the first part of " The Flower Garden."

THE MOTE IN THE SUNBEAM.

I lose me in the thought !
How great is God,—and I how merely nought !
What doth that Sun whence clearest splendours stream
Know of the mote that dances in his beam?
    Nay, if I may but ever live and move
    In the One Being who is perfect Love,
    Th' Eternal and the Infinite alone,
Let me forget all else, and all I deemed my own !
    Closer than my own self art Thou to me,
    So let me wholly yield myself to Thee ;

Be Thou my Sun, my selfishness destroy,
Thy atmosphere of Love be all my joy,
Thy Presence be my Sunshine ever bright,
My soul the little mote that lives but in Thy light!

WITHIN AND WITHOUT.

Out! out, away!
Soul, in this alien house thou hast no stay!
Seek thou thy dwelling in Eternity,
    'Tis there shall be
    Thy hiding-place, thy nest,
Where nor the world nor self can break thy rest.
    Within the heart of God,
    There is thy still abode,
There mayst thou dwell at rest and be at home,
Howe'er the body here may toil and roam.

———

    Within! within, O turn
    Thy spirit's eyes, and learn
Thy wand'ring senses gently to control;
Thy dearest Friend dwells deep within thy soul,
    And asks thyself of thee,
That heart, and mind, and sense He may make whole
    In perfect harmony.
    Doth not thy inmost spirit yield
And sink where Love stands thus revealed?
    Be still and veil thy face,
The Lord is here, this is His holy place!
Then back to earth, and 'mid its toil and throng
One glance within will keep thee calm and strong;
And when the toil is o'er, how sweet, O God, to flee
    Within, to Thee!

AT EVENING.

Lovely, shadowy, soft, and still
   Is the eventide,
Ah ! if but my heart and will
   Evermore might so abide !
God, Thy presence can alone
Make this lovely calm my own.

THE CROSS.

To praise the Cross while yet untried,
Comes oft of self-conceit and pride ;
But when it presses, to embrace
And love it, only comes of grace.

———

Nay ! not sore the Cross's weight,
   Save to souls the Cross that hate ;
Souls that can with love receive it,
Childlike to their Father leave it,
   May be still 'mid all its woe,
   And a strange deep gladness know.
   Only Self-love murmurs yet,
   Only Sense and Nature fret,
They repine, for they must perish
If the soul true life will cherish ;
   Light and dear the Cross shall prove,
   For it is the gift of Love.

THE TIRED CHILD.

Ah God ! The world hath nought to please ;
One loses strength and light and peace
In needful toil of sense and brain :
Would I might here with Thee remain !

I am sated with these things of nought,
Wearied with hearing, sight, and thought;
O Mother-Heart, to Thee I turn,
Comfort Thy child, for Thee I yearn:

Thy love, most gentle-innocent!
Would that each hour might there be spent,
That I absorbed in Thee might live,
And child-like to my Father cleave.

Like a parched field my soul doth lie
Pining beneath a sultry sky;
O Heavenly Dew, O gentle Rain,
Descend and bid it bloom again.

By far the most important new sect that was
founded at this time was that of the Moravians.
Properly speaking, indeed, the Moravian Church is the
living representative of that ancient Bohemian Church
whose hymns were the delight of Luther; but practically, its transplantation to German soil about the year
1722, and its rapid growth under the care of Count
Zinzendorf, constitute a new foundation of the society.
Zinzendorf grew up in the very bosom of Pietism.
Born at Dresden in 1700 of a noble, wealthy, and
religious family, he had Spener for his godfather, and
Franke for his tutor; while his maternal grandmother,
the Baroness von Gersdorff, whose house was his home
in childhood, was herself a woman of strict piety and a
writer of hymns. From his earliest years he had strong
religious impressions; as a child his favourite amusement was playing at preaching; as a boy at school
under Franke, he founded among his schoolfellows
the "Order of the Mustard-seed," the members of
which bound themselves in an especial manner to the

service of Christ, and above all to promote the conversion of the heathen. Some of his non-pietistic relatives insisted on his acquiring the accomplishments proper to his station in life, such as dancing, fencing, shooting, &c., and on his being sent to the orthodox university of Wittenberg to study law. He complied with their wishes, though he himself would have much preferred studying theology; and after his university course travelled for some years. Once, in passing through Dusseldorf, he saw in a gallery a picture of the Saviour crowned with thorns, over which was written, "All this have I done for thee; what dost thou for Me?" These words struck so deep into his heart that he never lost the impression; "from this time I had but one passion, and that was He, only He." At the age of twenty-one he returned to Saxony, accepted office under the government, married and settled down to the usual life of men of his order. He was a remarkably handsome man, tall, and exactly of what is termed aristocratic bearing and manners; he was also a ready speaker, with a clear ringing voice and graceful and imposing action. In private he was energetic and impetuous, but obliging in trifles, and full of vivacity and humour. Fortunately for him he had found a wife who entered heart and soul into all his plans, who travelled with him wherever he went, and managed his pecuniary affairs and the details of daily arrangements with a skill and prudence which he did not himself possess in such matters. It was just after his marriage that he first met with Christian David, a carpenter, thirty years of age, who had been born a Roman Catholic in Moravia; but reading by chance an evangelical book, had been converted and joined the Moravian Brethren. Since that time he had travelled in Hungary and Silesia, working at his trade; and observing how much peace and profitable instruction other evangelical Christians enjoyed, he had determined to urge his fellow-believers to emigrate into Protestant Germany. Just at this time he fell in with Count Zinzendorf and told him his wishes, and the Count immediately offered an asylum on one of his own estates near Dresden. Here in 1722 David felled the first tree and began to build the first house of what was afterwards the great Moravian settlement of Herrnhut. It increased rapidly; for not only did a number of emigrants come thither from Moravia, but many other persons were attracted to it, and in 1727 Zinzendorf resigned his office and went to live there himself, in order to superintend the growing community. After a time he saw that it would be necessary for him to take orders—an unheard-of thing then in a man of his rank—and he was entreated to do so by his friend Spangenberg, one of the leaders of the new body. He accordingly travelled *incognito* to Stralsund, passed the necessary examinations, and received ordination there. It was on his journey home that he learnt that his opponents, who viewed with extreme disgust the progress of the Brethren, had procured from the king an edict banishing him from Saxony on a charge of spreading false doctrine. It was ten years before he could return home, an interval employed by him in incessant journeyings and preachings, from St. Petersburg to the West Indies. He was twice in America, and founded various missions there, especially among the then wholly neglected negro slaves ; and he planted settlements of the Brethren in other parts of Germany, in Holland, and in England. From 1747, when the edict was recalled, he made

Herrnhut his head-quarters, but he once spent nearly four years in England organizing his communities here, and he obtained for them the recognition of Parliament. His private life was not without its trials ; he devoted the whole of his large fortune to the service of the cause, and himself died poor ; he lost all his sons, and finally his excellent wife ; but his courage never abated. He died in 1760, and by that time the United Brethren had not only spread within Europe, but had developed that remarkable missionary activity by which they have always been honourably distinguished, and the little Church had already its stations in Greenland, Lapland, Guinea, the Cape of Good Hope, Persia, and various parts of America.

In presence of a life of such self-devotion, achieving such results, we must acknowledge Zinzendorf to have been a noble apostle of the Lord ; but it is also true that he had, as he himself says, "a genius inclined to extravagances," and that these sometimes hindered his usefulness. His watchword was, "Christ and Him Crucified," but he carried this so far that he saw literally nothing else in Christianity but the one fact of the atoning sufferings of the Saviour. The life of Christ, the fatherhood of God, the morality of the Gospel, were all obscured to him behind this one central doctrine ; nay, he allowed himself to speak of them in a way that is most jarring, and that drew down on him severe censure from so warmly religious a man as Bengel. But it is to his credit that he profited by Bengel's attack, and modified his most extreme views, and the formal dogmatic expression of the Brethren's faith was left by him to his calmer and more sagacious friend Spangenberg. On hymnology the Moravians have had a powerful influence ; Zinzendorf himself, all the members of his family, and most of the early leaders of the Brethren wrote hymns ; singing was a prominent part of their worship, and they early began publishing hymn-books. These contained some of the old classical hymns, much abridged and altered to meet the taste of the new Church, and a large proportion of what are called " Brethren-hymns." The characteristics of the latter are a fervid affection and gratitude to the Saviour, a spirit of happy, childlike confidence, and a strong sentiment of Christian fellowship; but in many cases their poetical merit is not great, and they sometimes degenerate into a mere dwelling on physical sufferings, and a childish and extravagant style of expression. This was especially the case with many of the older hymns, which were afterwards rejected from their later collections ; some by Zinzendorf himself were among the worst offenders.[1] His hymns, of which he wrote more than two thousand, are of exceedingly different value ; some are fantastic and irreverent, some mere rhymed prose, others again have a real sweetness, fervour, and song in them. Among the best are the following; the first is taught in almost every religious German household to its children :—

FOLLOWING CHRIST.

Jesu, day by day
Lead us on life's way :
Nought of dangers will we reckon,
Simply haste where Thou dost beckon ;
Lead us by the hand
To our fatherland.

[1] Many of these hymns speak of the blood and wounds of Jesus, o making a bed in His wounded side, &c. in a way of which it is rea impossible to give instances.

Hard should seem our lot,
Let us waver not :
Never murmur at our crosses
In dark days of grief and losses ;
   'Tis through trial here
   We must reach Thy sphere.

When the heart must know
Pain for others' woe,
When beneath its own 'tis sinking,
Give us patience, hope unshrinking,
   Fix our eyes, O Friend,
   On our journey's end.

Thus our path shall be
Daily traced by Thee ;
Draw Thou nearer when 'tis rougher,
Help us most when most we suffer,
   And when all is o'er
   Ope to us Thy door.

THE KING'S FAVOURITES.

Such the King will stoop to and embrace,
Who when they no hope or path can trace,
         Sink at His feet,
And grace and guidance from His hand entreat

Such the King with blessing will secure,
Who when they behold one scorned and poor,
         Who is Christ's own,
Revere him more than princes on a throne.

Such the King will evermore defend,
Who accept the burden He doth send,
         And calmly sit,
Trusting to Him to raise it when 'tis fit.

Such the King will ever deign to teach,
Who can profit e'en by children's speech,
And gladly know
That they are only learners here below.

Of the Moravian hymn-writers, the best are Louisa
von Hayn, a convert of Zinzendorf's, and for many
years the superintendent of the Unmarried Sisters'
House at Herrnhut; Christian Gregor, the next bishop
of the Church after Spangenberg, who wrote that
touching hymn, "Ah, dearest Lord! to feel that Thou
art near;" Albertini, his successor in the episcopal
office, who died in 1831; and Garve, who died in 1842.
Of these Albertini ranks the highest as a poet; he was
a man of great and varied learning, and a friend of
Schleiermacher's, who asked to have Albertini's hymns
read to him on his death-bed. We give one:—

THE VIRGIN'S LAMP.

Lamp within me! brightly burn and glow,
Draw thy flame from Jesu's heart,
Whence a living fire doth ever flow,
Clearer flaming 'mid the sorest smart;
I will guard thy flame in stillness meek,
Nought so eagerly shall bid me seek
Him who can my wants supply,
As the fear thy light should die.

He will quench it not, but haste to pour
Oil from His exhaustless cruse;
Then the soul is filled with light once more
And the twilight's terrors she doth lose;
Safe she walks on her illumined way
Through the midnight, till the Voice shall say,

" Lo ! the Bridegroom and the feast are near;
    Virgins, haste to meet Him, He is here."

Well for those who in His strength have lived,
    Pure as He is pure within ;
Who with deep abhorrence aye have grieved
    O'er the slightest taint of sin,
Hearts that trembled at the smallest spot,
And till cleansed and pardoned, rested not ;
    Theirs the light that hath no shade,
    Theirs the wreath that cannot fade.

Pietism in its original shape had done its work.   Its
defects had become much more apparent in the second
and third generation than they were at first ; its
tendency to fix the attention of the Christian within,
on his own states of feeling and chances of salvation,
produced in some cases, when Pietism had become
fashionable and profitable, a hypocritical simulation
of such feelings ; in others a timid anxious tone of
mind, inclined to morbid self-scrutiny and religious
melancholy.   Its discouragement of many legitimate
forms of occupation as well as of recreation, which it
stigmatized as *worldly*, incapacitated it from keeping
abreast of the new tide of intellectual activity which
rolled through Germany towards the end of the
eighteenth century ; it had no place in its scheme of
life for the new learning, and art, and science.   And
for a time it seemed swept aside, but it had in it a
germ of true and deep spiritual life, and this never
died out ; it was handed down through a Lavater, a
Claudius, a Jung Stilling, an Arndt, a Falk, till in our
own days it is blossoming again in vast works of
Christian charity, which can spring only from a life
rooted through Christ in God.

CHAPTER XIII.

1750—1850.

THE religious poetry of Germany underwent a change in the course of this eighteenth century; it ceased to consist primarily of congregational hymns, and assumed the forms of the irregular lyric, the ode, and the epic. We have seen something of this change in the poems of Tersteegen and Arnold; it meets us more strongly in those of Gellert, Cramer, and Klopstock. The spirit of that age was not favourable to hymn-writing; for really good hymns must have in them something of the nature of the popular song; they must have its warmth, movement and melody; they must spring from a cordial, unquestioning faith, which has no misgivings about the response it will evoke from other hearts. The critical doubting religion of the eighteenth century, which even in its more earnest forms felt itself continually obliged to stand on the defensive, could not produce such hymns; nor could its stiff and artificial style furnish them with a fitting expression. The poetical diction of this time is indeed remarkably deficient in variety of rhythm and in musical flow; the traditional forms of metre and rhyme itself were despised, and great efforts were made to introduce new measures, of which but one, the hexameter, took any root.   But the old mastery over lyrical forms which distinguished German poetry in the days of its Minne-singers, the ringing melody which marked its popular songs, were quite lost; and we meet with nothing like them till we reach the days of Goethe. Even the classical hymns, though consecrated by association, could no longer satisfy the more pedantic taste of the age, and there sprang up a perfect mania for altering them, and for making new collections of such modernised versions for the various States.   These alterations generally consisted in watering down the old vigour,—substituting "virtue" for "holiness" or ": faith," "the Supreme Being" for "our faithful God," and so on;—and in planing away little unevennesses of metre so as to reduce hymns and tunes alike to a correct and tiresome flatness.   A large proportion of the State hymn-books still in use date from this period.

The one great step that was made in German hymnology at this time was the official introduction of vernacular hymns into the Roman Catholic churches of Southern Germany and Austria.   Many collections of hymns had already been made for private use; but now under the Emperor Joseph II. portions of the service of the mass itself were translated into German verse, and sung by the people while the priest was officiating; and even where the "Vienna Mass," as it was called, was not used, hymns in the mother-tongue were assigned to the various services and festivals.   The collections of hymns thus called into existence contain naturally a large proportion of translations from the Latin; they also possess a smaller number of original compositions, of which some have great sweetness and devotional feeling, while others are weak and overwrought; and they include a good many of the Evangelical hymns, modified where necessary to suit their new position.

The antagonism between the Roman Catholic and Protestant Churches which had been so fierce during the previous age, and which in another form has revived in our own, had in fact almost died out. The difference was regarded as one rather of birth and geographical position than of conviction; conversions from one Church to the other were generally censured as acts of disloyalty, but mixed marriages were common; while really serious Christians in either communion felt themselves strongly drawn together by the possession of a common faith in a time of scepticism. Thus a cordial and intimate correspondence on religious subjects was maintained between a circle of pious Protestants in Hamburg, of which Claudius and the Stolbergs were members, and similar circles on the Rhine and in Bavaria, which were composed of distinguished Roman Catholics, such as the Prince-Primate Dalberg the Princess Galitzin, and others. During the latter half of this century, Southern Germany possessed several Roman Catholics of high position and great abilities, who were also men of deep evangelical piety and strong national feeling, anxious to reform abuses within their own Church. Such men were Sailer, long a professor at Dillingen and Landshut and finally Bishop of Ratisbon, his great friend Feneberg, pastor of Seeg in Bavaria, and Von Wessenberg, the friend and coadjutor of Dalberg, and his successor in the bishopric of Constance. All three wrote hymns, which, if not of the first order, are yet good, earnest, and thoughtful; and all warmly promoted the use of such hymns in their own language among the people, both at home and in public worship.

Among the writers whose hymns were thus used by both Churches was Christian Fürchtegott Gellert, the immense popularity of whose writings in their own age shows how exactly they must have fulfilled its requirements. His life was uneventful enough. Born in 1715 in Saxony, the son of a country clergyman, he studied at the university of Leipsic, became a private tutor, and afterwards professor of poetry and moral philosophy there; and never left the city except for occasional visits to the baths and once to Berlin, until his death in 1769, at the age of fifty-four. In 1742, when he was a young man of seven-and-twenty, he joined with a number of his friends in bringing out a periodical called the "Contributions from Bremen" (*Bremer Beiträge*) which created a great sensation as being the first successful rebellion against the domination of Gottsched and the French school. Most of the men engaged in it were of some note in their day, but only two or three are now remembered, and among these Klopstock towers far above the rest. Gellert's contributions consisted of fables told with a spirit and fluency which made their humour and point all the more penetrating. He also wrote comedies, and his lectures at the university were famed for their charm of style and manner no less than for their clearness of thought and moral influence. Yet his life was not a joyous one: he suffered inces-

santly from ill health and from attacks of hypochon-
dria that was held in check only by his real piety and
excellence of conduct. For Gellert was a deeply
religious man, though rather of the old orthodox than
of the pietistic type; he was a most regular attendant
on religious services, and a great reader of devotional
works. In 1757 he published a volume of fifty-four
poems under the title of "Spiritual Odes and Songs,"
which were received with an enthusiasm almost like
that which greeted Luther's hymns on their first
appearance. His lectures also, and his habit of
interesting himself warmly in the personal conduct
and welfare of his students, gave him a remarkable influence over young men, who afterwards carried
the impression received in his class-room into every
part of Germany. Lessing and Goethe were each in
turn among his pupils, but his tendency to melancholy
and sentimentality, and his somewhat formal and
precise genius, were to them very uncongenial. Yet
Goethe, much the more kindly critic of the two, says:
"The reverence and affection which Gellert received
from all the young men was extraordinary. His lec-
ture-room was always crowded to the utmost; and
Gellert's beautiful soul, purity of will, his admonitions,
warnings and entreaties, delivered in a somewhat
hollow and sad voice, produced a deep impression.
A figure not tall, but slender without being thin, soft
rather mournful eyes, a very beautiful brow, all rendered his presence agreeable." Nor was his influence
confined to his class-room: a peasant one day laid a
load of firewood at his door as a thank-offering for
the pleasure derived from his fables; a young Prussian
officer sent him a sum of money, entreating him to

accept the gift from one whose heart had been raised by his writings ; and these were but instances of innumerable similar presents which Gellert used generally to bestow on the poor. Princes and great people of all kinds made pilgrimages to see him; even Frederick the Great had an interview with him, and pronounced him the most reasonable German professor he had ever come across. The general tone of his writings is that of a sincere Christian morality, kindly and a little formal, not very elevated or enthusiastic, but pure and honest, and coloured by a rather sentimental and pathetic view of life in general. His hymns, for the composition of which he always prepared himself by prayer, are correct and moderate, yet with a certain earnestness and pathos ; and though it is now the fashion to depreciate them as much as they were once admired, there is a merit not to be ignored in their rational piety and quiet good taste.

THE SOLACE OF THE LIFE TO COME.

When these brief trial-days are spent,
    There dawns a glad eternity ;
There, lost in measureless content,
    Our tears and sorrows cease to be ;
Here Virtue toils with earnest care,
Her glorious crown awaits her there.

True that the godly man may know
    Some happy moments e'en on earth ;
But joy is transient here below,
    Imperfect all and little worth ;
He is a man, and in his breast
Peace will but ebb and flow at best :

Now marred by sickness or by pain,
   Now by the world's incessant noise,
Now by the foes that yet remain
   Within him, whom no care destroys ;
Now others from without impose
The burden of their faults and woes.

For here, where virtue oft is sad,
   And vice as oft in splendour shines,
Where envy still pursues the glad,
   And sorrow in oblivion pines,
Here man can nevermore be free
From grief, nor from infirmity.

Here I must seek, there I shall find ;
   For there shall Virtue all unfold
Before my holier purer mind
   Her worth so great, so manifold ;
The God of Love, whom I adore,
I there shall worship more and more.

There shall His wise, foreseeing will
   Be all my joy, my choice alone ;
And loveliness and rapture fill
   My happy soul before His throne ;
While ever-new delights are given,
To bid me feel that this is heaven.

There in that light shall I discern
   What here on earth I dimly saw,
Those deep and wondrous counsels learn
   Whose mystery filled me here with awe ;
There trace with gratitude intense
The hidden links of Providence.

There at the footstool of my King,
   Where glimpses of His Face I gain,
Shall I the " Holy, Holy," sing,
   Unto the Lamb that once was slain,
While Cherubim and Seraphim
And all the heavens are praising Him.

Amid the holy angels placed,
   Like them in holy happy mood,
Shall I the unmixed pleasure taste
   Of godly converse with the good,
When each the other's rapture shares,
Their joy is mine, my gladness theirs.

And there shall I at last repay
   With million blessings on his head,
The guide who taught me first God's way
   And bade me boldly in it tread ;
There shall I find the friend once more
I found and treasured here of yore.

Perchance,—ah would that this might be !—
   Will some blest soul in that abode
Cry, " Hail ! for thou hast rescued me
   And won my heart to heaven and God !"
O God, what exquisite delight
To save a soul from sin and night !

Then what are ye, brief woes of Time,
   When weighed with glory such as this,
Destined to be our lot sublime
   From age to age of endless bliss ?
How nought, how merely nought appears
This moment full of cares and fears !

Another favourite religious poet of this time was
Johann Andreas Cramer, who was a friend of both

Gellert and Klopstock. He was a man of high character and considerable ability, who was considered in his day to be the greatest pulpit orator in Germany; for many years he was court-preacher at Copenhagen when Count Bernstorff was in power, and he died as chancellor of the university of Kiel in 1788 at the age of sixty-five. As a poet he does not hold a very high place; his poems resemble those of Gellert, but have less sweetness and feeling, and are more definitely didactic; they are, however, characteristic as embodying one type of the religion of this period, a type strongly contrasting with that of Zinzendorf, somewhat frigid and Deistic rather than Christian in its aspect, yet retaining a sincere attachment to Christianity and accepting it as an authoritative revelation from God. Cramer's favourite themes are the wisdom and goodness of God in nature and providence; the immortality of the soul,—not heaven, for he does not picture the future life to himself, but brings forward very good arguments for a belief in its existence; and the inculcation of specific Christian duties, such as cheerfulness, purity, usefulness, &c., in poems which at least have the merit of very good sense and sound morality. From the latter we choose the following poem on

THE DUTY OF THE SCHOLAR.

O ye, who from your earliest youth
Seek wisdom and would learn the truth,
Happy are ye if ye discern
Falsehood from Truth in all ye learn!

If ye with bold and eager mind
Cast prejudice and fear behind,

That so the Truth may set you free
From dreams and Error's slavery !

If to your comprehensive thought,
The lore that ancient sages taught
Is but the stepping-stone to more
And deeper truths unknown before !

Nor suffer fame to be your goal,
Still less to break the wise control
Of law and duty ; seek aright
To grow more perfect through more light.

Whoe'er on God's great works can cast
A clearer light than in the past,
And teach new eyes with awe to see
Their wonders,—ah, how happy he !

Learn ever clearer what adorns,
Ennobles life, and blunts its thorns ;
What in each nation, every State,
Has brought it low or made it great.

Learn too what shames us, what is base,
Virtue's whole worth and beauty trace,
Here and hereafter what the source
Of joys that cannot bring remorse.

And never deign to make for Vice
A league with Error, or with lies ;
Nor speak of Truth with careless scorn,
For every truth of God is born.

Whate'er ye learn, rejoice to share
With others, show them every snare
On learning's path where men have tript,
Be honest where yourselves have slipt.

KLOPSTOCK.

Forget not ye must live for aye,
Study not only for to-day,
Think of the reckoning ye must give,
And wisely, virtuously live.

All truth is God's as He is true,
Whate'er ye know He shows it you,
So let your knowledge as it grows
Draw you to Him more near and close.

Happy indeed is such a sage,
He shall be honoured in his age,
And fame shall follow where he trod,
For he, he is a light from God.

Friedrich Gottlieb Klopstock was born at Quedlin-
burg in 1724. His father was an official under the
Government—a clever, upright, crotchety man, given
to a belief in ghosts and the devil, with whom he considered himself to have had many personal encounters,
but a man who brought up his ten children to be
honest and hardy, religious and patriotic. Klopstock
was educated at a celebrated school at Schulpforta,
where he remained till he was twenty-one, and where
he already conceived the idea of his great epic the
"Messiah." The thought that France and England
had so far surpassed Germany in literature, filled him
even as a boy with indignation, and he solemnly
resolved that he would produce some great work
which should do his country honour. Various subjects,
such as the story of King Arthur, or of the early
German hero, Henry the Fowler, floated before his
mind, but at last it flashed on him that the work of
Redemption was the noblest subject on which the
human pen could be employed. Not long afterwards

Y 2

Milton's " Paradise Lost " fell into his hands ; he read it with rapture, and was more than ever confirmed in his choice of a theme.   From Schulpforta he went to Leipsic, where he soon became intimate with the set of young men who were bringing out the " Contributions from Bremen."   They urged him to join them, but he declined from modesty, until one day one of his friends named Schmidt drew out of a chest full of linen a manuscript, which proved to be the first three cantos of the "Messiah." Schmidt instantly carried them off to Cramer ; the friends read them with delight, and insisted on publishing them in the " Contributions " for 1748.   Several of his odes also appeared in the same volume, and the young Klopstock found himself suddenly famous all over Germany.   In 1750 he was invited to Zurich, and was honoured and caressed to the utmost in what was then the most literary town in Switzerland.   Throughout life he was a man of singularly pure and amiable character, and at this time he had much wit and liveliness, with a keen enjoyment of athletic sports, especially of skating, which from his example and praises became quite a rage in Germany during the next twenty years.   The consciousness of the great work in which he was engaged gave him however, as Goethe tells us, a certain dignity and self-control of manner which in later years, when the vivacity of youth was gone, increased to a sort of measured diplomatic courtliness.   It was about this time that he wrote most of his love poems and odes, inspired by a hopeless passion for Fanny, the sister of his friend Schmidt.   But ere long he consoled himself.   It was in 1751 that Count Bernstorff, then prime minister to the King of Denmark, invited him to reside at Copenhagen, and offered him a pension, which should enable him to complete the " Messiah " undisturbed by pecuniary cares. Klopstock accepted it, and on his way northwards made the acquaintance at Hamburg of a certain Meta Moller, the daughter of a merchant, a clever, ardent-minded girl, who was a correspondent of Richardson and Young, and had already conceived a great admiration for the author of the " Messiah." A correspondence ensued, which terminated in 1754 in a marriage. Nothing could be happier than this union, but it lasted little more than four years, when Meta died in childbirth. Her death was a terrible blow to Klopstock, and for a time seems to have diverted his thoughts altogether from his great work. Ten cantos had already been given to the world, but during the next nine years, when Klopstock was a man between thirty and forty, only minor poems appeared, chiefly of a religious character.

After Meta's death he lived in Count Bernstorff's house, but he was in the habit of spending long periods of time among his friends in or near Hamburg ; and on the retirement of Bernstorff in 1770, he removed there altogether, and took up his abode in the house of a Herr von Winthem, who had married Meta's niece. Hamburg was at this time a sort of literary capital of Germany, and more particularly of its northern half, as Weimar became some years later. Lessing and Klopstock, then the greatest names in German literature, made it their residence ; Herder visited it occasionally ; and a number of lesser lights, such as Voss, Claudius, Reimarus, the Stolbergs, &c. gathered round the chief luminaries. Klopstock enjoyed a sort of reverence not unlike that paid to Dr. Johnson in England, but in some respects more flattering, as he was a man of whom it was much easier to make a popular, and especially a ladies' hero. Here the "Messiah" was at last completed in 1773; a complete edition of his odes and lyrics was brought out; and here he devoted the autumn of his long life to the study and purification of the German language and its grammar. He had always been a passionate lover of his country, but this did not prevent him from taking the keenest interest in the American War of Independence and the opening of the French Revolution. He was among those who, like our own Wordsworth, hailed its earlier years with eager sympathy and the hope of a coming brighter era for humanity, and who afterwards underwent the bitterness of profound disappointment. The National Assembly had marked their recognition of his friendship for the French people by according him the rights of a French citizen; but when the terrible massacres of 1793 took place he sent back to them his diploma.

In his sixty-seventh year he married for the second time, choosing the Frau von Winthem, who had meanwhile become a widow, and who survived him. He died in 1803, in his seventy-ninth year, retaining all the vigour of his faculties to the last, and was buried by Hamburg with royal honours.

The "Messiah," which as we have seen occupied twenty-seven years in its composition, is a poem in twenty cantos, written in hexameters except where certain choral songs occur in the unrhymed lyrical measures employed by Klopstock for his odes. The

action opens after the triumphal entry into Jerusalem, when the Messiah withdraws from the people,
and alone on the Mount of Olives renews His
solemn vow to the Almighty Father to undertake the
work of Redemption ; it closes when that work is
completed, and He sits down at the right hand of
God. Around the central figure of the God-man are
grouped an infinite variety of spectators and actors:
angels and seraphs, among whom Eloa and Gabriel
are especially appointed to attend on the Divine Suf-
ferer ; evil spirits who conspire against Him, but one
of whom, Abbadonna, repents and at last obtains
mercy ; Adam and Eve and the patriarchs, who watch
with profound interest and gratitude the reparation
of the Fall ; and the inhabitants of another world,
like in nature to man, but unfallen, who are permitted
to know what is taking place among their sinful
kindred. Even the Father himself is introduced as
speaking, and the scene is sometimes laid in the
highest heaven. The earthly actors are the mother and
disciples of Jesus, the Jews and the Romans who lead
Him to death, and a number of those who have come
in contact with Him in His ministrations, among whom
the most clearly drawn are two female figures, both
named Cidli : one, the wife of Gedor, is a reminiscence
of Meta, and her death is an exact transcript of
Meta's deathbed ; the other is the daughter of Jairus,
between whom and Semida, the youth of Nain, there
exists a pure but ardent attachment, which at last finds
satisfaction in heaven. The immense number of per-
sonages thus introduced produces a confusing impression ; everything is described by one or other of them,
and talked over at length ; scarcely anything actually

takes place before the reader; there is an absence of local colouring and of character, and very few of the actors have any distinct individuality at all; while the effort to keep the whole tone of the poem at the highest possible pitch of intensity and awe gives rise to an overstrained inflation of both thought and style, which becomes in the long-run inexpressibly fatiguing. Yet Klopstock's poem has made for itself and for him a place in the literature of his country which does not depend on the number of readers it now attracts. Its subject is linked by a thousand invisible fibres to the whole Christian thought of centuries past, while its spirit of mercy, forgiveness, and tolerance, of Redemption in a word, is essentially characteristic of the later developments of Christianity. To treat such a theme worthily at all—to embody it in a form which, however full of defects, yet possesses a certain dignity and real genius—marks its author as a great poet, if not one of the greatest, and gives him a place historically even higher perhaps than he has a right to command as an artist.

Klopstock also wrote scriptural dramas, which, however, speedily fell into oblivion. Much finer are his odes, which indeed show the most fire and originality of any of his works; though some of these too suffer from their length and elaboration. He also recast, not always very successfully, many of the older hymns, and composed a number of his own, of which a good many are adopted into the hymn-books, though in general their style is too stilted and declamatory to be genuinely popular. As specimens we give one of his odes, one of his psalms, and a hymn: it is impossible within a short compass to give extracts from the " Messiah " which could really convey any idea of the work.

THE VISION OF GOD.[1]

Trembling I rejoice
Nor should dare to believe,
Were not the Promiser
God the Eternal !
For I know it, I feel it,
I am a sinner !
I must know it, and feel it,
E'en had not light from God
Streamed on my conscience, and shown
My soul to herself,
Clearly unveiling
Her form that sin hath wounded and defaced.

With low-bended knee,
With deep adoring amazement,
I rejoice :
I shall behold Him !
Soul, ever drawing nearer the body's grave,
Thyself immortal,
Pursue this all-divinest thought
Which thy thought can conceive.
Not that thou darest
To enter yet into the holiest place !
Within that sanctuary dwell
Joys unconceived, unpraised, unsung as yet.

[1] In this ode the translation follows the original line by line, imitating as exactly as possible the accent and number of syllables in each. In the psalm that follows it a little more licence in metre is taken, as the original has also a more condensed and regular rhythm.

Only from far I hail one mild and softened beam,
Softened to let me live ;
One gleam that earthly darkness tempers here,
Of glory I may see.

How great the Prophet was who dared implore,
" If I have found grace in Thy sight, now let me
Behold Thy glory !"
So to the Infinite might pray, and find a hearing !
To the land of Golgotha came he not,
An earlier death avenged the fault
That once, but once, his God he trusted not ;
How great the Prophet shows this very doom !
Him the Father concealed in a deep gloom of the mountain,
When before a mortal passed the Glory of the Son ;
When the trumpet was silent on Sinai
And the voice of the thunder, as God spake of God.
No longer wrapt in night,
But in a daylight's splendour
That needs no shadows to enhance its brightness,
He now beholds, so we believe, for ages already
Far o'er the limits of Time,
Unconscious of moments that ever
Are followed by moments,—he gazes
On Thee, O Holy, Holy, Holy Lord !

Most nameless delight of my soul,
Thought of the Vision to come,
Thou art my mighty Reliance,
Thou art the Rock, whereon I stand and gaze up to heaven,
When the terrors of Sin
And the terrors of Death
Fearfully threaten
To whelm me below !

Upon this Rock, O Thou
Whom now the dead in God behold,
Let me stand when the power
Of Death irresistibly hems me around !

   Arise, O my soul, above this mortality,
Look up and gaze, and thou wilt behold
The Father's Brightness
Beam from the Face of Jesus Christ.
Hosanna ! Hosanna ! the fulness of the Godhead
Dwells in the Man Jesus Christ !
Scarce ringeth the Cherubims' harp here, it quivers,
Scarce sound on their voices, they tremble, they tremble !
Hosanna ! Hosanna !
The Godhead in fulness
Dwells in the Man
Jesus Christ.
Even then, when one of the beams from God to our world
Illumined more clearly the prophecy, when 'twas fulfilled,
When He was despised and afflicted
As no son of man had been despised and afflicted before,
E'en then, mortals could not discern,
But the Cherubim saw
The Father's Brightness
In the countenance of the Son.

   I see, I see him, that witness,
Seven long appalling midnights
Hath he doubted, and painfully wrestled
With the saddest of sorrows.
I see him !
To him appeareth the Risen One,
He layeth his hands in the print of the wounds,
Heaven and earth are vanishing round him :

He beholds the Father's Brightness in the Face of the Son,
I hear, I hear him ! he cries——
Heaven and earth are vanishing round him—he cries :
My Lord and my God !

PSALM.[1]

Round their planets roll the moons,
Planets round their sun,
All the hosts of suns revolve
Round one mighty Sun,
Thee " Our Father," Thee " who art in heaven !"

On all these worlds, light-beaming, light-receiving,
Are dwelling souls of diverse powers and forms,
But all contemplate God, rejoice in God :
" Hallowed be Thy name !"

But He the Highest who alone
Can wholly know Himself,
Wholly rejoice in God, 'twas He conceived
The scheme profound to bless all creature-minds :
" Thy kingdom come !"

O well for them that He, and not themselves,
Orders their Present, and their Future too ;
O well for them, and well for us !   " Thy will
Be done on earth, as 'tis in heaven," O God !

He lifts the ear upon its golden stalk,
Matures the blushing apple, purple grape ;
Pastures the lamb upon the field,
The wild-deer in the woods :
But His thunder rolleth around,
And its bolts may beat down the corn and the bough,
May destroy in the fields and the woods !
Then, " Give us to-day our daily bread !"

[1] This psalm was sung at Klopstock's funeral.

Perchance that high above the thunder's course
Sinners and mortals dwell like those on earth?
There too the friend may change to foe?
There too the dearest part in death?
" Forgive us," Lord, " our debts
As we forgive our debtors."

Various the paths to one exalted goal,
To endless happiness :
Through lonely wastes there are that wind their course,
Yet e'en on these, some joys beside the way
Will blossom and refresh the fainting soul :
" Lead us not," then, " into temptation," Lord,
" But deliver us from evil."

Thee we adore, who hath the central Sun
Compassed with suns and planets and their moons ;
Who didst create all souls intelligent,
And plan their blessedness ;
Raisest the fruitful ear, and dost command
Or stay the bolt of death :
Who leadest to the goal through deserts lone,
And cheerest weary wanderers on their way ;
Thee we adore !
" For Thine is the kingdom, the power, and the glory,
For ever and ever ! Amen !"

The following hymn is very commonly used at
funerals or at Easter services :—

THE RESURRECTION.

Rise again ! yes, rise again wilt thou
My dust, though buried now !
To life immortal
Is this brief rest the portal :
Hallelujah !

For the seed is sown again to bloom
　　Whene'er the Lord shall come,
　　　His harvest reaping
　　In us who now are sleeping :
　　　　　　Hallelujah !

Day of praise, of joyful tears the Day,
　　Thou of my God the Day,
　　　When I shall number
　　My destined years of slumber,
　　　　　　Thou wakenest me !

Then shall we be like to those that dream,
　　When on us breaks the beam
　　　Of that blest morrow ;
　　The weary pilgrim's sorrow
　　　　　　Is then no more.

Then the Saviour leads us of His grace
　　Into the Holiest Place,
　　　Where we for ever
　　Shall praise His Name who doth deliver !
　　　　　　Hallelujah !

With Klopstock this short survey of the course of
German religious poetry must end.   He has brought
us within the entrance of that modern revival of literature which rendered the close of the eighteenth century
as remarkable for its brilliancy as the opening of it
had been for its barrenness.   Germany had once more
woke up to life ; and perhaps because political and
practical life offered no career to attract her ablest
minds, their energies were all the more thrown into the
field of thought, of literature and philosophy, criticism
and research.   To a great extent this new intellectual

activity made for itself other channels quite apart
from that peculiarly Christian form of literature which
we have been following ; yet not wholly so. Klopstock marked the opening of the new era by the
greatest religious epic that Germany possesses ; Herder
not only wrote religious poems of merit himself, but
did better service by his works on ancient national
poetry, and especially that of the Hebrews, which
taught men afresh what they ought to seek and care
for in this kind of literature. The writers of the
so-called Romantic school, and of the patriotic songs
which flew over Germany during the wars with
Napoleon, furnished a few really fine religious poems
and hymns, such as those of Novalis, Ernst Moritz
Arndt, Schenkendorf, and Fouqué, whose name is best
known to us by his lovely little romance of "Undine."
Then followed a time which produced very little of
this kind. With the exception of a few illustrious
names—such as those of Neander, Rothe, Bunsen, or
Nitzsch—the two tendencies most easily recognisable
in the religious thought of Germany of later years
have been an aggressive or a quietly contemptuous
scepticism, confronted by a narrow and arrogant ortho-
doxy which has allied itself to whatever was least
progressive in the political world. But by the side of
these there has also been an undergrowth of a genuine
religious life which has not as yet asserted itself in the
field of thought, but has shown itself almost exclusively
in that of active Christian charity and devotional feeling. It is to this spirit that the country owes that
remarkable development of philanthropic agencies
which find their bond of common work in the "Inner
Mission," and no less the reform of its hymn-books,

and the rise of a large new school of hymn-writers. Within the last thirty years the hymnology of Germany, both before and since the Reformation, has been the subject of the most careful research; several important historical works on the subject have been written, and many thoroughly good collections of hymns have been published; while even the authorized State hymn-books are by slow degrees sharing in the improvement.   At present the best is that of Wurtemberg.   The original religious poetry of the present day is very considerable in quantity, but varies much in character.   Among the Roman Catholic writers, Spee, with all the defects no less than the beauties of his style, affords the most frequent model, while the most usual theme is the praise of Mary.   The Evangelical authors, on the other hand, take the earlier Lutheran school for their pattern in congregational "church-songs," and if they do not attain quite the force and condensed pregnancy of the classical hymns, they have at least much sweetness, earnestness, and simplicity; while their poems not intended for congregational use are often graceful and touching. The best among them are those of Spitta, Knapp, Victor Strauss, and Gerok, Luise Hensel and Meta Haüszer.   Of the recent lyrical poets of Germany, one of the most distinguished, Friedrich Rückert,[1] is a religious as well as a secular poet, and with two of his poems we will wind up this long series of Christian singers.   It began, a thousand years ago, with the monk whose great work was to present the Life of Christ to the German people in their own tongue; it ends with the modern lyric poet and scholar whose

[1] Died in 1866.

favourite study has been the wisdom of the Brahmins and Persians, and who yet finds that all these centuries have not exhausted the meaning that lies in Bethlehem and Calvary.

MIDNIGHT.

At dead of night
Sleep took her flight.
I gazed abroad, no star of all the crowds
That people heaven, was smiling through the clouds
To cheer my sight
That dreary night.

At dead of night
I scaled the height
Of giddy question o'er our mortal lot;
My searchings found no answer, brought me not
One ray of light
In that deep night.

At dead of night
In still affright
I turned and listened to my throbbing heart;
One pulse of pain alone, whose ancient smart
Had dimmed sweet light,
Beat there that night.

At dead of night
I fought the fight
Humanity, of all thy pain and woes;
My strength could not decide it, and my foes
O'erwhelmed me quite
At dead of night.

At dead of night
All power and might
I yielded, Lord of life and death, to Thee,
And learnt Thou watchedst with me, and that we
Are in Thy sight
In deepest night!

BETHLEHEM AND CALVARY.

In Bethlehem the Lord was born
  Whose birth has brought us life and light,
On Calvary that death of scorn
  He died, that broke Death's cruel might:
I wandered from a western strand
And sought through many an eastern land,
Yet found I greater nought than ye,
O Bethlehem and Calvary!

Ye wonders of the ancient world,
  How hath your pomp been swept away,
And earthly strength to ruin hurled
  By power that knows not of decay!
I saw them scattered far and wide,
The ruined heaps on every side;
But lowly glory still I see
Round Bethlehem and Calvary.

Ye Pyramids are but a tomb
  Wherein did toiling mortals build
Death's utter darkness; 'tis his gloom,
  Not peace, wherewith your depths are filled.
Ye Sphinxes, to the world of old
Could Life's enigma ne'er unfold;
'Tis solved for ages yet to be
In Bethlehem and Calvary!

O Syria's earthly Paradise,
  Fair Schiraz' gardens of the rose,
Ye palmy plains 'neath Indian skies,
  Ye shores where soft the spice-wind blows,
Death stalks through all that looks so fair,
I trace his shadow everywhere ;
Look up, and Life's true Fountain see
In Bethlehem and Calvary !

Thou Kaaba, black desert-stone,
  Against which half the world to-day
Still stumbles, strive to keep thy throne
  Lit by Thy Crescent's pallid ray ;
The moon before the sun must pale,
That brighter Sign shall yet prevail,
Of Him whose cry of victory
Is Bethlehem and Calvary !

O Thou, who didst not once disdain
  The childish form, the Manger poor ;
Who once to take from us our pain
  All pain didst on the Cross endure ;
Pride to Thy Manger cannot bend,
Thy Cross doth haughty minds offend,
But lowly hearts draw close to Thee
In Bethlehem and Calvary !

The Kings approach, to worship there
  The Paschal Lamb, the Shepherd race ;
And thitherwards the nations fare
  As pilgrims to the Holy Place ;
The storm of warfare on them breaks,
The World but not the Cross it shakes,
When East and West in strife ye see
For Bethlehem and Calvary.

O not like those, with weaponed hand,
    But with the Spirit let us go
To conquer back the Holy Land,
    As Christ is conquering still below;
Let beams of light on ev'ry side
Speed as Apostles far and wide,
Till all the Earth draws light from thee,
O Bethlehem, O Calvary!

With pilgrim hat and staff I went
    Afar through Orient lands to roam,
My years of pilgrimage are spent,
    And this the word I bring you home;
The pilgrim's staff ye need not crave
To seek God's Cradle or His Grave,
But seek within you, there shall be
His Bethlehem and Calvary!

O Heart, what helps it to adore
    His Cradle where the sunrise glows?
Or what avail to kneel before
    The Grave whence long ago He rose?
That He should find in thee a birth,
That thou shouldst seek to die to earth
And live to Him;—this, this must be
Thy Bethlehem and Calvary!

THE END.